# Seminars in Psychiatric Genetics 616.89

# College Seminars Series

## Series Editors

**Professor Hugh Freeman**, Honorary Professor, University of Salford, and Honorary Consultant Psychiatrist, Salford Health Authority

**Dr Ian Pullen**, Consultant Psychiatrist, Royal Edinburgh Hospital

**Dr George Stein**, Consultant Psychiatrist, Farnborough Hospital, and King's College Hospital

**Professor Greg Wilkinson**, Editor, *British Journal of Psychiatry*, and Professor of Psychiatry, The London Hospital Medical College

## Other books in the series

*Seminars in Child and Adolescent Psychiatry*. Edited by Dora Black & David Cottrell

*Seminars in Basic Neurosciences*. Edited by Gethin Morgan & Stuart Butler

*Seminars in Psychology and the Social Sciences*. Edited by Digby Tantam & Max Birchwood

**Forthcoming titles**
*Seminars in the Psychiatry of Learning Disabilities*. Edited by Oliver Russell

*Seminars in Adult Psychiatry*. Edited by George Stein & Greg Wilkinson

*Seminars in Forensic Psychiatry*. Edited by Derek Chiswick & Rosemarie Cope

*Seminars in Drug and Alcohol Misuse*. Edited by Jonathan Chick & Roch Cantwell

*Seminars in Psychiatry for the Elderly*. Edited by Brice Pitt & Mohsen Naguib

*Seminars in Psychopharmacology*. Edited by David King

# Seminars in Psychiatric Genetics

By
Peter McGuffin, Michael J. Owen,
Michael C. O'Donovan,
Anita Thapar & Irving I. Gottesman

GASKELL

**British Library Cataloguing in Publication Data**

McGuffin, Peter
  Seminars in Psychiatric Genetics. -
  (College Seminars Series)
  I. Title  II. Series
  616.89

ISBN 0-902241-65-6

Distributed in North America
by American Psychiatric Press, Inc.
ISBN 0 88048 628 7

Gaskell is an imprint of the Royal College of Psychiatrists,
17 Belgrave Square, London SW1X 8PG
The Royal College of Psychiatrists is a registered charity, number 228636)

The views presented in this book do not necessarily reflect those of
the Royal College of Psychiatrists, and the publishers are not
responsible for any error of omission or fact. College Seminars are
produced by the Publications Department of the College; they should
in no way be construed as providing a syllabus or other material for
any College examination.

Printed in Great Britain

# Contents

The authors      vi
Foreword. *Series Editors*      vii
Preface      viii

1   The cell and molecular biology      1
2   Quantitative genetics      30
3   Linkage and association      55
4   Mental retardation      66
5   Schizophrenia      87
6   Affective disorders      110
7   Neurotic disorders      128
8   Personality disorders and criminal behaviours      146
9   Alcoholism      161
10   Childhood disorders      174
11   Dementia      192
12   Genetic counselling and ethical issues      218

Index      226

# The authors

Peter McGuffin, Professor of Psychological Medicine, University of Wales College of Medicine, Department of Psychological Medicine, Heath Park, Cardiff CF4 4XN

Michael J. Owen, Senior Lecturer, University of Wales College of Medicine, Departments of Psychological Medicine and Medical Genetics, Heath Park, Cardiff CF4 4XN

Michael C. O'Donovan, Senior Lecturer, University of Wales College of Medicine, Department of Psychological Medicine, Heath Park, Cardiff CF4 4XN

Anita Thapar, MRC Fellow, University of Wales College of Medicine, Department of Psychological Medicine, Heath Park, Cardiff CF4 4XN

Irving I. Gottesman, Commonwealth Professor of Psychology, Department of Psychology, University of Virginia, Charlottesville, USA

# Foreword

## *Series Editors*

The publication of *College Seminars*, a series of textbooks covering the breadth of psychiatry, represents a new venture for the Royal College of Psychiatrists. At the same time, it is very much in line with the College's established role in education and in setting professional standards.

*College Seminars* are intended to help junior doctors during their training years. We hope that trainees will find these books useful, on the ward as well as in preparation for the MRCPsych examination. Separate volumes will cover clinical psychiatry, each of its subspecialties, and also the relevant non-clinical academic disciplines of psychology and sociology.

*College Seminars* will also make a contribution to the continuing medical education of established clinicians.

Psychiatry is concerned primarily with people, and to a lesser extent with disease processes and pathology. The core of the subject is rich in ideas and schools of thought, and no single approach or solution can embrace the variety of problems a psychiatrist meets. For this reason, we have endeavoured to adopt an eclectic approach to practical management throughout the series.

The College can draw upon the collective wisdom of many individuals in clinical and academic psychiatry. More than a hundred people have contributed to this series; this reflects how diverse and complex psychiatry has become.

Frequent new editions of books appearing in the series are envisaged, which should allow *College Seminars* to be responsive to readers' suggestions and needs.

*Hugh Freeman*
*Ian Pullen*
*George Stein*
*Greg Wilkinson*

# Preface

In about 1977, one of us, then a psychiatric registrar, had a conversation with one of his teachers, an eminent professor of social psychiatry, about an essay just submitted for Part I of the University of London MPhil in Psychiatry. This reviewed work by various groups, including the registrar and his colleagues, on possible associations between HLA and schizophrenia, and contained a proposal for a genetic linkage study with HLA and other markers. "Extraordinarily arcane," was the professor's judgement, carrying with it the implication that a young Maudsley doctor should find better things to do with his time.

Seventeen years on, there is still no replicated genetic linkage in schizophrenia, but recombinant DNA technology has revolutionised our understanding of many other diseases. The gene for Huntington's disease has been identified, and three different loci definitely involved in the aetiology of Alzheimer's disease are the subject of intense investigation. So-called positional cloning approaches are successfully being applied to complex non-Mendelian disorders such as familial cancers and coronary heart disease, and there is much justifiable optimism that there will soon be important advances in schizophrenia, manic depression, and perhaps other disorders.

Our aim in writing this book has been to try to convey some of the current excitement about prospects for molecular genetic research in psychiatry, while not overlooking the pitfalls. At the same time, we wish to stress that the subject has arrived at the threshold of a new molecular phase, having been carried there by the cumulative advance of older, pre-molecular technologies. Furthermore, although family, twin, and adoption studies have been extensively exploited in disorders such as schizophrenia and manic depression, their usefulness has still not been exhausted and their systematic application in some other disorders has scarcely begun.

Like other volumes in the *College Seminars Series*, this book is mainly aimed at trainee psychiatrists, but takes them beyond what they need to know about genetics simply for the purpose of passing postgraduate examinations. We hope that the book, although necessarily concise, is sufficiently comprehensive to be also of interest to qualified psychiatrists, as well as to geneticists, clinicians and researchers in allied fields. It is a measure of the current vigour of research in psychiatric genetics that quite a few essential new references have had to be added at the proof stage, and despite our best efforts, some sections will almost certainly become out of date fairly soon after publication. Finally, we hope that this book will help contribute to the positive and growing general interest in the genetics of psychiatric disorders that has been evident in recent years, and help do away with any lingering idea that research in the area is only for lovers of the obscure.

PMcG, MJO, MCO'D, AT
*Cardiff, Wales*
IIG
*Charlottesville, Virginia*

*January 1994*

# 1   The cell and molecular biology

---

*The chromosomal basis of heredity • Cytogenetic techniques and their application • The molecular basis of heredity • Genomic phenomena that decrease familial resemblance • Recombinant DNA technology and the new genetics • The application of molecular genetics to the study of disease • The study of gene expression in the central nervous system*

---

## The chromosomal basis of heredity

### Chromosomes

Chromosomes are so called because they stain deeply with various biological dyes. They can be seen as thread-like structures within the dividing nucleus. Each chromosome consists of a linear deoxyribonucleic acid (DNA) molecule which is complexed with proteins to form *chromatin*. Genetic information is encoded within the DNA and a gene is a length of DNA that specifies the structure of a particular protein product. Genes are arranged along the chromosomes in a linear order, with each having a precise position or *locus*. Alternative forms of a gene that can occupy the same locus are termed *alleles*. Each chromosome bears only a single allele at a given locus, though in the population as a whole there may be many alleles, any one of which can occupy that locus.

### *The human karyotype*

The chromosomes of each species have a characteristic number and morphology known as a karyotype. Each chromosome has a long and a short arm separated by a constricted region known as the *centromere*, which is important in cell division. Normal human somatic cells contain 46 chromosomes consisting of 23 homologous pairs. The members of homologous pairs have the same genetic loci in the same order, although at any one locus they may have either the same alleles – and are therefore said to be *homozygous* – or different alleles – in which case they are said to be *heterozygous*.

### *Autosomes*

One member of each pair of chromosomes is inherited from the father, the other from the mother, and one of each pair is transmitted to each child. Twenty-two pairs are present in both males and females and are known as autosomes.

1

*Sex chromosomes*

The remaining pair, the sex chromosomes, differ in male and female and play a major role in sex determination. Normally the members of a pair of autosomes are microscopically indistinguishable. This is also true for sex chromosomes in females, who possess two X chromosomes. However, in the male, the sex chromosomes differ from one another. One is an X, identical to Xs of the female, while the other is smaller and is called the Y chromosome. Normally, sexual development in the embryo depends upon whether or not a Y chromosome is present.

In the female each cell contains only one active X chromosome. The inactivated X chromosome can be revealed as a densely staining area, the *Barr body*, in cells from a buccal smear. It is conventional to indicate the total number of chromosomes per cell by an Arabic numeral and, if relevant, the constitution of sex chromosomes by one X and/or Y for each chromosome. Thus the normal male and female karyotypes are written as 46XY and 46XX respectively, while Klinefelter's males are 47XXY and Turner's females are 45X0.

## The behaviour of chromosomes during cell division

There are two kinds of cell division:

(1) *mitosis*, by which the body grows and replaces dead or injured cells
(2) *meiosis*, resulting in the production of reproductive cells (*gametes*).

Observation of the behaviour of chromosomes during the processes of cell division and gametogenesis allowed the physical bases of Gregor Mendel's empirical laws to be understood.

*Mitosis*

Mitosis is show diagramatically in Fig. 1.1. Before cell division each nuclear chromosome duplicates to form two identical chromatids. These subsequently separate to become chromosomes in their own right, thus doubling the normal chromosome complement of the cell. When the cell divides, one of each pair of chromatids segregates into each daughter cell. The result is that the original chromosome number and composition of the parent is exactly duplicated in the progeny.

*Meiosis*

Meiosis is shown diagramatically in Fig. 1.2. In gametogenesis two cell divisions occur in the parent cell. However, because the chromosomes only duplicate once, the number of chromosomes in the final progeny is reduced to half that in the parent. Not only are sister chromatids paired during the first division but homologous chromosomes also come together giving rise to a quadruple structure. During the ensuing two divisions both sister chromatids and homologous pairs are separated and passed to different daughter cells. *Gametes* therefore have only one representative of each chromosome pair and are said to be *haploid*. In contrast, somatic cells contain both members of each homologous pair and are called *diploid*. The union of sperm and egg at fertilisation normally restores the diploid state.

During the first meiotic division, the two members of each homologous pair separate, with one member going to each pole. The different chromosome pairs assort themselves independently of one another so that the chromosomes received originally as a paternal and maternal set are now sorted into random combinations of paternal and maternal chromosomes with one representative of each pair going to each pole. The disjunction of paired homologous chromosomes is the physical basis of *segregation*, and the random assortment of paternal and maternal chromosomes in the gametes is the basis of *independent assortment* (see

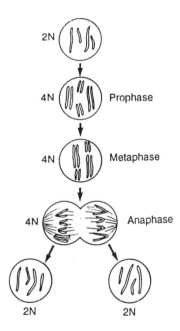

**Fig. 1.1** Mitosis, somatic cell division, results in two identical daughter cells that each have the same number of chromosomes as the parent cell. Somatic cells contain both members of each homologous pair of chromosomes (diploid). For the sake of simplicity, the behaviour of only two homologous pairs is shown. During prophase each duplicates to form two identical chromatids.

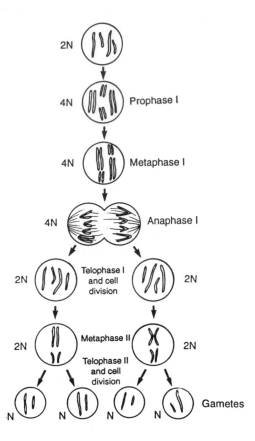

(a)

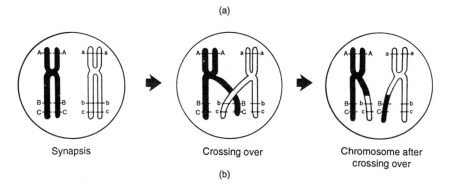

(b)

**Fig. 1.2** (a) Meiosis, sex cell division, results in four daughter cells (gametes) that each have half the number of chromosomes of the parent cell (haploid). (b) Crossing-over (or recombination). The allelles of genes A and B assort independently. In contrast, the alleles of B and C, which are close together, are inherited together (they are linked).

Chapter 2). Thus the behaviour of chromosomes in the first meiotic division provides the physical basis for Mendelian inheritance.

### Recombination

One might suppose that alleles on the same chromosome would fail to assort independently. However, as can be seen from Fig. 1.2, the metaphase chromatids of homologous chromosomes exchange segments by breakage and recombination. This is known as crossing over (or recombination). It causes chromosomes to become reorganised into new combinations of alleles and therefore increases genetic variability in the next generation. It also has the effect of producing independent assortment of genes on the same chromosome. However, the probability of recombination occurring is a function of the propinquity of two genetic loci; therefore departures from independent assortment do occur when two loci are sufficiently close together, resulting in *genetic linkage* (see Chapter 3).

## Cytogenetic techniques and their application

Chromosomal analysis is usually carried out upon white blood cells, since these are capable of growth and rapid division in culture and are readily accessible. White blood cells are separated from the other components of blood and stimulated to divide by a mitogenic agent such as colchicine. This culture is then incubated until the cells are dividing well (usually about 72 hours). At this point a dilute solution of colchicine is added to the medium. This effectively stops mitosis at metaphase, and cells in metaphase therefore accumulate in the culture. The cells are then fixed, spread on slides and stained by one of several techniques.

Longer-term chromosome cultures can be obtained from skin biopsies. Foetal cells from amniotic fluid obtained by amniocentesis can also be cultured using similar methods.

### Karyotyping

Chromosome spreads are examined under a microscope, a process known as karyotyping. There are a variety of staining techniques available but broadly speaking these can be divided into *solid staining*, in which each chromosome is stained uniformly darkly, and *banded staining*. The latter uses dyes that differentially stain parts of the chromosome resulting in a characteristic pattern of bands across the width of each chromosome. Chromosomes that have been stained in this way are easily distinguished from their non-homologous neighbours, thus allowing gross analysis of chromosomal number and composition.

Chromosomes are now classified according to both their size and banding pattern. Moreover each chromosome and each chromosomal band are numbered according to a standard system. The Paris classification is shown in Fig. 1.3.

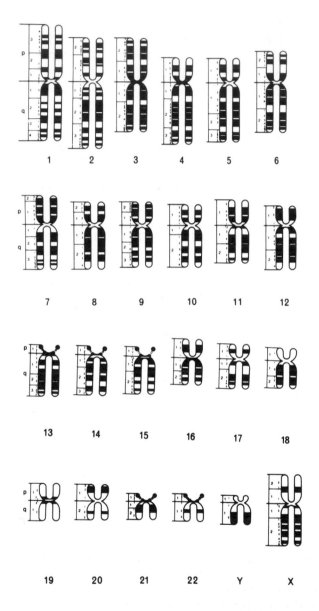

**Fig. 1.3** The Paris classification of chromosomes. Each chromosome has a long (q) and a short (p) arm separated by a centromere. Particular chromosomes are identified by their size, the relative lengths of the p and q arms, and by their banding pattern.

The pattern shown in Fig. 1.3 is based upon staining of metaphase spreads. When prophase and prometaphase chromosomes are stained they reveal a much larger number of bands. Such *high-resolution banding* can be helpful in pin-pointing precise breakpoints or in showing small alterations in chromosome structure that could not otherwise be observed.

## Chromosomal abnormalities

A number of different chromosomal abnormalities can be detected by karyotyping. These include various *aneuploidies* – alterations in the number of the sex chromosomes or autosomes. In addition, a whole series of abnormalities can arise as a consequence of the breakage of chromosomes. These are *deletions*, where a segment of chromosome is lost; *inversions*, where a piece of chromosome becomes detached then re-attached in the opposite orientation; and *duplications*, where a segment of chromosome is included twice over. *Reciprocal translocations* occur when chromosomes of two different pairs exchange segments. The term *Robertsonian translocation* is used to describe the fusion of two chromosomes at their centromeres. The role of chromosomal abnormalities in syndromes of mental handicap is described in Chapter 4.

So-called *fragile sites* are present on several human chromosomes. In particular there is one on the distal long arm of the X chromosome that is seen in a proportion of cultured cells from males with a specific type of familial, X-linked mental retardation known as *fragile X syndrome* (see Chapter 4). Demonstration of the fragile site depends upon culturing cells under conditions of thymidine deprivation either by using a medium low in thymidine and folic acid or by adding an inhibitor of thymidine synthetase to the culture. As we shall see in Chapter 4, the molecular basis of this fragile site has recently been determined and it can now be detected directly by molecular genetic techniques.

## Applications of cytogenetic techniques

There are many applications of cytogenetic techniques; perhaps the most important are in clinical diagnoses where chromosomal abnormalities are suspected. The chromosomal abnormalities that are of major relevance to psychiatry are those that lead to mental handicap (see Chapter 4). Chromosome analysis can also be helpful in determining the causes of infertility or repeated abortions. A very high incidence of chromosome abnormalities is found in foetuses from spontaneous abortions occurring during the first trimester. However, only a small proportion of couples with infertility or repeated abortion have a chromosomal abnormality that could account for their reproductive difficulties. There is an association between chromosomal abnormalities and late maternal age.

The karyotype of the foetus can be determined with relative ease and safety using amniocentesis. An alternative approach is chorionic villous sampling, which allows even earlier fetal karyotyping. Familial chromosome abnormalities can also be detected prenatally. There is also a range of research applications of cytogenetics, in particular, the study of cytogenetic abnormalities in neoplasia has been of great importance.

# The molecular basis of heredity

## The structure of DNA

DNA is made up of two chains of *nucleotide* bases wrapped around each other in the form of a double helix which is held together by hydrogen

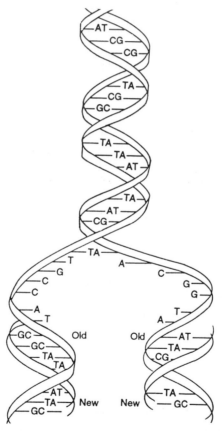

**Fig. 1.4** The structure of DNA. DNA consists of two anti-parallel strands in the form of a double helix. The four bases in DNA are adenine (A), guanine (G), cytosine (C) and thymine (T). In the bottom half of the figure the two strands of the parental double helix have unwound and each is specifying a new daughter strand by the base pairing rule. In this way, identical daughter double helices are generated through semi-conservative replication of DNA.

bonds between the bases (Fig. 1.4). There are four bases in DNA:

adenine (A)
guanine (G)
cytosine (C)
thymine (T)

These can lie in any order along the sugar-phosphate backbone. Because of their particular steric properties A always pairs with T and C with G. This means that one strand contains a sequence of bases that is complementary to the other, and that each strand can always be copied using the complementary strand as a template. This allows the duplication of the double helix by the unwinding and copying of each strand to produce a complementary sequence according to the base pair rule (Fig. 1.4). Genetic information is encoded by the sequence of bases along the DNA molecule. For genetic information to be expressed it must first be read (*transcription*) and then decoded (*translation*).

## Gene structure and expression

### Ribonucleic acid (RNA)

Genetic information is transported from the cell nucleus to the cytoplasm by a type of ribonucleic acid (RNA) known as messenger RNA (mRNA). The primary structure of RNA is similar to that of DNA except that it contains a different sugar and that the base uracil occurs in place of thymine. Messenger RNA is synthesised directly from one strand of the DNA (Fig. 1.5). Each molecule of mRNA therefore contains bases in a sequence complementary to that found on the portion of the DNA molecule (gene) from which it was copied. The transfer of genetic information from the gene to mRNA is known as transcription. Once in the cytoplasm mRNA then acts as a template from which protein molecules are assembled. This is accomplished using the protein synthetic machinery of the cell, its basic unit being the ribosome. Protein synthesis is based simply upon the sequential reading of groups of three bases, each triplet sequence coding for a particular amino acid, with some acting as start or stop signals. Amino acids, which are the building blocks of proteins, are themselves polymerised sequentially until the protein product is completed. The end result is the conversion of linear genetic information encoded in DNA into either an enzyme or a structural protein. The rule that the flow of genetic information is from DNA, to RNA, to protein is often called the 'central dogma' of molecular genetics.

### Introns and exons

Early insights into the structure of genes came from the study of bacteria, which are *prokaryotic* (i.e. they do not contain a nucleus), and genes were

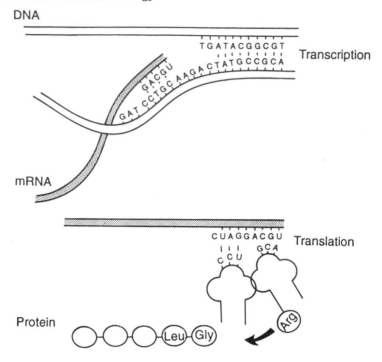

**Fig. 1.5** Genetic information in the cell flows from DNA to RNA to protein. Genetic information contained in the base sequence of DNA is converted into structural information by the process of transcription of DNA to mRNA, followed by translation of mRNA into protein (LEU is leucine, GLY is glycine and ARG is arginine).

viewed simply as segments of DNA containing the code for the amino acid sequence of the protein molecule. However, more recent work on *eukaryotic* cells (those with nuclei) has established that the structure of genes is more complex than this and that the process of gene expression is correspondingly more involved, especially in higher eukaryotes. In many genes of man and other vertebrates the coding regions, called *exons*, are interrupted by stretches of non-coding intervening sequences or *introns*. On transcription of the gene the initial RNA transcript is processed in a complex manner which involves *splicing out* non-coding regions as well as other post-transcriptional modifications such as the addition of a poly (A) tail before the mature mRNA is released into the cytoplasm (see Fig. 1.6). The exons and introns of genes are flanked by regions that are important in the regulation of gene expression.

### Classes of DNA in the genome

There are an estimated 50 000 – 100 000 genes in man, which range in size from 1000 to more than 2 000 000 base pairs (bp) in size. These constitute

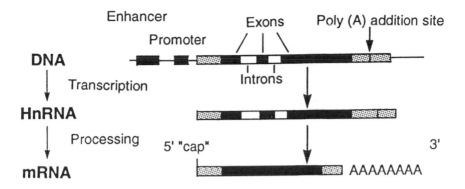

**Fig. 1.6** Schematic representation of a typical eukaryotic gene. Gene expression is regulated by a promoter close to the start of transcription as well as enhancer sequences which may be at various sites upstream, downstream or even within the gene itself. After transcription the large heteronuclear RNA (HnRNA) molecule is processed to produce mRNA which then passes from the nucleus to the cytoplasm. This processing includes splicing out non-coding regions, addition of a poly (A) tail and addition of a 5' cap which is essential for efficient translation of mature mRNA.

only a small percentage of the 3 x $10^9$ bp that is estimated to be contained by the human haploid genome.

The function of much of the remaining DNA is unknown but some of it exists to regulate the expression of coding regions such as the so-called *enhancer* or *promoter* regions contained within the flanking regions of genes. Other non-coding DNA may play a role in DNA replication and chromosome pairing and recombination. It also seems likely that much DNA serves no function at all – so-called 'junk' DNA.

The organisation of DNA sequences in higher organisms can be classified into three kinds.

(1) *Unique sequences*. These are present in a single or only a few copies in the genome and make up approximately 60–70% of the total DNA. The majority of protein coding sequences (genes) fall into this category

(2) *Highly repetitive sequences*. These consist of small tandemly repeated elements that are not transcribed. They are present in hundreds of thousands of copies in the human genome. They tend to be clustered at the centromeres of human chromosomes as well as in other regions

(3) *Moderately repetitive sequences*. These can be either dispersed or clustered and make up some 20–30% of the human genome.

## DNA mutation and variation

*Point mutations*

Changes in the sequence of bases in genes can have significant effects on cellular structure and metabolism. For example, point mutation, which is the substitution of one base for another, is common and can cause an amino acid substitution in the protein which may change its chemical properties. Similarly, production of a stop signal will cause premature termination of protein synthesis. Changes outside coding regions can have a profound effect on gene expression. For example, a mutation at a promoter sequence may abolish transcription of a gene, and one at a splice junction may result in aberrant processing of the mRNA. Point mutations are themselves just one of a number of ways in which the structure and function of genes can be disrupted. Others include:

(1) *deletions* (loss of a sequence of bases)
(2) *insertions* (the gaining of a piece of DNA)
(3) *frame shift mutations* (the loss of one base, causing the triplet code to be read out of frame)
(4) *translocations* (the breaking of a chromosome and its rejoining at a different site).

These deleterious changes will tend to be selected against in the ensuing population due to reduction in fitness of the organism.

Not all changes in DNA are deleterious however. Rarely, changes may be advantageous to the organism, for example if they improve the properties of an enzyme. These will confer a selective advantage upon the progeny of the organism and hence will tend to increase in the population.

*Neutral mutations*

There is also another class of mutations, those that have little or no effect and are called *neutral*. Some base substitutions will not change the amino acid composition of a particular protein due to the redundancy of the genetic code; many amino acids are coded for by more than one triplet. Similarly, some amino acid changes may not change protein function, particularly if one amino acid is replaced by another with similar chemical and physical properties. It is also evident that changes in non-coding regions of DNA may also have no net effect.

Such neutral changes in DNA may be carried passively in the population, their frequency changing through random processes. A proportion of sequence variation is also probably maintained in the population through recurrent mutation. The result of these processes is that comparison of any one person's DNA with another's reveals a difference in base sequence approximately every $10^3$ base pairs.

This individual variation has proved extremely useful in the study of genetic disease, as we shall see later, and also forms the basis of so-called genetic fingerprinting, which has many applications in such areas as paternity testing and forensic medicine.

# Genomic phenomena that decrease familial resemblance

Many traits and diseases, including many psychiatric disorders, do not exhibit clear patterns of Mendelian transmission and display phenomena such as incomplete penetrance and variable expressivity, which will be described in later chapters. Conventionally these have been seen as reflecting the co-action or interaction of several or many genes and/or the influence of environmental factors. However, recent research has revealed a number of genomic phenomena which can cause departures from simple Mendelian inheritance patterns.

## Mutations

New *germ line mutations* (i.e. those occurring in parental gametes) appear to be a frequent cause of some single-gene disorders of psychiatric relevance such as tuberous sclerosis (see Chapter 4) (Sampson *et al*, 1989). Up to half of cases of this condition, known to be dominantly inherited (see p. 36), occur in people with unaffected parents. Genetic mutations can also arise in somatic cells that are actively dividing. For example, in hereditary retinoblastoma a mutation occurs in a gene, on the long arm of chromosome 13, called RB1. An individual inheriting one defective copy of the RB1 gene has a high risk, but not a certainty, of developing retinoblastoma. Two defective copies of RB1 need to be present in a cell before there is uncontrolled proliferation leading to retinoblastoma, so that the 'first hit', an inherited defective gene on chromosome 13, must be followed by a 'second hit' in the same gene on the homologous chromosome due to a *somatic mutation* before retinoblastoma develops (Knudson, 1986).

It is reasonable to speculate that a more general 'two-hit' hypothesis might be applicable to some psychiatric disorders, where the first hit is inheritance of a gene, or set of genes, predisposing to illness and the second is a somatic mutation, or series of mutations, occurring early in development at a time when there is active division of neuronal stem cells. Environmental factors could of course contribute to such mutations but they might also occur completely randomly.

## Unstable DNA sequences

A number of pathological mutations have now been shown to involve variations in the copy number of tandemly repeated DNA leading to a disruption of gene function. For example, the first exon of the human androgen receptor gene normally contains about 20 repeats of the sequence CAG. However, in X-linked spinal and bulbar muscular atrophy this region is expanded and many such repeats are found. Unstable DNA trinucleotide sequences have also been observed in fragile X syndrome (Chapter 4), myotonic dystrophy (Harley *et al*, 1992) and most recently in Huntington's disease (see Chapter 11).

Broadly speaking, it appears that variations in repeat length are correlated with phenotypic variations such as in severity and age of onset. In Chapter 4 we discuss how the irregular pattern of inheritance in fragile X syndrome can be accounted for in terms of expansion of an unstable trinucleotide repeat.

In myotonic dystrophy (MD) the phenomenon of *anticipation*, whereby successive generations show a lower age of onset and/or increasing severity, can be explained by the expansion of a trinucleotide repeat sequence in the MD gene (Harper *et al*, 1992). Clearly, the existence of such genes could explain phenotypic variability and even the occurrence of unexpressed genotypes in psychiatric disorders. It is of particular interest that the four diseases in which unstable DNA sequences have been implicated show disruption of brain function.

### Genomic imprinting

Genomic imprinting refers to the phenomenon whereby the expression of a gene or set of genes differs according to whether the relevant chromosomes are of maternal or paternal origin. The precise mechanisms by which this occurs are not well understood but are thought to involve methylation of DNA (Reik *et al*, 1987) which is known to be an important modifier of gene expression that is both heritable and reversible. The best known examples of genomic imprinting of psychiatric relevance are in the Prader–Willi and Angelman syndromes, which are described in Chapter 4. A less striking but nevertheless important example is in Huntington's disease where early onset is associated with transmission from the father (Ridley *et al*, 1988). It has been pointed out that imprinting might be a phenomenon of more general relevance that could account for the irregular patterns of transmission observed in other disorders (Hall, 1990) and may therefore be of importance in psychiatric conditions.

## Recombinant DNA technology and the new genetics

### The study of DNA

All the cells of an individual have essentially the same genotype, apart from in the exceptional instances described above. DNA can be obtained and prepared most conveniently from peripheral blood leukocytes.

However, one of the daunting aspects of the study of this genetic material is its sheer size in molecular terms – about $10^8$ base pairs of DNA per chromosome. One particular characteristic of DNA, however, has proved particularly useful in its study. This is the concept of complementarity between two DNA strands, which was discussed above. DNA has the property that above a certain temperature it 'melts' or *denatures*, in other words the two strands of the helix will separate. This is a reversible process, and under the correct conditions the strands will *hybridise* or *reanneal* back together again. However, because of the constraints of base pairing (A–T and G–C), a certain sequence of DNA will only recognise, and hence hybridise to, its corresponding complementary partner, although a certain amount of mismatch is possible. Thus, in general, a purified, single-stranded sequence of DNA will recognise only its complementary sequence of DNA even in a complex mixture. Similarly, a purified RNA sequence will recognise only the DNA sequence from which it was transcribed and vice versa. Thus purified sequences can be used as detectors or *probes* for the corresponding sequence in a mixture of nucleic acids *in vitro*. These properties of DNA have been known for a long time, but several developments have allowed us to exploit them.

## Restriction enzymes

A key development in modern molecular genetics has been the discovery in bacteria of restriction enzymes, or restriction endonucleases. In bacteria, these enzymes serve the function of breaking down infecting viral DNA molecules. Several hundred such enzymes are now known. These cut DNA not at random but where specific base sequences occur in the molecule. Each restriction enzyme recognises a different sequence of bases. This results in fragments of easily manageable size (usually $10^3$–$10^4$ base pairs). It is relevant to note that this size is of the order of that expected for many genes and therefore restriction enzyme digestion enables genes to be handled more or less in isolation rather than as parts of very long molecules.

## Molecular cloning

The second major development has been in the ability to purify specific pieces of DNA. This allows them to be studied further, for example by DNA sequencing, and in particular to be used as DNA probes.

There are two main types of DNA probe:

(1) those made from genomic DNA extracted and digested with restriction enzymes
(2) those made from complementary DNA (cDNA), which is synthesised from mRNA by the action of an enzyme called reverse transcriptase.

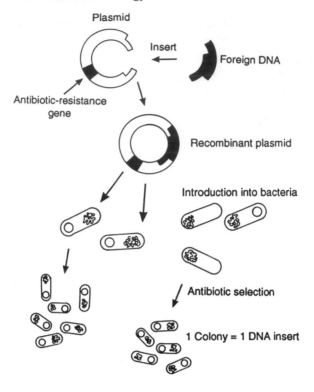

**Fig. 1.7** DNA cloning into bacteria. Foreign DNA is inserted following digestion by a restriction enzyme into a bacterial plasmid which contains an antibiotic resistance gene. The recombinant plasmids are then introduced into bacteria. Bacteria that contain recombinant plasmid are able to grow in the presence of antibiotics whereas those without them cannot.

The cDNA probes therefore represent copies of the coding sequences of genes. Following restriction enzyme digestion, these pieces of DNA can be inserted into the genome of vectors such as bacterial plasmids or bacteriophages, which have the ability to replicate freely within bacteria such as *Escherichia coli* and from which they can be recovered.

The resultant molecules are known as *recombinant DNA* molecules since they contain DNA sequences from different organisms. The preparation can be treated in such a way that only one DNA fragment is inserted into each bacterium. If the collection of bacteria is then diluted and plated out, individual bacteria will give rise to bacterial colonies each containing many copies of the DNA fragment which was inserted into the founder. This process is known as *molecular cloning* and can be considered as a process of biological purification and amplification of specific DNA fragments (see Fig. 1.7). The collection of bacterial colonies from a

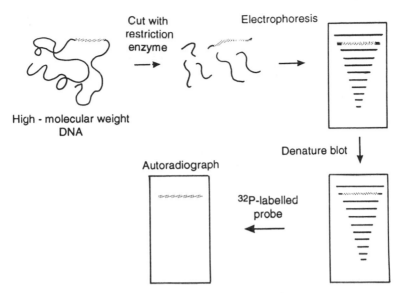

**Fig. 1.8** Southern blotting. Genomic DNA is cut with a restriction enzyme and subjected to agarose gel electrophoresis. The gel is then blotted onto a membrane producing a replica that can be hybridised to a suitable radiolabelled probe. The probe will bind to its complementary sequence and the position of this particular fragment will show up on subsequent autoradiography.

particular source is termed a *library*, in which there is a certain probability that any given sequence from the starting DNA mixture will be represented.

## Southern blotting

These technological advances are combined in one of the most fundamental techniques of molecular genetics which is called Southern blotting after its inventor E. M. Southern. First, genomic DNA is cut with a restriction enzyme. This produces a large number of different-sized DNA fragments which can be separated, according to their size, by electrophoresis on an agarose gel.

Because of the specificity of the enzyme, only a few particular fragment sizes will contain the DNA region of interest. In order to detect these fragments, the DNA has to be treated with alkali to denature it to single-stranded DNA. It is then transferred to a membrane sheet of either nitro-cellulose or modified nylon by a blotting procedure. This results in a copy of the gel which retains the electrophoretically produced arrangement of DNA fragments. The blot is then exposed to a radioactively labelled DNA probe. The DNA probe will bind to that part of the filter containing its complementary sequence, but surplus DNA probe will not bind elsewhere and can be washed away. The position on the membrane of the fragments containing the region of DNA to be analysed, whose sequence corresponds to that of the probe, can then be determined by autoradiography (see Fig. 1.8).

Southern blotting can therefore detect a sequence of interest in a starting sample of DNA and can also provide information about the surrounding region in terms of the size of the DNA molecule contained between the flanking restriction enzyme recognition sites.

## DNA sequencing

The complete characterisation of a piece of DNA requires knowledge of its exact base sequence. Once again, until recently this was a daunting prospect, but techniques are now available to determine the base sequence of any purified piece of DNA by either chemical or enzymatic means. The only factor limiting the analysis of base sequence is that it is labour intensive and time consuming, which sets an upper limit of about $10^5$ base pairs on the size of DNA conveniently studied. This has not deterred the proposal that the whole of the human genome should be sequenced in the near future, and with this in prospect attempts are being made to speed up the process of DNA sequencing, by several orders of magnitude, using already developed automated technology.

## The polymerase chain reaction

The polymerase chain reaction (PCR) (White *et al*, 1989) is an important new technique that has many applications in molecular genetics (Fig. 1.9). It allows a sequence of interest to be amplified selectively against a background of a large excess of irrelevant DNA. This method allows a sequence of up to 5 kbp or more in genomic DNA to be amplified $10^5$ to $10^6$-fold. PCR requires that unique sequences flanking the sequence of interest are known, so that specific oligonucleotide primers can be constructed. These are then used to prime DNA synthesis using a heat-stable DNA polymerase, such as that from *Thermus aquaticus*. Amplification is achieved by running approximately 30 cycles of reaction, one after the other, in an automated machine.

Following amplification the products can be separated by gel electrophoresis and genomic target sequences visualised directly under ultraviolet light following staining with ethidium bromide. Direct inspection can show the presence or absence of a target sequence. If the target sequence contains a polymorphic restriction enzyme site then this can be detected following digestion of the PCR products without the need for a probe or radio-labelling. PCR-amplified DNA can also be sequenced directly, without cloning, which allows mutations in known genes to be characterised with much greater ease.

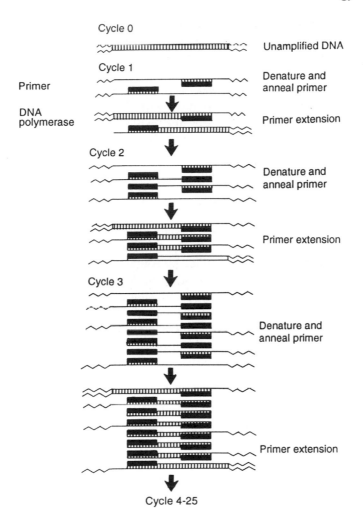

**Fig. 1.9** Diagrammatic representation of the polymerase chain reaction (PCR). Denaturation, annealing and extension take place at different temperatures.

The identification of mutations has also been greatly facilitated by the development of a number of techniques that allow the presence of mutations in small stretches of PCR-amplified DNA (*c.* 200–400 bp) to be detected (Strachan, 1992). These can be used as rapid screens for known mutations or to narrow down the location of an unknown mutation prior to sequencing. PCR is also extraordinarily sensitive and has also been used successfully to amplify denatured DNA from such diverse sources as Egyptian mummies, brain slices preserved in paraffin, and formalin-fixed tissue.

# The application of molecular genetics to the study of disease

As described above, there is considerable genetic variation between individuals at the level of the base sequence of DNA, most of which is undetectable phenotypically. A powerful aspect of the new genetic techniques is their ability to detect and exploit these variations. We are therefore able not only to study the mutations which give rise to a particular defect, but also to use genetic variation to mark the location of mutations without detailed knowledge of the molecular pathology.

## The identification of causal mutations

With diseases for which a genetic locus has already been identified, it is relatively straightforward to characterise the abnormality at the molecular level. Gross deletions may be identified by Southern blotting, from alterations in the size of the band detected by a probe for the disease gene.

Point mutations may be detected by DNA sequencing. Alternatively, where a specific mutation is known to exist in the population, short oligonucleotide probes can be synthesised which can distinguish between the normal and mutated DNA sequence by their hybridisation characteristics. This is based on the observation that mismatches between probes and a particular sequence tend to lower the melting temperature of the hybrid molecule, an effect that is more marked the shorter the probe length. Appropriate washing conditions can be selected which will 'melt off' mismatched hybrids, but leave perfect matches intact. This technique has been used in the prenatal diagnosis of phenylketonuria. More recently a number of techniques based upon PCR have been developed that allow known mutations to be identified. These include denaturing gradient gel electrophoresis, chemical cleavage, single-strand conformation analysis, and heteroduplex analysis (Strachan, 1992).

## DNA markers and disease

DNA variation can also be exploited to give rise to a number of types of genetic marker which can be used to distinguish specific alleles of a particular DNA sequence. These markers may not be directly related to the mutation causing a particular disorder but are useful in several ways. First, they may enable carriers of a disease mutation to be detected prenatally where the marker is close to a known mutation site even if the detailed molecular pathology is not known. Secondly, polymorphic DNA markers enable the location of a disease gene to be determined without any prior knowledge as to its specific chromosomal whereabouts using the techniques of linkage and association (see Chapter 3).

We have seen that restriction enzymes cleave DNA at specific base sequences. However, as already discussed, there is considerable variation in base sequence between individuals (except in identical twins). The result of this is that fragments produced by digestion of one individual's DNA by a restriction enzyme will not be the same as those produced by digestion of DNA from someone else. This is due to two mechanisms:

(1) the gain or loss of restriction enzyme recognition sites because of base changes
(2) variation in the number of bases between the same recognition sites, resulting often from variable lengths of tandemly repeated DNA

This is illustrated in Fig. 1.10.

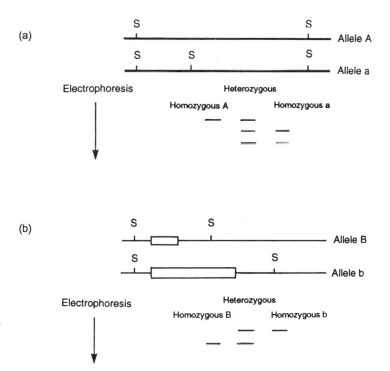

**Fig. 1.10** Restriction fragment length polymorphisms (RFLPs). There are two main types of RFLP. (a) A single base change in this piece of DNA has resulted in the formation of two alleles. Allele A contains two recognition sites (S) for a particular restriction enzyme. Allele a has an additional recognition site. Restriction enzyme digestion therefore produces one fragment from allele A, but two smaller fragments from allele a. These fragments can be separated on an agarose gel, subjected to Southern blotting and detected by a radio-labelled probe. (b) In this case variation in the number of bases between the same recognition sites occurs, often as a result of variable lengths of tandemly repeated DNA. ☐ = tandemly repeated DNA.

*Restriction fragment length polymorphisms*

Variations in the size of specific restriction fragments labelled by a given probe after Southern blotting are termed restriction fragment length polymorphisms (RFLPs). In such instances, the polymorphic site is either within or, more usually, close to the sequence recognised by the probe. Since they are generally inherited in a simple Mendelian fashion, RFLPs can be used as genetic markers; the different alleles of the markers can be distinguished and their inheritance followed through families or studied in populations.

*Linkage analysis*

Linkage analysis relies upon the ability to detect co-segregation of marker alleles with those of the disease gene. In order for a marker to be 'informative' for a particular meiosis, the individual concerned must be heterozygous at both the marker and the disease locus. Consequently, the usefulness of a given genetic marker for linkage analysis, known as 'informativeness', depends upon the frequency with which it is heterozygous within the population.

The majority of RFLPs arise from single base substitutions and are bi-allelic, which limits their informativeness. However, markers which rely upon length polymorphisms of tandemly repeated sequences (variable number of tandem repeats, VNTRs) are often extensively polymorphic. The use of probes detecting VNTRs typically generates multi-allelic systems that are highly informative. Unfortunately, VNTRs are not distributed uniformly: most are located close to telomeres. More recently (Weber & May, 1989), it has been discovered that a class of repeated DNA sequence known as *microsatellite repeats* or *simple sequence repeats* such as $(AC)_n$ (i.e. the sequence AC, repeated $n$ times where $n$ is a variable number), are highly polymorphic and more uniformly distributed. Moreover they can readily be detected on polyacrylamide gels after amplification of the region concerned by PCR (Fig. 1.11).

Recently a 'second generation' linkage map of over 800 such markers spread throughout the genome has been published (Weissenbach *et al*, 1992). We can now contemplate the availability within a few years of a set of very closely spaced microsatellite markers covering the entire genome which will be invaluable in mapping the genes responsible for complex disorders such as the common psychiatric diseases.

**Linkage studies with DNA markers**

The principles of linkage analysis will be described in Chapter 3. For studies using DNA markers, DNA is extracted from leukocytes taken from

**Step 1** Amplify region of repeat from genomic DNA using PCR primers P1 and P2

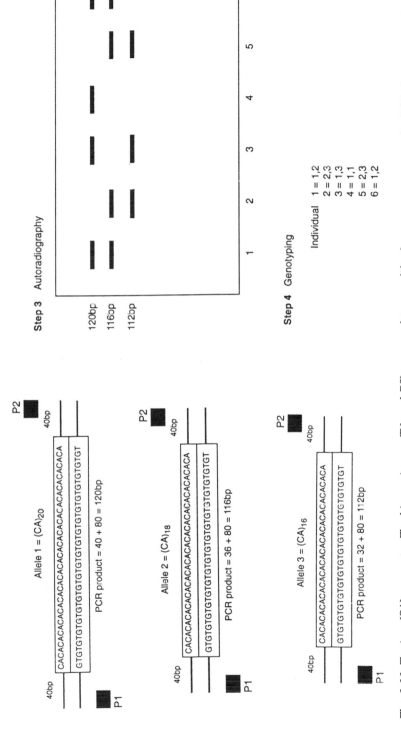

Allele 1 = (CA)₂₀

40bp CACACACACACACACACACACACACACACACACA
GTGTGTGTGTGTGTGTGTGTGTGTGTGT
P2 40bp
P1

PCR product = 40 + 80 = 120bp

Allele 2 = (CA)₁₈

40bp CACACACACACACACACACACACACACACACA
GTGTGTGTGTGTGTGTGTGTGTGTGT
P2 40bp
P1

PCR product = 36 + 80 = 116bp

Allele 3 = (CA)₁₆

40bp CACACACACACACACACACACACACA
GTGTGTGTGTGTGTGTGTGTGT
P2 40bp
P1

PCR product = 32 + 80 = 112bp

**Step 2** Denature PCR products and size fractionate on polyacrylamide gel

**Step 3** Autoradiography

120bp
116bp
112bp

1   2   3   4   5   6

**Step 4** Genotyping

Individual   1 = 1,2
             2 = 2,3
             3 = 1,3
             4 = 1,1
             5 = 2,3
             6 = 1,2

**Fig. 1.11** Typing (CA)ₙ repeats. Flanking primers (P1 and P2) are used to amplify the repeat sequence by PCR. In step two the PCR products are size fractionated on a polyacrylamide gel. In step three, autoradiography reveals the genotypes of each individual.

members of families containing several individuals with the disease in question. Briefly, the aim is to find a DNA marker whose alleles tend to segregate with the illness. In other words, one variant of the polymorphism will be present in affected but not unaffected members of a particular family more often than would be expected by chance. If this happens, it suggests that the marker locus and the pathological gene are close enough on the same chromosome to render separation during meiosis (recombination) unlikely. Thus, within certain limits the frequency of recombination is an approximate measure of the physical distance separating the two loci.

Broadly speaking, there are two strategies that can be employed to find linkage using DNA markers – the 'positional cloning' and 'candidate gene' approaches.

## Positional cloning

Positional cloning describes a set of techniques by which disease genes are identified through their position in the genome rather than through their function (Collins, 1992). In its initial stages this approach can rely upon a systematic search of the genome for linkage. This has been made possible by the availability of systematically constructed linkage maps of the human genome. These consist of DNA markers whose chromosomal positions have been mapped, which are polymorphic and which have been assembled so that they are approximately evenly spaced throughout the genome.

Many of these markers are 'anonymous' in the sense that they are not known to be within, or close, to genes. The important point is that they are separated at a distance which allows detection of linkage between them and the disease gene. This enables a systematic search to be make for linkage, a strategy that has been successful in the study of diseases such as Friedreich's ataxia (Chamberlain *et al*, 1988) and cystic fibrosis (Strachan, 1992).

In many cases positional cloning has been facilitated by clues from cytogenetic abnormalities that implicate a particular part of the genome such as a particular chromosome or chromosomal region in the pathogenesis of a disease. For example, the association between Down's syndrome and Alzheimer's disease led to the finding of linkage in familial Alzheimer's disease on chromosome 21 (Goate *et al*, 1989) (see Chapter 11).

Another way in which interest may be focused upon a particular chromosomal region is when cases of a disease are identified in association with a gross, cytogenetically identifiable, chromosomal abnormality such as a translocation or a deletion. The study of cases with deletions greatly facilitated the identification of the gene for Duchenne muscular dystrophy (Monaco *et al*, 1985). It was the discovery of two related individuals with schizophrenia associated with an unbalanced translocation of chromosome 5 (Bassett *et al*, 1988) that prompted investigators to look for linkage to markers from this region (see Chapter 5). This approach offers a potentially powerful method of locating disease genes without the need for a lengthy, labour-intensive, genome search. However, there is always the danger that researchers will be misled either by a chance association or in cases where there is a more complex causal relationship between the chromosomal abnormality and the disease in question.

Once linkage has been detected, it is possible to use a number of molecular genetic techniques to characterise the region in question further and ultimately to identify the genetic defect responsible. Detailed description of these methods is beyond the scope of the present chapter (see Collins, 1992; Strachan, 1992). In outline, they consist of the generation of more genetic markers from the region in the hope of isolating markers that are closer to the disease gene than existing linked markers. In time, markers flanking the disease locus can be identified and subsequent genetic mapping will result in the progressive reduction of the region known to contain it. This region can then be characterised by a number of molecular genetic techniques in order to detect genes within it and then to test for the presence of mutations in diseased individuals.

Once the disease causing mutation, or mutations, have been characterised, it is then possible to determine the structural or metabolic pathology that is responsible for the disease. The power of positional cloning lies in the fact that it can be conducted in the absence of *a priori* knowledge as to the disease pathogenesis. In reality, such knowledge is often available and useful in guiding molecular genetic research, and there is often a complex interplay between positional cloning and candidate gene approaches.

**Candidate gene approach**

In the candidate gene approach a polymorphism that is close to or within a gene whose involvement in the disease is suspected *a priori* is used as a genetic marker. For example, genes coding for various enzymes involved in the biosynthesis and metabolism of monoamine neurotransmitters might be relevant to psychiatric disorders such as schizophrenia and bipolar affective disorder. Obviously the likely success of this approach depends upon how well the disease pathogenesis is understood. As we shall see in Chapter 11, this approach has been successful in both Alzheimer's disease and 'prion dementia', with mutations being discovered in the amyloid precursor protein gene on chromosome 21 and the prion protein gene on chromosome 20, respectively.

**DNA markers in association studies**

The methodology of association studies is described in Chapter 3. Association studies simply compare the frequency of a marker in samples of patients and controls. In general they have played a lesser part in the recent successes of molecular genetics in Mendelian disorders than linkage studies. However, as attention is turned increasingly towards diseases with complex patterns of inheritance, association studies may assume a greater importance (Owen & McGuffin, 1992).

It is worth noting that at present the genetic map is not sufficiently dense to allow a systematic search for association to be undertaken. This would require at least 1850 evenly spaced markers (see Chapter 3). However, where candidate genes are available, association studies may well prove to be useful as in other common diseases such as insulin dependent diabetes (Cavan *et al*, 1992). Moreover, as we have seen, a number of PCR-based techniques are now available that allow the detection of allelic variation within cloned genes. This will allow association studies of variations that affect protein structure or expression in candidate genes (Sobell *et al*, 1992) which will not be dependent upon the maintenance of linkage disequilibrium between a genetic marker and the susceptibility locus.

# The study of gene expression in the central nervous system

The structure and function of an organ such as the brain depends upon the pattern of protein synthesis in its constituent cells. This in turn depends upon the pattern of gene expression within each cell. All the cells in the body contain essentially the same genes. It follows that differences in cell phenotypes must depend upon mechanisms that alter the expression of particular genes and hence the production of particular proteins. These processes will be important both during development and in response to the various stimuli that impinge upon each cell.

The study of gene expression and protein synthesis in the central nervous system (CNS) can therefore be expected to have an important role in understanding psychiatric disease. This is likely to be so not only for diseases with a major genetic component, where studies of this kind will help to bridge the gap between studies of DNA and the abnormal phenotype, but also in diseases that do not have a major genetic component, where such studies can be expected to throw light upon the pathophysiological mechanisms suggested by established neurochemical, neuropharmacological and neuropathological methods.

## Northern blotting

Messenger RNA can be extracted easily from tissue, including brain. As in the case of DNA, the complexity of the resulting mixture of molecules used to be a severe handicap to its analysis. However, the ability to isolate individual species using molecular cloning has made the task easier. Purified RNA can be separated on agarose gels and transferred to a membrane, a process known as Northern blotting! Specific RNAs can be detected by hybridisation with a radio-labelled complementary sequence. Northern blotting or similar hybridisation experiments in solution (O'Donovan *et al*, 1991) can be used to perform qualitative and quantitative comparisons of the expression of particular 'candidate' genes between brain regions or between normal and diseased brains. mRNA mixtures may also be analysed by first using them to direct protein synthesis in a cell-free system. The protein products can then be analysed themselves by two-dimensional gel electrophoresis. This may enable a specific protein or proteins involved in the pathogenesis of the disease to be identified.

Messenger RNA that has been extracted from brain can be used to construct cDNA libraries. These can be used to compare the pattern of gene expression in different situations. For example, both disease-specific changes and drug-induced effects can be studied.

## *In situ* hybridisation histochemistry

The techniques described so far are limited to the analysis of gene expression in whole brains or regions of brains. In contrast, *in situ* hybridisation histochemistry (ISHH) allows gene expression to be studied at the cellular level. In ISHH, as in Northern blotting, a labelled length of DNA or RNA is used as a probe to hybridise to, and hence detect, a complementary mRNA strand coding for a particular protein. However, in this case, hybridisation is assessed in fixed tissue sections. Thus gene probes can be used as cytochemical markers in a similar fashion to antibody probes in immunocytochemistry. However, because proteins may be transported along neuronal processes to different sites, the two techniques give complementary information. ISHH identifies the cells making a mRNA at a particular time, whereas immunocytochemistry establishes the distribution of the protein product.

## Animal studies

Unfortunately, the CNS is relatively inaccessible in living patients. It follows that the majority of studies of gene expression in the brain must be conducted on experimental animals. The application of this work to human psychiatric disease is hampered by the absence of convincing animal models. However, mRNA is surprisingly stable post-mortem and human brain tissue from autopsy can be used for studies of gene expression, including those employing ISHH. It should be remembered that gene expression can be influenced by factors such as age, medication and agonal state, for which strict controls are needed.

Another potential difficulty arises from the possibility that some mental illness may result from abnormalities of gene expression that only occur at certain stages (including prenatal) of neural development. However, in spite of these problems, the study of gene expression when used in combination with other approaches such as DNA analysis, neuro-pharmacology, neurochemistry and neuropathology should help to elucidate the connection between molecular events in neurones and disease phenotypes.

# References

Bassett, A.S., McGillivray, B.C., Jones, B.D., *et al* (1988) Partial trisomy chromosome 5 cosegregating with schizophrenia. *Lancet, i*, 799-801.

Cavan, D., Bain, S., Barnett, A., *et al* (1992) The genetics of type I (insulin dependent) diabetes mellitus. *Journal of Medical Genetics*, **29**, 441-446.

Chamberlain, S., Shaw, J., Rowland, A., *et al* (1988) Mapping of mutation causing Friedreich's ataxia to human chromosome 9. *Nature*, **334**, 248-250.

Collins, F.S. (1992) Positional cloning: let's not call it reverse any more. *Nature Genetics*, **1**, 3-6.

Goate, A.M., Haynes, A., Owen, M.J., *et al* (1989) Predisposing locus for Alzheimer's disease on chromosome 21. *Lancet, i*, 352-355.

Hall, J.G. (1990) Genomic imprinting: review and relevance to human diseases. *American Journal of Human Genetics*, **46**, 857-853.

Harley, H.G., Brook, J.D., Rundle, S.A., *et al* (1992) Expansion of an unstable DNA region and phenotypic variation in myotonic dystrophy, *Nature*, **355**, 545-546.

Harper, S., Harley, H., Reardon, W., *et al* (1992) Anticipation in myotonic dystrophy: new light on an old problem. *American Journal of Human Genetics*, **51**, 10-16.

Knudson, A.G. (1986) Genetics of human cancer. *Journal of Cell Physiology*, **7** (suppl. 4), 7-11.

Monaco, A.P., Bertelson, C.J., Middlesworth, W., *et al* (1985) Detection of deletions spanning the Duchenne muscular dystrophy locus using a tightly linked DNA segment. *Nature*, **316**, 842-845.

O'Donovan, M.C., Buckland, P.R. & McGuffin, P. (1991) Simultaneous quantification of several mRNA species by solution hybridisation with oligonucleotides. *Nucleic Acids Research*, **19**, 34-46.

Owen, M.J. & McGuffin, P. (1992) The molecular genetics of schizophrenia. *British Medical Journal*, **305**, 664-665.

Reik, W., Collick, A., Norris, M.L., *et al* (1987) Genomic imprinting determines methylation at parental alleles in transgenic mice. *Nature*, **328**, 248-251.

Ridley, R.M., Frith, C.D., Crow, T.J., *et al* (1988) Anticipation in Huntington's disease is inherited through the male line but many originate in the female. *Journal of Medical Genetics*, **25**, 589-595.

Sampson, J., Scarhill, J., Stevenson, J., *et al* (1989) Genetics of tuberous sclerosis in the West of Scotland. *Journal of Medical Genetics*, **26**, 28-31.

Sobell, J.L., Heston, L.I. & Sommer, S.S. (1992) Delineation of genetic predisposition to multifactorial disease: a general approach on the threshold of feasibility. *Genomics*, **12**, 1-6.

Strachan, T. (1992) *The Human Genome*. Medical Perspectives Series.

Weber, J. & May, P.E. (1989) Abundant class of human DNA polymorphisms which can be typed using the polymerase chain reaction. *American Journal of Human Genetics*, **14**, 388-396.

Weissenbach, J., Gyapay, G., Dib, C., *et al* (1992) A second generation linkage map of the human genome. *Nature*, **359**, 794-801.

White, T.J., Arnheim, N. & Erlich, H.A. (1989) *Trends in Genetics*, **5**, 185.

# 2 Quantitative genetics

*Family studies • Twin studies • Adoption studies • Formal genetics: patterns of transmission • Path analysis: estimating h² and c² • Multiple thresholds and heterogeneity • Model fitting*

In essence human genetics is the study of traits that show quantitative or qualitative variability in the population and familial aggregation. This aggregation or resemblance can occur because of shared genes, shared environment or a combination of the two. Although the main focus traditionally has been on genetic causes of familial resemblance, it is unwise when dealing with complex traits such as psychiatric disorders to focus entirely on nature and ignore nurture. Therefore the task of psychiatric genetics is twofold:

(1)  there is a need to discover *whether* genes contribute to psychiatric disorders or other traits of interest
(2)  it is necessary to discover *how* genes result in disorder (i.e. to understand their mechanisms of action and to unravel the modes of coaction and interaction with environment and experience).

The traditional methods of study in psychiatric genetics involve investigations of families, twins, and adoptees. Family studies allow us to say whether familial aggregation occurs and to what extent, while twin and adoption studies provide two forms of 'natural experiments' which enable us to tease apart the effects of shared genes and shared environment.

## Family studies

Family studies compare the frequency of a disorder (or trait) in the relatives of affected index cases, or *probands*, with the frequency in a sample of individuals drawn from the general or control population. Alternatively a comparison is made with the frequency of the disorder in relatives of healthy control probands or the relatives of patients suffering from an entirely different disease. The easiest and least expensive approach is to take a history from the proband but this usually underestimates the frequency of psychopathology among relatives (i.e. most people know much more about themselves than do any of their family). The accuracy of the *family history* method can be improved by interviewing first-degree relative informants in addition to the proband. However, the most

---

**Box 2.1 Weinberg's shorter method of age correction**

Let number of affected relatives of a certain class (e.g. siblings, offspring, etc.) = *A*, and number of unaffected relatives of the same class = *U*.

Uncorrected frequency (*F*) of affected relatives = $A/(A+U)$

However, the *U* relatives are of three types: (a) $u_1$ are younger than the age of risk, (b) $u_2$ are within the period of risk (say, 15–55 years for a disorder such as schizophrenia), (c) $u_3$ are older than the period of risk.

Thus *F* provides an underestimate of lifetime incidence. This can be corrected by assigning weights to the number of unaffected persons in each age group as follows: (a) 0, (b) ½, (c) 1.

Then the corrected frequency of affected relatives, or morbid risk (MR), is given by:

$$MR = A/(A + \tfrac{1}{2} u_2 + u_3)$$

The corrected denominator is often referred to as the *Bezugsziffer*, or BZ.

---

satisfactory approach is to interview personally all available relatives: *the family study method.* Nowadays it is usual to use structured or semi-structured interviews and to apply reliable operational diagnostic criteria. In addition, register-based material may be useful, such as national or local case registers, and it is essential to scrutinise hospital notes if they are available.

## Ascertainment

Careful thought must also be given to how probands are *ascertained* or selected for inclusion in the sample. The most important principle is that each proband is ascertained independently of all other probands. This does not usually present a problem when a disorder is comparatively uncommon and where the probability of ascertainment is low. Here there is never more than one proband in any family, a situation described as *single* ascertainment.

Where a disorder is comparatively common and where the systematic method of sampling entails, for example, collecting a consecutive series of patients with a certain disorder referred to a certain district hospital, then it is quite possible for some families to contain more than one proband. This is referred to as *multiple incomplete ascertainment* to distinguish it from the (rarely achieved) situation of *complete ascertainment,* when all affected individuals within a certain population are included in the sample.

### Prevalence

A further problem in genetic research is that it is of more interest to know the proportion of individuals who have *ever* had a disorder at any time in their life up to the time of interview (*lifetime prevalence*) than merely to discover the proportion who are ill at the time of interview (*point prevalence*). But even lifetime prevalence is not a wholly satisfactory statistic since some family members at the time of the study will be unaffected but may develop the disorder at a future date and others may have already died while unaffected. The probability of this occurring will depend upon the age of the individual and the extent to which he/she has lived through the period of risk for the disorder.

The most useful way of expressing rates of illness in relatives is as *morbid risk*, which is also sometimes called *lifetime incidence* or *lifetime expectancy.* Various methods of age correcting have been devised to estimate morbid risk but the most straightforward is the shorter method devised by Weinberg, a German physician. Here the lifetime prevalence, or total $n$ of relatives ever affected/total $n$ of relatives, is converted into a morbid risk by correcting the denominator downwards to approximate the number of observed lifetimes at risk. The corrected denominator, or *Bezugsziffer* (BZ), is calculated by assigning weights to the relatives, dependent on their age at the time of study. This is summarised in Box 2.1.

Other methods of age correcting include the Slater–Strömgren method, which is an elaboration of the shorter Weinberg approach, life tables, for example the longer Weinberg morbidity table, and a method proposed by Kaplan & Meier.

# Twin studies

Identical or monozygotic (MZ) twins are the products of the fertilisation of a single egg by a single sperm and therefore have 100% of their genes in common, whereas fraternal or dizygotic (DZ) twins, like full siblings, are from two eggs and two sperms and share on average, 50% of their genes. Assuming both types of twin share common environmental effects to an approximately similar extent, any greater similarities for a particular trait shown by MZ pairs compared with DZ pairs will be due to genetic influences. DZ twins may be of the same or opposite sex and the frequency of DZ twins varies around the world. However, in Western European populations about 1 delivery in 100 results in a pair of twins (roughly 2 DZ to every MZ pair).

For continuous traits such as IQ or personality test scores that have normal distribution (i.e. bell shaped or Gaussian) in the population, similarity within pairs is expressed by the *intra-class correlation coefficient*.

## Concordance

For dichotomous or present/absent traits such as a full-blown psychiatric disorder, similarity between probands and co-twins is expressed as a concordance rate. Sometimes a *pair-wise concordance* rate is reported, signifying the number of pairs both having the diagnosis divided by the total number of pairs. However, it is preferable to report *proband-wise concordance*. This is where the number of affected twins is divided by the total number of co-twins. It is a common source of confusion that these methods may give somewhat different answers. This is because the proband-wise method is appropriately applied when there has been systematic ascertainment from a twin register. Consequently, it sometimes occurs that both members of a concordant pair are included independently in the same series as probands and hence such pairs are counted twice. The aim here is not to inflate the concordance rate spuriously or exaggerate the evidence of a genetic effect; in fact it is quite the reverse.

Twin series ascertained in a non-systematic way tend to be biased towards including the most memorable or conspicuous pairs of twins. For example, if a researcher invites colleagues to refer twins with a certain disorder there is likely to be an excess of pairs who are both MZ and concordant. Ascertainment via a hospital register which lists consecutively all new patients who are twins or from a national or district-based register guards against this bias.

A further possible source of error is mis-specification of zygosity. In some earlier studies this was simply based on similarity of appearance, but there is an obvious hazard if a single investigator diagnoses both psychopathology and zygosity. The problem is best overcome by using objective methods. In the past, fingerprint pattern and ridge count or anthropometric measure have been used. However, it is preferable to rely on red cell types or other genetic markers in the blood or best of all to perform 'DNA fingerprinting' which makes use of minisatellite polymorphisms and is a method of simultaneously examining 30 or more marker loci (see Chapter I).

A less expensive and reasonably reliable alternative is simply to use a similarities questionnaire (e.g. "Were you as alike as two peas in a pod? Are you often mistaken for each other? Do you have the same eye/hair colour?" etc.) (Goldsmith, 1991).

As in family studies, a standardised method of recording and interpreting clinical data is desirable in twin studies and so, where possible, investigators now use structured interviews and apply operational diagnostic criteria. It is also important to try to reduce bias by having blind diagnoses, where each twin is examined by an investigator ignorant of the zygosity or the clinical details of the co-twin. In practice this may be difficult to achieve and the problem of blindness is at least partially overcome by preparing detailed case abstracts from which identifying information and zygosity are removed and having these assessed by independent raters.

## Environment

One of the most frequent criticisms of twin studies is that MZ pairs may be treated more alike by their parents, may dress more alike, and may share a special 'micro-environment' to a greater degree than DZ pairs. There have been various attempts to study this problem. For example, Loehlin & Nichols (1976) asked the parents of MZ and DZ twins to rate their similarity on environmental factors. As expected, the MZ twins proved to be slightly more similar than the DZ pairs but within the MZ group there appeared to be no relationship between degree of similarity for environmental sharing and the size of correlation for cognitive traits and personality. Similarly McGuffin *et al* (1993), using a brief structured interview to assess family environment, found evidence of slight but significant differences regarding early environmental sharing in MZ compared with DZ twins in a study of depression in adults. However, differences in environmental sharing could not account for the differences between MZ and DZ twins regarding concordance for depressive disorder.

An interesting way of assessing the effects of environmental sharing is to study twins who are mistaken about their zygosity and who have assumed that they are dizygotic when they are actually monozygotic or vice versa. In a study of adolescent twin pairs a surprisingly high proportion, nearly 40%, were mistaken (Scarr & Carter–Saltzman, 1979). However, non-identical (DZ) twins who thought they were identical (MZ) were no more alike in cognitive tests than DZ pairs who were correct about their zygosity. Similarly, identical (MZ) pairs who incorrectly believed themselves to be non-identical showed only slightly greater differences than MZ pairs who were not mistaken about their zygosity.

A more radical method of overcoming the alleged problem of environmental sharing is to study monozygotic twins reared apart (MZA). Unfortunately MZA pairs are rare, the degree of separation is often incomplete, and with a few exceptions the methods of ascertainment in MZA twin studies have been haphazard, involving, for example, advertisements in newspapers, television or radio. Nevertheless, cautiously interpreted against a background of evidence from other sources, studies of MZA twins have provided confirmatory information in such areas as the study of intelligence, personality and psychosis.

Finally, isolated case reports of twins or of two or three pairs are not uncommon in the literature, especially when dealing with relatively rare conditions. The value of these is somewhat limited and again there is a tendency to be biased towards 'conspicuous' (MZ-concordant) pairs. Therefore it is important to be wary in interpreting 'twin series' which are actually compilations of twin reports from various sources. Nevertheless, a report of a single discordant MZ pair who have lived through the period of risk for a disorder provides strong evidence that the condition is not entirely genetically determined. By the same token, studies which concentrate on discordant MZ pairs can potentially provide important information about non-genetic contributors to a disease (Torrey *et al*, 1994).

Other new variations on twin strategies can be found in the overview by Kendler (1993).

## Adoption studies

For some tastes adoption studies provide a cleaner, crisper separation between the effects of genes and those of family environment. The approach is to focus on individuals who have been fostered or adopted in early life and on both their adopted and biological families. There are three commonly used designs:

(1) *the adoptee study* – the adopted away offspring of affected parents are studied and compared with control adoptees of normal parentage
(2) *the adoptee's family study* – the index cases are adopted people who have developed a disorder of interest; the rates of illness are then compared in their biological and adopted relatives
(3) *the cross-fostering study* – the rate of illness in adoptees who have affected biological parents but who were raised by unaffected adopting parents, are compared with the rates of illness in the offspring of normal parents brought up by adopting parents who themselves become affected (this is the least common design).

Adoption studies have the potential benefit of allowing investigation of both genetic endowment and environment of rearing in circumstances where these are clearly separate. In particular, if cross-fostering designs are applied it is possible to study gene–environment interactions. As with family and twin studies, it is desirable to use explicit standardised methods of diagnosis. However, one of the drawbacks of adoption studies is that adoption is in many senses an abnormal event and such studies tend to find higher general rates of psychopathology (especially antisocial traits), even among control adoptees, than in the population at large. A further complication is that placement of adoptees is not random and there may be a tendency for adoption agencies to seek what they regard as a good match for physical, social, ethnic or other characteristics between the adoptee and prospective parents. Nevertheless, adoption studies have proved useful in confirming a genetic contribution to IQ and have been particularly influential in the evidence they provided for genetic contributions to schizophrenia and to alcoholism.

# Formal genetics: patterns of transmission

We have already noted that most psychiatric disorders are complex traits where if genes play a part, they do so in concert with the environment (including prenatal environment). Family, twin and adoption studies may converge to allow us to infer whether or not there is a genetic contribution to a disorder and can be interpreted in this simple way without much knowledge of formal genetics. However, in order to understand more fully how characteristics are passed on from one generation to the next we need to discuss mechanisms and patterns of genetic transmission. The modern study of formal genetics began with the botanical experiments of Gregor Mendel, which were published in 1866. Mendel was an Augustinian abbot who worked in comparative isolation and obscurity in Brno, Moravia (now in the Czech Republic) and his results were almost totally ignored for more than 30 years. When they were rediscovered in 1900 they initiated a revolutionary effect and signalled the beginning of a new science which in 1905 William Bateson named 'genetics'. The term 'gene' for Mendel's causal units was coined in 1909 by Wilhelm Johannsen, who also made the important distinction between *phenotype*, the observed trait, and *genotype,* the genetic endowment.

## Mendel's laws

Mendel in reaching his particulate theory of inheritance chose to work with clear-cut dichotomous phenotypes in pea plants. These included characteristics such as smooth versus wrinkled coat and tall versus short (which, we should note, is not a simple dichotomous trait in humans). He first observed that there was *uniformity* of outcome in the first generation (F1) of offspring when parents of different types (e.g. smooth *versus* wrinkled) were crossed (Table 2.1).

Mendel inferred that uniformity occurred because one phenotype was *dominant* and the other *recessive*, such that all *homozygous* parents of the types AA and aa produce *heterozygous* offspring, Aa, and resemble the AA parent rather than displaying a phenotype that is intermediate between those of the parents.

However, when an intercross was carried out between pairs of F1 generation plants, *segregation* could be demonstrated with the ratio of

**Table 2.1** Mendelian laws

| Laws | | Comments |
|---|---|---|
| *Uniformity* | | |
| Parents | AA x aa | Two alternative genes (alleles), A, a, at one locus. Each parent has a double dose of different alleles (homozygotes) |
| Offspring | Aa | All offspring are of the same type (heterozygotes) |
| *Segregation* | | |
| Parents | Aa x Aa | Parents both heterozygotes |
| Offspring | AA Aa aA aa | Three possible types of offspring with probability of occurrence = 1:2:1 |
| *Independent assortment* | | |
| Parents | AaBb x aabb | Two loci with alleles A, a and B, b, double heterozygote x double homozygote parents |
| Offspring | AaBb aaBb Aabb aabb | Four possible types of offspring, each with equal probability of occurrence |

offspring (F2) showing the recessive character to those showing the dominant character being 1:3. At the genotypic level Mendel inferred there were three possible types of F2 offspring, with the probability of occurrence of 1:2:1.

Finally, Mendel showed that if two different traits are studied at the same time they generally show *independent assortment*. We now know this law holds when the traits are coded for by two or more alternative genes, or *alleles*, which occupy points on a chromosome, or *loci*, which are either far apart or are on completely different chromosomes. Independent assortment can be most clearly shown in a series of so-called double backcross matings where one set of parents are doubly heterozygous, having different alleles at each of the pair of loci, while the other parents are doubly homozygous, having the same alleles at both loci. There are four possible, equally frequent genotypes in the offspring (Table 2.1).

## Sex-linked traits

We also need to consider the special cases of Mendelian inheritance when the locus is on the X chromosome. Normal females have a pair of X chromosomes while normal males have one X and one Y chromosome. Males are therefore effectively *hemizygous* for any characteristic on the X chromosome and this can only be received from their mother. Hence a recessive trait carried on the X chromosome, for example colour blindness, will always be expressed in males who inherit such a chromosome. In turn, all of the daughters of such an affected male will be unaffected *carriers* (assuming their mother is neither affected nor a carrier) but none of his sons will be either affected or carriers (since only a Y chromosome is transmitted from father to son).

On average, half of the male offspring of a carrier female will be affected, assuming that their father is unaffected. Dominant X-linked transmission is rare, but has sometimes been invoked as a possible mode of transmission of bipolar affective disorder (see Chapter 6). Again, the essential hallmark of a potential X-linked pedigree is absence of father–son transmission.

## Recessive disease

In practice most diseases showing simple Mendelian inheritance are comparatively uncommon individually, but collectively they impose a large burden (McKusick, 1992). Recessive disorders usually arise in the offspring of two unaffected 'carrier' parents and on average show a ratio of affected to unaffected individuals of 1:3. Phenylketonuria (PKU) (1 in 10 000) and Wilson's disease (1 in 30 000) are two well known examples of recessive disease of psychiatric relevance (see Chapter 4). The frequency of recessive disorder is increased in populations where there are high rates of consanguineous (e.g. cousin–cousin) marriage. Such *inbred* populations will tend to show a higher frequency of homozygosity at all loci and hence higher rates of recessive disease.

## Dominant disorders

In dominant disorders the most common occurrence is that one parent is an affected heterozygote and the other an unaffected homozygote. Offspring are then produced in the ratio of affected to unaffected of 1:1. Therefore, unlike recessive conditions, dominant traits do not 'skip' generations, and if a typical dominant condition arises in someone with unaffected parents it must be inferred that this is either a fresh mutation or a *phenocopy* (i.e. a phenotypically indistinguishable disorder in the absence of the genotype). Huntington's disease (HD) (1 in 20 000) and acute intermittent porphyria (1 in 30 000) are dominant conditions which may commonly present with psychiatric symptoms. Other examples of dominant conditions causing mental handicap are discussed in Chapter 4. 'Fragile X' syndrome is the commonest (1 in 1250 males) condition carried on the X chromosome resulting in low intelligence and Lesch–Nyhan syndrome (<1 in 1 000 000 males) is an example of a rarer but more typically clear-cut X-linked recessive disorder resulting in low intelligence and self-mutilation (see Chapter 4).

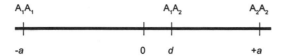

**Fig. 2.1** A phenotype measured on a continuous scale, resulting from a single gene with two alleles, A$_1$ and A$_2$.

## Continuous phenotypes

Many measurable human characteristics such as height, weight, blood pressure or scores on IQ tests are continuously distributed and it is difficult at first sight to reconcile the possibility of genetic transmission with Mendelian principles which, after all, were based upon the study of dichotomous characteristics. Let us therefore consider the case of a single locus with two alleles A$_1$ and A$_2$, coding for a phenotype measured on a continuous scale as shown in Fig 2.1.

As before, there are three possible genotypes but their respective phenotypes, rather than being qualitative (or discontinuous), now differ quantitatively with respect to their values on the phenotypic scale. A$_1$A$_1$ has a value of -$a$ and A$_2$A$_2$ a value of +$a$ while the heterozygote A$_1$A$_2$ has a value of $d$. When $d = 0$, i.e. A$_1$A$_2$ is exactly mid-way between two homozygotes, we can say that the genetic contribution to the phenotype is entirely *additive*. If $d = -a$ then this would in effect be the same as A$_2$ being a classically recessive gene with respect to A$_1$ whereas if $d = +a$ the reverse is true and A$_2$ is completely dominant. If on the other hand d lies somewhere between 0 and -$a$, or between 0 and +$a$ then both *dominance* and *additive* effects have to be considered in accounting for phenotypic variation.

Let us suppose for the sake of simplicity that we have purely additive gene effects and that the two alleles A$_1$ and A$_2$ have frequencies in the population of $p$ and $q$ respectively which add up to 1 (hence $q = 1 - p$). Assuming that there is no inbreeding and no migration, mutation or selection against any genotypes, they would be distributed in the population as follows:

genotypes:  A$_1$A$_1$    A$_1$A$_2$    A$_2$A$_2$

frequency:  $p^2$    $2pq$    $q^2$

This is known as the *Hardy–Weinberg equilibrium* (discovered independently by Hardy, a British mathematician, and the same Weinberg who described age correction). Let us simplify further and assume that

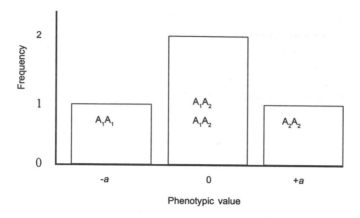

**Fig. 2.2** Frequency of phenotype values of a continuous trait: one locus.

$p = q = 0.5$. We would then have three phenotypic values distributed in the population in the relative frequencies of 1:2:1 and shown in Fig. 2.2.

Let us now extend this idea to a continuous trait with contributions from two loci each having two alleles of equal frequency and additive effect. What then would be the distribution in the population? This is shown in Fig. 2.3, where we see that there are now five possible phenotypic

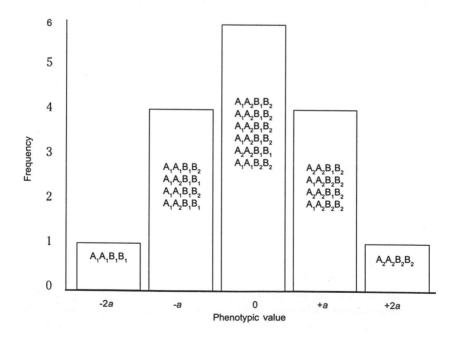

**Fig. 2.3** Frequency of phenotypic values of a continuous trait: two loci.

values occurring in the relative frequencies of 1:4:6:4:1. In general, if there are $n$ loci there are $2n + 1$ possible phenotypic values. Hence it is possible to envisage that as the number of loci contributing to the overall phenotypic distribution increases then the closer is the approximation to a normal distribution. It is thought that most continuously distributed inherited traits are *polygenic,* resulting from the mainly additive combination of many genes at different loci. When the phenotype is due to the combination of polygenes as well as environmental contributors the term *multifactorial* inheritance is used.

## Components of variation in quantitative traits

We have already stated that any phenotype (P) must be considered as resulting from the combination of genotype (G) and the environment (E) to which that genotype is exposed. This can be summarised as:

$$P = G + E$$

In quantitative genetics the aim is usually to explain the variation of a phenotype $(V_p)$ in the population and so we can rewrite the equation as

$$V_p = V_g + V_e$$

where $V_g$ is the genetic variance and $V_e$ is the variance due to environment. (In fact, this is an oversimplification, since we have left out the non-additive terms due to gene–environment covariance and gene–environment interaction. We shall ignore these for now but come back to them later.)

As we have seen earlier, the genetic contributions to a continuous trait comprise both additive and dominance components, so that $V_g$ is made up of variance due to additive gene effects $(V_a)$ and dominance variance $(V_d)$.

The *heritability* $(h^2)$ of a trait is defined as the proportion of total phenotype variance accounted for by additive gene effects, i.e. $h^2 = V_a/V_p$. It may be of interest to know the degree of total genetic determination of a trait, $V_g/V_p$. This is also often referred to as the *broad heritability,* but of course if the genetic effects are purely additive, heritability and broad heritability are the same.

It is also important to recognise that there are two main contributors to environmental variance. These are variance due to common or shared family environment $(V_{ce})$ and environment which is specific to the individual and not shared with other family members $(V_{ns})$. Just as it may be of interest to estimate heritability we might also wish to know how much of the phenotypic variance of a trait is contributed by common environment within families. This is usually denoted by $c^2$, where:

$$c^2 = V_{ce} / V_p$$

A trait may be familial because $h^2$, or $c^2$, or both are greater than 0. However, it is important to note that the terms $h^2$ or $c^2$ refer to the proportion of variance accounted for in a *population*. Thus heritability does not have a simple meaning at the individual level. For example, suppose that we found a heritability for IQ of 0.5 in a certain population. We cannot then take an individual member of that population and declare that half of his IQ score is determined by his genes. Similarly heritability is specific to the population in which it is estimated and other populations may differ with respect to $V_g$ or $V_e$ or both, and hence heritabilities will differ too.

## Path analysis: estimating $h^2$ and $c^2$

Various ways have been devised to estimate the size of genetic and environmental components of variance but probably the most straightforward and easy to grasp, because it is based on simple diagrams, is called path analysis. For example, the phenotype of an individual, P, is contributed to by his genotype, G, environment shared with his family, CE, and non-shared environment, NS, as shown in Fig. 2.4. The letters ($h$, $c$ and $s$) alongside the arrows from these variables to the phenotype are called path coefficients. (For readers familiar with multiple regression analysis, these are the same as partial regression coefficients or 'beta weights'.)

Let us now consider a pair of siblings (phenotypes $P_1$ and $P_2$) and, keeping the diagrams simple, we will just concentrate on the factors causing them to resemble each other, i.e. their genotypes, $G_1$ and $G_2$, and their shared environment CE. These are represented in Fig. 2.5. The simple rules of path analysis dictate that the correlation between $P_1$ and $P_2$, $r_{12}$, is given by the sum of the connecting paths, thus:

$$r_{12} = B \times h \times h + c \times c = B\,h^2 + c^2$$

where $B$ is the correlation between genotypes.

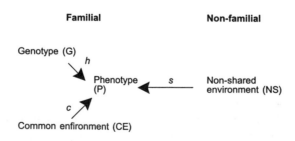

**Fig. 2.4** Contributions to the phenotype P – a path diagram.

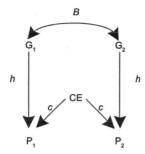

**Fig. 2.5** A simple path model of the sources of resemblance between twins or pairs of siblings. $G_1$ and $G_2$ are genotypes with correlation $B$, CE is common environment, $P_1$ and $P_2$ are phenotypes and $h$ and $c$ are path coefficients.

We know that the genotypic correlation between full siblings or DZ twins is 0.5, i.e. on average they have 50% of their genes in common. Similarly MZ twins have 100% of their genes in common and so their genetic correlation is 1. Therefore if we have carried out a twin study, let us say of IQ, we would expect the correlation for DZ twins, $r_{DZ}$, to be:

$$r_{DZ} = \tfrac{1}{2} h^2 + c^2$$

and the correlation for MZ twins, $r_{MZ}$, to be

$$r_{MZ} = h^2 + c^2$$

By substitution and rearrangement it is easy to show that

$$h^2 = 2\ (r_{MZ} - r_{DZ})$$

and

$$c^2 = 2\ r_{DZ} - r_{MZ}$$

hence we can use twin data to estimate what proportion of the variation in a trait can be explained by genes ($h^2$), shared environment ($c^2$) and residual or non-shared environment ($1 - [h^2 + c^2]$).

In Table 2.2, we set out some examples of how, for a variety of traits, correlations on pairs of twins can provide estimates of these various components. The IQ data are taken from a compilation by Bouchard & McGue (1981) and the correlations are weighted means from a large number of studies of twins reared together. They suggest a pattern that the reader may intuitively expect, that IQ scores are influenced by both genetic factors and shared environment together with some unshared or residual affects. However, the personality test scores for extraversion provide a

**Table 2.2** Variance components for continuous traits (see text for sources of data)

| Trait | $r_{MZ}$ | $r_{DZ}$ | $h^2$ | $c^2$ |
|---|---|---|---|---|
| IQ | 0.86 | 0.6 | 0.52 | 0.34 |
| Extraversion (E) | 0.51 | 0.21 | 0.60 | 0.00 |
| Bulimia | 0.28 | 0.26 | 0.04 | 0.24 |
| Religious involvement | 0.60 | 0.58 | 0.04 | 0.56 |

$r_{MZ}$, $r_{DZ}$ = monozygotic and dizygotic twin correlations, respectively.
$h^2$ = heritability.
$c^2$ = proportion of variance explained by family (shared) environment.

different pattern of correlations (from Martin & Jardine, 1986). Here the $h^2$ component is substantial but the common environmental component is zero. (In fact, the above formula for $c^2$ results in a negative value but this is statistically meaningless and the value in the table is therefore set at 0.)

This result of an environmental contribution consisting entirely of non-shared effects will probably look surprising to most readers who are new to behaviour genetics. However, it is completely consistent with almost all genetic studies of personality traits conducted so far (Plomin *et al*, 1991) (see also Chapter 8). The two other characteristics, bulimia scores on an eating disorder inventory (Rutherford *et al*, 1993) and religious involvement (Loehlin & Nichols, 1976) provide examples of traits which appear to be familial ($c^2$ of 0.24 and 0.56, respectively) but where there is a negligible genetic contribution. This again demonstrates that some traits may show familial resemblance but are not necessarily genetic.

## Non-additive effects

In practice the interplay between genes and environment is often more complex than the simple additive situation just described. We have already mentioned that non-additive genetic effects may include dominance. However, there is also a possibility of *epistasis* or gene–gene interactions between different loci. Similarly there may be gene–environment *interactions* as opposed to just simple genes + environment *co-actions*. The phenomenon of gene–environment interaction is well described in experimental animals. For example, pure-bred strains of mice differ markedly on certain tasks such as time taken to find food in a maze. Henderson (1970) has shown that all of several strains perform better when reared in an enriched environment than when reared in a standard environment. However, the degree of improvement differed greatly. Some genotypes showed a pronounced difference in performance in the two environments while others showed only a modest improvement in the enriched environment. If the gene–environment combination was purely additive a parallel improvement across all genotypes would have been seen. However, in this instance mouse genotypes permit individualised phenotypic *reaction ranges* (Gottesman, 1963) when exposed to different environments.

A further possibility is that genotype and environment are correlated. For example, we could speculate that in certain circumstances bright children might elicit responses in their parents or teachers which cause them to provide more educational stimulation than is usually given to less bright children. Therefore the overall variation in intelligence in children might have a component due to *gene–environment covariance*, that is, the genotype influences the type of environment to which it is exposed.

## Irregular phenotypes and threshold models

Common familial disorders typically do not show Mendelian segregation with obvious 25% or 50% risks in siblings, and therefore are sometimes described as irregular phenotypes. Neither can they be described as continuous traits, since in the population people are classified as either affected or unaffected. However, psychiatric disorders and many common medical disorders can be thought of as *quasi-continuous* in the sense that the affected portion of the population can often be graded along a mild to severe continuum. We might go further and postulate that there is an underlying *liability to develop the disorder* which is continuously distributed in the population even though it cannot be directly measured. Only those whose liability at some stage exceeds a certain *threshold* manifest the condition. This is illustrated in Fig. 2.6. If the underlying liability is polygenic

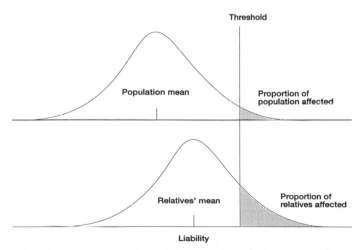

**Fig. 2.6** A polygenic or multifactorial (MF) threshold model of disease transmission.

or multifactorial (MF) then it can be reasonably assumed to have a normal distribution (or one that can be transformed to a normality). Relatives of affected individuals have an increase in their mean genetic liability compared with the general population and hence their overall distribution is shifted to the right in Fig. 2.6 with the resultant increase in the frequency of being affected compared with the general population. Knowing the proportion of affected individuals in the general population and the proportion of affected relatives of probands it is possible to estimate the *correlation in liability* between pairs of relatives (Falconer, 1965; Reich *et al*, 1972).

An alternative explanation of apparently non-Mendelian patterns of transmission is of single major locus (SML) inheritance modified by *variable expression* or *incomplete penetrance*. Neurofibromatosis is a good example of a gene showing variable expression which may range from a full-blown disorder to just a few *cafe-au-lait* spots on the skin. *Penetrance* is the probability of manifesting a trait given a certain genotype, and for Mendelian disorders this is always either 0 or 1. Irregular patterns of transmission however may occur because of *incomplete penetrance* where the probability of manifesting the trait is greater than 0 but less than 1. Both regular Mendelian and irregular non-Mendelian patterns can be thought of as subforms of the general single major locus (SML) model summarised below (Table 2.3).

If a trait is influenced by environmental factors we can again consider the SML model as a type of liability/threshold model and this is illustrated in Fig. 2.7, where the three genotypes have differing mean liabilities with variation about the mean contributed by non-familial environment. Note the lack of determinism or 'inevitability' implied by this model. Even though one locus is very important in the aetiology, some $A_2A_2$ people are spared the illness and some $A_1A_2$ people become affected.

**Table 2.3** Penetrances (probabilities of being affected) in simple Mendelian and general single major locus (SML) models of disease

| Model | Genotypes | | |
|---|---|---|---|
| | $A_1A_1$ | $A_1A_2$ | $A_2A_2$ |
| Recessive | 0 | 0 | 1 |
| Dominant | 0 | 1 | 1 |
| General | $0 \leq f_1 \leq 1$ | $0 \leq f_2 \leq 1$ | $0 \leq f_3 \leq 1$ |

Note: A penetrance of 1 means that all individuals of this phenotype are affected while zero penetrance means that none are affected. However, in the general model the penetrances ($f_1$, $f_2$, $f_3$) can theoretically take any value between 0 and 1.

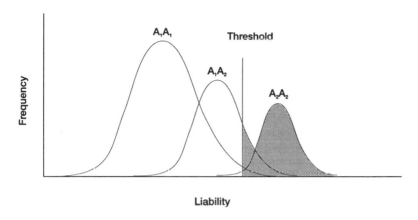

**Fig. 2.7** A general two-allele single major locus (SML) model. Only those beyond the threshold are affected.

An SML kind of model has been put forward as a possible explanation of transmission of schizophrenia, bipolar affective disorder, and familial or early-onset forms of Alzheimer's disease as well as a variety of other common conditions such as diabetes mellitus. As we will see later, the SML model provides the theoretical basis for the application of genetic linkage strategies to the study of complex disorders. However, it is important to note than in its pure form the SML model states that a single gene is the *only* source of resemblance between relatives, i.e. that family environment and polygenic or 'background' genetic effects do not exist. As a more comprehensive alternative which may seem more plausible, the notion of 'mixed model' inheritance has been put forward (Morton, 1982) where both a major gene and polygenic and/or multifactorial environment may contribute to the familiality of a trait. In other words the penetrance of the major gene is influenced by the action of polygenes and/or multifactorial environmental effects. Lastly it may be that irregular phenotypes such as schizophrenia result from the co-action or interaction of a handful of genes (Gottesman & Shields, 1972; Risch, 1990). Such *oligogenic* models are difficult to distinguish statistically from mixed or classical polygenic models that assume many loci. However, resolution by linkage analysis is a feasible prospect, as we discuss in Chapter 3.

## Multiple thresholds and heterogeneity

It seems likely that most psychiatric disorders, like other common familial illness, will turn out to be heterogeneous. For example, there are already strong suggestions from linkage studies of the existence of more than one type of what we currently lump together as Alzheimer's disease (see Chapter

11). Similarly, recent studies suggest that there are early-onset genetic forms of common cancer (e.g. breast, colon) which may differ aetiologically from later-onset non-familial types. Diabetes mellitus has for some time been subdivided into insulin dependent and non-insulin dependent types on clinical grounds, but association studies, first with human leukocyte antigen (HLA) types and more recently with other genetic markers, have firmly established the existence of genetic heterogeneity.

The place of linkage and association studies in psychiatry will be discussed in Chapter 3. Here we will briefly consider statistical approaches to resolving heterogeneity using *multiple threshold* analysis. In doing this we need to remember that the opposite of genetic heterogeneity (one syndrome, many causes) is pleiotropy (one cause having multiple effects). For example, let us consider a disorder which appears to segregate in families in two or more forms. We might have one common, mild form of disorder (the broad form) and another less common but more severe type (the narrow form). If we assume that the two disorders actually occupy the same continuum of liability, we could invoke a multiple threshold model where we would expect more affected relatives in the families of narrow-form probands than in the families of broad-form probands (Fig. 2.8). It has been found for example that the relatives of typical or 'nuclear' schizophrenics are more often affected than are the relatives of those suffering from less severe or 'peripheral' schizophrenia (Kallman, 1938) and that the proportions are those predicted by a simple two-threshold model (McGuffin *et al*, 1987).

Similarly, it has been pointed out (Carter, 1969) that where a familial disorder is more common in one sex than the other, then probands of the less commonly affected sex might be expected to have more affected relatives than probands of the more commonly affected sex. An ingenious set of variations on the theme of multiple threshold models has been devised by Reich *et al* (1979) and have been used to show, for example,

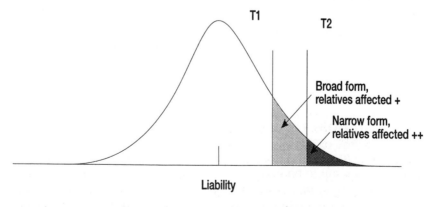

**Fig. 2.8** A two-threshold model, with thresholds T1 and T2

that the differences in prevalence of alcoholism between men and women needs to be explained by a more complex model where the increased risk in men is contributed by non-familial environmental exposure (Reich *et al*, 1979; Cloninger *et al*, 1983). Similarly an application of threshold models was used to demonstrate that alcoholism and affective disorder, although sometimes observed to cluster in the same families, are independent conditions which do not occupy the same continuum of liability (Cloninger *et al*, 1979). Independence (i.e. aetiological heterogeneity) can be inferred in threshold analysis if the cross-correlations between the two forms of disorder do not differ significantly from zero.

# Model fitting

The advent of high-speed computers has led to considerable advances in the investigation of complex modes of transmission of common familial disorders. Although the details of the statistical approaches are complicated, the general principles are fairly straightforward and can be understood without recourse to any complicated mathematics. Broadly, there are two rather different aims in fitting statistical models. The first is to use observations on the resemblance between relatives for particular traits to attempt to fit multiple threshold models like those just discussed, or to *partition the variation* in the phenotype using path analytic models. The second aim is to attempt to resolve major gene effects and to determine, for example, whether a disorder is most likely to be explained by polygenic inheritance, an SML model, or a combination of the two, so-called mixed-model inheritance. This is achieved by a set of techniques called *segregation analysis*. We will briefly consider each of these in turn.

## Path analysis with model fitting

The main drawback of applying path analytical models in the simple way that we did earlier in this chapter is that it will not tell us how confident we can be about our estimates of the influence of genetic and environmental factors, or indeed whether we could explain the data just as well by dropping out one or other of these factors. The traditional way of dealing with this problem is of course to calculate the standard errors and hence produce confidence limits for the estimates of the parameters. However, with modern computers it has become relatively easy and practicable to apply a more satisfactory approach involving *iteration* (i.e. carry out a repetitive search) to obtain the best fit.

In iterative model fitting the main program uses a subprogram called an optimisation routine to obtain the most satisfactory solution to the problem. The researcher provides the main computer program with the relevant data and supplies the starting values for the parameters that are effectively

**Table 2.4**  Fitting a simple additive model to twin data on hospital-treated depression

|  | Parameter estimates | | | |
|  | $h^2$ | $c^2$ | $x^2$ | $P$ |
|---|---|---|---|---|
| No transmission | {0} | {0} | 548.31 | 0.000 |
| Additive genetic effects | | | | |
|   only (G) | 0.99 | {0} | 38.38 | 0.000 |
| Shared environment | | | | |
|   only (C) | {0} | 0.77 | 11.82 | 0.006 |
| G & C | 0.43 | 0.46 | 0.0 | |

$h^2$ = heritability.
$c^2$ = proportion of variance explained by family (shared) environment: parameters in brackets are fixed.
From McGuffin *et al* (1991).

his or her best guess what the 'correct' values should be. This information determines the initial value of a mathematical function supplied by the investigator, the form of which depends upon the model being tested. Usually the mathematical function is either a $x^2$ or a log likelihood. Iteration ceases when the maximum likelihood or the minimum value of $x^2$ is obtained, so providing the 'best fit' estimates of the model parameters.

An example of this type of data analysis based on a sample of twins is summarised in Table 2.4. Here the probands had all received hospital treatment for major depression, and a broad definition of concordance was used, consisting of any form of depression in the co-twin, providing hospital treatment was also received (McGuffin *et al*, 1991). The probandwise concordance for MZ twins was 57 out of 84 (68%) and for DZ twins it was 56 out of 130 (43%). Assuming a population morbid risk up to age 65 for hospital-treated depression of 8.9% (Sturt *et al*, 1984), we can calculate correlations in liability and use these in the model-fitting exercise. A full model, allowing for both genetic and shared environmental effects, provides a perfect fit, with a $x^2$ of 0, an $h^2$ of 43% and $c^2$ of 46%. However, if we attempt to explain the data in terms of shared environmental effects alone, the minimum $x^2$ is 11.82, which is a very poor fit. (The significance level for one degree of freedom is 0.006.) On the other hand, if we hypothesise that the data can be explained by additive genetic effects only, the fit is even poorer, with a $x^2$ of 38.38. Lastly, we can test the hypothesis of no transmission, with both $h^2$ and $c^2$ fixed at zero; here the minimum $x^2$ becomes huge, and we can conclude this is a very poor fit indeed. In summary, then, we can conclude that there is familial transmission of depression (broadly defined as above) and that both genetic effects and family environment are significant contributors to this familiality.

It should be noted that in this example the computer program minimised a $x^2$ function. An alternative procedure is to maximise a log likelihood. Comparison of models is then carried out using a *likelihood ratio test*. This depends on the fact that if $L_1$ is the log likelihood for a certain model and $L_2$ is the log likelihood of the second model, which is a subset of the first, then -2 $(L_1 - L_2)$ is approximately distributed as a $x^2$.

## Segregation analysis

Methods such as path analysis use incidence data on pairs of relatives. However, if the aim is primarily to discover the most likely mode of transmission and to resolve major gene effects, rather than partition sources of variation, information from entire pedigrees is used to carry out complex segregation analysis. Currently the most commonly applied procedures are based upon the mixed model of Morton & MacLean (1974), where it is postulated that *liability* to develop the disorder depends upon the combination of a major gene effect, a residual environmental component and a multifactorial effect. As mentioned earlier, this is effectively a combination of the multifactorial (MF) threshold model and the general SML model. The mixed model is illustrated in Fig. 2.9. The defining parameters are a gene frequency ($g$), a displacement between the mean liability values of the two homozygotes ($t$) and a dominance deviation that gives the heterozygote mean value relative to the means of the two homozygotes ($d$). The multifactorial effect is defined by a single parameter ($H$), the proportion of variance in liability contributed by non-major gene

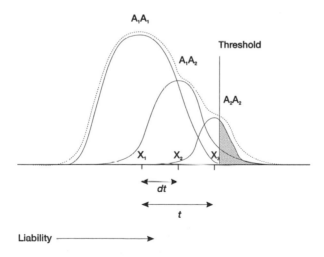

**Fig. 2.9** The mixed model: a multifactorial 'background' (broken line) and three major genotypes having mean liabilities of $X_1$, $X_2$ and $X_3$, where $X_1$ and $X_3$ are $t$ standard deviations apart, and dominance is measured by parameter $d$.

familial effects, also called 'multifactorial heritability'. Again, full use is made of the potential of iterative model-fitting approaches, and the standard procedure is to test the full mixed model against reduced models (MF or SML) which are its subsets.

Segregation analysis has greatest power to resolve major gene effects when the phenotype can be measured on a continuous scale (see for example Rice *et al*, 1984). The power is also increased by analysing extended pedigrees rather than just nuclear families (i.e. parents and children alone). However, even with extended pedigree data, there are certain weaknesses in analysing dichotomous (present/absent) traits so that, for example, in bipolar disorder segregation analysis has provided suggestive but not convincing evidence of a major locus involved in transmission (Rice *et al*, 1987; O'Rourke *et al*, 1983). In schizophrenia the findings have been even less conclusive and the ability to distinguish between any of the models has been poor (see for example Vogler *et al*, 1990). Even more misleading is the fact that segregation analysis can sometimes point to the conclusion that there is a major gene where common sense suggests that this is unlikely. For example, a recent study where mixed model analysis was carried out (McGuffin & Huckle, 1990) suggested that attendance at medical school among the relatives of medical students could best be explained by the segregation of a recessive gene!

Despite these problems and the fact that attempts to resolve the major gene effects by purely statistical methods have been disappointing, such studies can provide useful information about the plausible models to be invoked in the transmission of psychiatric phenotypes. For example, a study of the transmission of Alzheimer's disease suggested that both a major gene and multifactorial contributions were present and suggested that the major effect may exist in only a minority of families (Farrer *et al*, 1991). This might help explain some of the inconsistencies in recent linkage studies (see Chapter 11). Studies of this type can be seen as a necessary preliminary step before proceeding to more ambitious work which seeks to establish the molecular basis of inheritance.

# References

Bouchard, T. J. & McGue, M (1981) Familial studies of intelligence: a review. *Science*, **212**, 1055–1059.

Carter, C. O. (1969) Genetics of common disorders. *British Medical Bulletin*, **25**, 52–57.

Cloninger, C. R., Rice, J. & Reich, T. (1979) Multifactorial inheritance with cultural transmission and assortative mating III. Family structure and the analysis of separation experiments. *American Journal of Human Genetics*, **31**, 366–388.

——, Reich, T., Suarez, B., *et al* (1985) The principles of genetics in relation to psychiatry. In *The Scientific Foundations of Psychiatry* (ed. M. Shepherd). Cambridge: Cambridge University Press.

Falconer, D. S. (1965) The inheritance of liability to certain diseases, estimated from the incidence among relatives. *Annals of Human Genetics*, **29**, 51–76.

Farrer, L. A., Myers, R. H., Connor, L., *et al* (1991) Segregation analysis reveals evidence of a major gene for Alzheimer's disease. *American Journal of Human Genetics*, **48**, 1026–1033.

Goldsmith, H. H. (1991) A zygosity questionnaire for young twins: a research note. *Behavioural Genetics*, **21**, 257–269.

Gottesman, I. I. (1963) Genetic aspects of intelligent behaviour. In *The Handbook of Mental Deficiency: Psychological Theory and Research* (ed. N. Ellis), pp. 346–347. New York: McGraw-Hill.

—— & Shields, J. (1972) *Schizophrenia. A Twin Study Vantage Point.* London: Academic Press.

Henderson, N. D. (1970) Genetic influence on the behaviour of mice can be observed by laboratory rearing. *Journal of Comparative Physiological Psychiatry*, **72**, 505–511.

Kallmann, F. J. (1938) *The Genetics of Schizophrenia*. New York: J. J. Augusta.

Kendler, K. S. (1993) Twin studies of psychiatric illness: current status and future directions. *Archives of General Psychiatry*, **50**, 905–915.

Loehlin, J. C. & Nichols, R. C. (1976) *Heredity, Environment and Personality: a Study of 850 Sets of Twins*. Austin, Texas: University of Texas Press.

Martin, N. G. & Jardine, R. (1986) Eysenck's contribution to behaviour genetics. In *Hans Eysenck: Consensus and Controversy* (eds S. Modgil & C. Hodgil), pp. 13–27. Philadelphia: Falmer.

McGuffin, P., Katz, R. & Bebbington, P. (1987) Hazard, heredity and affective disorder: a family study. *Journal of Psychiatric Research*, **21**, 365–375.

—— & Huckle, P. (1990) Simulation of mendelism revisited. The recessive gene for attending medical school. *American Journal of Human Genetics*, **46**, 994–999.

——, —— & Rutherford, P. (1991) Nature, nurture and depression. A twin study. *Psychological Medicine*, **20**, 329–335.

——, ——, Rutherford, J., *et al* (1993) Twin studies as vital indicators of phenotypes in molecular genetic research. In *Twins as Tools of Behavioral Genetics* (eds T. J. Bouchard & P. Propping), pp. 243–256. Chichester: Wiley.

McKusick, V. A. (1992) *Mendelian Inheritance in Man* (10th edn). Baltimore: Johns Hopkins Press.

Morton, N. E. (1982) *Outline of Genetic Epidemiology.* Basel: Karger.

—— & MacLean, C. J. (1974) Analysis of family resemblance. III. Complex segregation analysis of quantitative traits. *American Journal of Human Genetics*, **26**, 489–503.

O'Rourke, D. H., McGuffin, P. & Reich, T. (1983) Genetic analysis of manic–depressive illness. *American Journal of Physical Anthropology*, **62**, 51–59.

Plomin, R., DeFries, J. C. & McClearn, G. E. (1990) *Behavioral Genetics: a Primer* (2nd edn). New York: W. H. Freeman.

Reich, T., James, J. W. & Morris, C. A. (1972) The use of multiple thresholds in determining the mode of transmission of semi-continuous traits. *Annals of Human Genetics*, **36**, 163–184.

——, Cloninger, C. R., Wette, R., *et al* (1979) The use of multiple thresholds and segregation analysis in analyzing the phenotypic heterogeneity of multifactorial traits. *Annals of Human Genetics*, **42**, 371.

Rice, J., McGuffin, P., Goldin, L. R., *et al* (1984) Platelet monoamine oxidase (MAO) activity: evidence for a single major locus. *American Journal of Human Genetics,* **36**, 36–43.

——, Reich, T., Andreasen, N. C., *et al* (1987) The familial transmission of bipolar illness. *Archives of General Psychiatry,* **44**, 441–447.

Risch, N. (1990) Linkage strategies for genetically complex traits: III The effect of marker polymorphism analysis on affected relative pairs. *American Journal of Human Genetics,* **46**, 242–253.

Rutherford, J., McGuffin, P., Katz, R. J., *et al* (1993) Genetic influences in eating attitudes in a normal female twin population. *Psychological Medicine,* **23**, 425–436.

Scarr, S. & Carter-Saltzman, L. (1979) Twin method: defense of a critical assumption. *Behavior Genetics* **9**, 527–542.

Slater, E. & Cowie, V. (1971) *The Genetics of Mental Disorders.* London: Oxford University Press.

Sturt, E. (1986) Application of survival analysis to the inception of dementia. *Psychological Medicine,* **16**, 583–593.

——, Kamakura, N. & Der, G. (1984) How depressing life is – lifelong morbidity risk for depressive disorder in the general population. *Journal of Affective Disorders,* **7**, 109–122.

Torrey, E. F., Taylor, E., Bowler, A., *et al* (1994) *Schizophrenia and Manic Depressive Disorder. The Biological Roots of Mental Illness as Revealed by the Landmark Study of Identical Twins.* New York: Basic Books.

Vogler, G. P., Gottesman, I. I., McGue, M. K., *et al* (1990) Mixed model analysis of schizophrenia in the Lindelius Swedish pedigree. *Behaviour Genetics,* **20**, 461–472

# 3   Linkage and association

*Linkage • Linkage studies and complex disorders • Affected relative pairs • Association*

In Chapter 2 we discussed statistical methods for studying the mode of transmission of psychiatric disorders. Studies using genetic markers offer a more direct approach to the identification and localisation of genes and the eventual understanding of the molecular basis of disease. Genetic markers are reliably measured characters which have a simple mode of transmission and are *polymorphic*, that is, there are two or more alleles with a gene frequency of at least 1%. Until the beginning of the 1980s there were relatively few markers available for study, and they included blood groups, histocompatibility (HLA) antigens, red cell enzymes, certain plasma proteins and chromosomal banding patterns demonstrable by high-resolution staining techniques. Even with good collaboration between a number of laboratories, it was rarely feasible to mount a linkage study using more than about 30 of these so-called 'classical' markers. The situation dramatically changed with the introduction of restriction fragment length polymorphisms (RFLP) and more recently other types of DNA markers (described in Chapter 1), such as dinucleotide repeat polymorphisms. The new molecular biological technology has resulted in literally many hundreds of markers becoming available to serve as reference points throughout the human genome and enabling linkage studies to commence in earnest both for Mendelian disorders and more complex phenotypes.

## Linkage

In linkage studies the co-segregation of a genetic marker and a disorder is investigated with the aim of *detecting* departure from independent assortment and of *estimating* the amount of recombination between the marker and the main trait (or disease).

This is best understood by again considering a double back-cross mating, just as we did in discussing independent assortment (Chapter 2). Let us further postulate that in the double heterozygote parent shown overleaf in Fig. 3.1, A and B are on the same chromosome while a and b reside on the other member of the homologous pair. This will mean that offspring of type aaBb or Aabb must result from *crossing-over* between the homologous pair of chromosomes during meiosis (see Chapter 1). Such offspring are known as *recombinants,* while offspring of the same type as

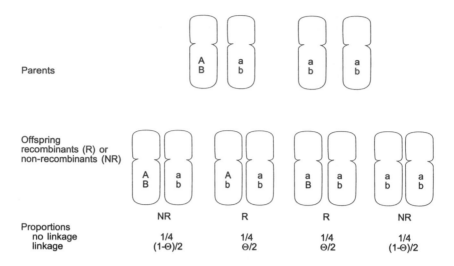

**Fig. 3.1** Possible types of chromosomes from a double back-cross mating

the parents, AaBb or aabb, are *non-recombinants.* The *recombination fraction*, Θ, is simply defined as the number of recombinants divided by the total number of offspring.

If two loci are on different chromosomes or are very widely separated on the same chromosomes, then independent assortment takes place and Θ = ½ (i.e. there is a 50:50 chance of offspring being either recombinants or non-recombinants). However, when two loci are close together, assortment is no longer independent and recombination fractions of less than ½ are observed. Within certain limits, the size of the recombination fraction is proportional to the physical distance between the two loci, so that for loci very close together, recombination becomes infrequent and Θ approaches zero. By convention genetic distances are measured in centimorgans (cM), where 1 cM is equivalent to recombination occurring once in every 100 meioses (i.e. a recombination fraction of 0.01).

Although in plants and often in laboratory animals it is possible to carry out the relevant crosses and simply count the number of recombinants and non-recombinants, human beings are much more awkward from the viewpoint of genetic research. Statistical methods for the detection of linkage and the estimation of recombination are required.

Again methods based upon maximum likelihood have been particularly useful and the usual approach is to calculate *lod scores* (Morton,1955). A lod (or log of the odds) score is the common log of the likelihood that the recombination fraction has a certain value, Θ', divided by the likelihood that Θ is ½,

$$\text{lod } (\Theta') = \log_{10}\{ \text{ likelihood } (\Theta = \Theta') \text{ /likelihood } (\Theta = 0.5) \}$$

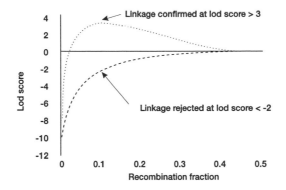

**Fig. 3.2** Hypothetical two point lod scores between loci which are linked
( · · · · · ) and unlinked (– – – – – –)

A range of values for the lod score is calculated between $\Theta' = 0$ and
$\Theta' = 0.5$, and the point at which the lod score reaches its highest value is
taken as the maximum likelihood estimate of the recombination fraction,
$\hat{\Theta}$. This is shown graphically in Fig. 3.2.

Conventionally, a lod score of at least 3, representing odds on linkage
of 1000:1, is the accepted level for concluding that the linkage has been
detected. This sounds highly conservative, but there is a low prior
probability of two loci selected at random being linked (of the order of
about 1 in 50) (Edwards, 1991). Thus a lod score of 3 corresponds to a
posterior probability of *reliability* of about 95% (Clerget-Darpoux, 1991).
Again by convention, a lod score of -2 (or odds of 100:1 against) is taken
as the level at which linkage may be confidently excluded.

A recent extension of likelihood methods is to carry out *multipoint linkage
analysis* (Ott, 1991). Here, instead of the conventional two-point analysis,
where the co-segregation of the disease and a single marker is studied,
multiple markers lying reasonably closely together on the same
chromosome are studied. This may enable greater precision in the most
likely positioning of the disease locus, or may allow *exclusion* of the disease
locus from a particular region of chromosome.

## Linkage studies and complex disorders

One of the problems of linkage studies is that they were originally conceived
as a means of studying unambiguously defined traits with known Mendelian
transmission. However, it has now become common to apply linkage
methods in studies of familial disorders where there is evidence of a major

gene with incomplete penetrance, or even where the mode of transmission is completely unknown but the involvement of a major gene is a possibility. The presence of incomplete penetrance reduces the efficiency of lod score methods, so that large sample sizes are required. However, computer program packages are now widely available, for example LINKAGE (Lathrop *et al*, 1984), which can easily cope with the increased mathematical complexity of incomplete penetrance and even of variable age of onset. The model of disease transmission assumed in such packages is the general SML model. Even though this is unsatisfactory in explaining the transmission of disorders such as schizophrenia (McGue *et al*, 1985, and also see Chapter 5) this does not present insuperable problems. Recent work suggests that if schizophrenia is an oligogenic disorder or has a mixed mode of transmission with a major gene plus polygenic correlation among relatives, then linkage analysis making the simpler assumptions of SML inheritance should not necessarily produce misleading results (Ott, 1991). Mis-specifying the model in other ways, for example entering incorrect penetrances in the computer analysis, does not usually result in inflation of the lod score or false positives (i.e. detection of linkage when in fact no linkage exists). However, mis-specification of the mode of transmission can result in false negatives (i.e. the exclusion of linkage when linkage in fact is present) (Clerget-Darpoux,1991).

There has been much confusion in the recent literature concerning claims of positive linkage findings in schizophrenia and in manic depression (see Chapters 5 and 6) that were closely followed by failures of replication, even though the original evidence appeared to be strong, with lod scores well in excess of the conventional level of 3. Can such high lod scores sometimes represent false positives? The factors that increase the risk of false positives in linkage studies of psychiatric disorders include the use of multiple diagnostic schemes and the exploration of multiple genetic models of transmission. Together these result in the problem, familiar to statisticians, of multiple hypothesis testing. This will tend to inflate the lod score and increase the probability of falsely positive results. Therefore it is prudent to take this effect into account, and it may be advisable to apply a correction factor for multiple tests (Ott, 1991). However, the most convincing evidence that linkage is present is if independent replication can be achieved (McGuffin *et al*, 1990).

A further problem when dealing with disorders with variable ages of onset, such as schizophrenia or manic depression, is that phenotypes may change over time. That is, previously well individuals may become affected and this can result in a change in the lod score if the initial calculation was carried out under the mistaken assumption that such individuals did not carry a 'disease' allele. For example, a study of manic depression in a multiply affected family in the United States suggested linkage between the disorder and markers on chromosome 11p (Egeland *et al*, 1987). However, on follow-up, two key individuals who were previously thought to be well became affected. Their status therefore changed from being probable non-recombinants to recombinants. This, together with information on an extension of the pedigree, resulted in a marked lowering of the lod score and a virtual disappearance of what had initially been a promising positive finding (Kelsoe *et al*, 1989) (see also Chapter 6).

## Linkage studies with heterogeneity

Last is the problem of genetic heterogeneity. This comes in various guises. The first, which poses few real difficulties for linkage analysis, is *allelic heterogeneity*, where two or more mutant alleles can exist at the same locus. These can result in clearly different phenotypes, as for example in Duchenne muscular dystrophy and the less severe Becker-type muscular dystrophy, which both result from mutations at the same locus in the X chromosome (Kunkel *et al*, 1986).

Second, there may be *locus heterogeneity*, that is, there are two or more loci at which mutations result in similar phenotypes. This is true for example of retinitis pigmentosa, tuberous sclerosis and Charcot-Marie-Tooth (CMT) neuropathy, all of which can result from a number of distinct mutations on different chromosomes (Strachan, 1992). Sometimes the different types of disorder may be easily differentiated by their modes of transmission. For example, one form of CMT is X-linked; however, two other forms are autosomal dominant and the loci are on different chromosomes. If homogeneity was assumed and linkage analysis carried out on a collection of families containing a mixture of the two autosomal forms of CMT, the results could be misleading and linkage might be overlooked.

Third, only a minority of cases of a disorder might be due to a major locus but the majority of cases are either polygenic or not genetic at all. This seems to be true for some inherited cancers, for example carcinoma of the breast (Easton *et al*, 1993) as well as Alzheimer's disease (see Chapter 11), where early-onset familial cases have been shown by linkage studies to be dominant conditions with nearly complete penetrance, whereas later-onset cases show less obvious familial aggregation and no evidence of linkage to the markers found linked to early-onset forms. Again, linkage analysis carried out on a mixture of forms and assuming homogeneity could produce falsely negative results.

Fortunately, methods exist to test statistically for the presence of locus heterogeneity. The details of these are beyond the scope of this book, but the underlying principle is straightforward (see Clerget-Darpoux, 1991, for a fairly non-technical account and Ott, 1991, for a more comprehensive description). This consists of computing likelihoods under the hypotheses of no linkage with homogeneity, linkage with homogeneity, and linkage with heterogeneity. Pairwise comparison of each of the three hypotheses is then carried out using likelihood ratio tests (see Chapter 2).

## Affected relative pairs

Because of the problems in correctly specifying the mode of transmission in studies of complex disorders, it may be preferable to apply a 'model-free' method of analysis. In common with non-parametric statistics used elsewhere, model-free linkage tests such as *affected sib pair analysis* (e.g. Green & Woodrow, 1977; Suarez *et al*, 1978) are robust but are comparatively lacking in statistical power. That is, such methods will perform satisfactorily even when the researcher is completely ignorant of the mode of transmission of the disorder, but this is at the expense of being less sensitive to the detection of linkage than model-dependent methods. Even model-free methods of linkage analysis require the assumption that a gene of major effect is segregating at least in a proportion of families. In this context what is meant by 'major effect' is rather vague, and it is probable that with a sufficient sample size (e.g. 200 sib pairs), even a gene accounting for a small proportion of variance in liability (10% or less) can be detected. It should be noted, however, that affected sib pair methods only allow detection of linkage. They do not provide a way of estimating the recombination fraction which, as we have discussed, is necessary if the researcher wants to have an idea of how far apart are two linked loci.

Recent elaborations of this approach have included pairs of relatives other than just sibs (Risch, 1990). The general feature of such methods is that they rely on comparing expected and observed numbers of affected relatives sharing marker alleles inherited from common ancestors, that is, alleles that are identical by descent (IBD). For example, in the absence of linkage, affected siblings sharing two, one or no marker alleles would be expected to occur in the ratio 1:2:1. Any statistically significant departure from this ratio suggests a relationship between the marker locus and the disease. An alternative strategy which has recently been introduced in an attempt to increase the scope and applicability of affected relative methods is simply to use information on marker alleles identical by state (IBS), that is, to count shared alleles, whether or not they are known to come from a shared ancestor (Weeks & Lange, 1988). This relies heavily on having accurate information on the frequency of the marker alleles in the general population, since the crucial question is whether affected relatives share alleles simply by chance. For this reason IBS methods are still somewhat controversial, and positive results based on such methods alone are to be treated cautiously.

## Association

For disorders of unknown mode of transmission where several or even many loci may be involved, an alternative or complementary strategy is to search for *allelic association*. Typically, association studies are done on

**Table 3.1** Marker–disease association in a population

| Marker | *n* affected | *n* unaffected |
| --- | --- | --- |
| Present | *c* | *d* |
| Absent | *e* | *f* |

populations where a comparison is made of the frequency of marker phenotypes in a sample of patients and a sample of healthy controls, as in the classic example where patients with duodenal ulcer were found to have a higher frequency than expected of blood group O. In essence they are therefore much simpler than linkage studies and the typical analysis is of a 2 x 2 contingency table as shown in Table 3.1.

The appropriate significance test is a $x^2$ with one degree of freedom. It may also be useful to have a measure of the *strength of the association* such as the *relative risk*. Within a population, this is the proportion of those who carry the marker who are ill, $P_1 = c/(c + d)$, divided by the proportion of those who do not carry the marker who are ill, $P_2 = e/(e + f)$. When, as in the usual case, only a small proportion of the population is affected, then *c* is small relative to *d*, and *e* is small relative to *f*, so that $P_1/P_2$ approximates to $(c \times f)/(d \times e)$. Strictly speaking, this is an *odds ratio* or cross-product ratio, but it is often (somewhat confusingly) referred to simply as the relative risk.

### Equilibrium and disequilibrium

Linkage between a marker and a disease gene within families does not usually result in allelic association within populations. Thus, if we refer back to Fig. 3.1, and suppose that A is a mutant (disease) allele linked to a second locus at which we have allele B on the same chromosome, while the homologous chromosome carries allele a and allele b. In the offspring of the AB/ab parent, the proportion of A and B alleles found together has reduced to $(1 - \Theta)$ and there is a subsequent reduction of the proportion of associated alleles of the same magnitude every successive generation. Thus if linkage between the two loci is fairly loose, *equilibrium* is rapidly reached where chromosomes of the types AB or ab are no more frequent than chromosomes of the types aB or Ab. However, if linkage is very tight (for example a recombination fraction of 0.01 or less) equilibrium takes many generations to achieve and so a population study may find allelic association arising because there is still *linkage disequilibrium* between the two loci. The detection of linkage disequilibrium therefore requires that the marker and the disease susceptibility locus lie very close together.

## Pleiotropy

Another cause of allelic association is if the marker allele itself has some direct effect on susceptibility to the disease. This is the phenomenon of *pleiotropy*, where the same gene has two or more apparently different effects. For example, we have mentioned the long-established association between blood group O and susceptibility to a duodenal ulcer, and this may occur because the same gene confers both the red cell type and the disease susceptibility (Emery, 1988).

## Stratification

Apparent allelic associations can also arise because of sample *stratification*. This occurs when there have been recent admixtures of populations or when a population actually consists of several subpopulations without much intermarriage. For example, most of the Afro-Caribbean population in south London have arrived there within the past generation or two, and Afro-Caribbeans and the southern English have rather different distributions of genetic polymorphisms such as HLA types. If an association study was carried out in which the patient and control samples contained greatly different proportions Afro-Caribbean and white subjects, then a spurious association between HLA type and the disease might be found. To avoid being misled by a stratification effect association studies need to be carefully planned and carried out in ethnically homogeneous populations. Alternatively, the simple but ingenious approach suggested by Falk & Rubenstein (1987) can be adopted, where a series of affected individuals and their unaffected parents are studied. Here the parental allele frequencies inherited versus those not inherited provides an inbuilt control which is robust to stratification effects.

## Size of the genetic effect

One advantage of association studies is, as we have already hinted, that they provide a means of using genetic markers to detect genes of only small effect. For example, Edwards (1965) showed that, although it is well replicated, the blood type O association accounts for little more than 1% of the variation in liability to develop duodenal ulcer. Using the Edwards approach, which assumes a multifactorial liability/threshold model of transmission, it can be shown than even some of the stronger HLA/ disease associations that are now very well replicated (e.g. with ankylosing spondylitis or juvenile diabetes) may only account for a small proportion of the liability to the disorder (McGuffin & Buckland, 1991).

It has been argued that since all behavioural traits can be considered as quantitative (either as directly measured or threshold traits) then the most rational approach is to assume at the outset the presence of multiple genes and look for ways of detecting so-called quantitative trait loci (QTL) (Plomin, 1990). This general strategy has proved successful in plant genetics, where for example multiple genes for quantitative characteristics of tomato fruit have been identified (Paterson *et al*, 1988). Similarly, genes contributing to the variation in blood pressure in rats have been localised (Hilbert *et al*, 1991).

A search for QTL in humans is limited by the inability to carry out experimental back-crosses; however, association strategies may offer a way forward. Association studies can be regarded as 'near sighted'. While they can detect genes of very small effect, they can, for the reasons discussed earlier, only detect those that are very close to the marker. By contrast, linkage studies are capable of detecting genes some distance from the marker, but only those of relatively large effect. This means that it is theoretically feasible to perform a systematic search of the human genome for QTL providing there is a very detailed map available with close reference points, such that no QTL is more than 1 cM from a marker (Owen, 1992). Assuming that the human genome is about 3700 cM in length (Strachan, 1992), there is then a need for around 1850 evenly spaced polymorphisms. This has yet to be achieved but is technically feasible. A 'second generation' linkage map consisting of over 800 simple sequence repeat polymorphisms all of the $(AC)_n$ type (see Chapter 1) has been published (Weissenbach *et al*, 1992) and current work mapping the genome is progressing very rapidly so that a map with 1–2 cM resolution is not far off.

**VAPSE**

Another set of technical developments which is of particular interest consists of methods to detect gene variations affecting protein structure or expression (VAPSE) (Sobell *et al*, 1993). To date, most DNA markers used in association studies have been presumed to result from variations in non-coding regions. Hence any association detected will reflect linkage disequilibrium between the marker allele and a disease susceptibility locus. However, there are now many genes that have been identified and cloned which encode for proteins involved in neurotransmission, for example neuroreceptors or enzymes involved in neurotransmitter metabolism (Owen & McGuffin, 1992). The aim of searching for VAPSE in such genes is therefore to detect a variation which itself has a direct (or pleiotropic) effect on disease susceptibility. As discussed in Chapter 1, there are, in addition to direct DNA sequencing, various new methods of detecting variations of potential functional significance in so-called 'candidate' genes. These hold much future promise in psychiatric genetics, particularly if advances can be made in understanding the pathophysiology of mental disorders.

# References

Clerget-Darpoux, F. (1991) The uses and abuses of linkage analysis in neuropsychiatric disorder. In *The New Genetics of Mental Illness* (eds P. McGuffin & R. Murray), pp. 44-57. Oxford: Butterworth-Heinemann.

Easton, D. F., Bishop, D. T., Ford, D., *et al*, and the Breast Cancer Linkage Consortium (1993) Genetic linkage analysis in familial breast and ovarian cancer: results from 214 families. *American Journal of Human Genetics*, **52**, 678-701.

Edwards, J. H. (1965) The meaning of the association between blood groups and disease. *Journal of Human Genetics*, **29**, 77-83.

—— (1991) The formal problems of linkage. In *The New Genetics of Mental Illness* (eds P. McGuffin & R. Murray), pp. 58-70. Oxford: Butterworth-Heinemann.

Egeland, J. A., Gerhard, D. S., Pauls, D. L., *et al* (1987) Bipolar affective disorders linked to DNA markers on chromosome 11. *Nature*, **325**, 783–787.

Emery, A. E. H. (1988) *Methodology in Medical Genetics*. Edinburgh: Churchill Livingstone.

Falk, C. T. & Rubenstein, P. (1987) Haplotype relative risks: an easy reliable way to construct a proper control sample for risk calculations. *Annals of Human Genetics*, **51**, 227-233.

Green, J. R. & Woodrow, J. C. (1977) Sibling method for detecting HLA-linked genes in disease. *Tissue Antigens*, **9**, 31-35.

Hilbert, P., Lindpainter, K., Beckman, J. S., *et al* (1991) Chromosomal mapping of two genetic loci associated with blood-pressure regulation in hereditary hypertensive rats. *Nature*, **353**, 521-529.

Kelsoe, J. R., Ginns, E. I., Egeland, J. A., *et al* (1989) Re-evaluation of the linkage relationship between chromosome 11q loci and the gene for bipolar affective disorder in the old order Amish. *Nature*, **325**, 238-243.

Kunkel, L. M., Hejtmancik, J. F., Caskey, C. T., *et al* (1986) Analysis of deletions in DNA from patients with Becker and Duchenne muscular dystrophy. *Nature*, **322**, 73-77.

Lathrop, G. M., Lalouel, J. M., Julier, C., *et al* (1984) Strategies for multilocus linkage analysis in humans. *Proceedings of the National Academy of Sciences, USA*, **81**, 3443-3446.

McGue, M., Gottesman, I. I. & Rao, D. C. (1985) Resolving genetic models for the transmission of schizophrenia. *Genetic Epidemiology*, **2**, 99-110.

McGuffin, P., Sargeant, M., Hett, G. *et al.* (1990) Exclusion of a schizophrenia susceptibility gene from the chromosome 5q11-q13 region. New data and a reanalysis of previous reports. *American Journal of Human Genetics*, **47**, 524-535.

—— & Buckland, P. R. (1991) Major genes, minor genes and molecular neurobiology of mental illness - a comment on 'quantitative trait loci and psychopharmacology'. *Journal of Psychopharmacology*, **5**, 18-22.

Morton, N. E. (1955) Sequential tests for the detection of linkage. *American Journal of Human Genetics*, **7**, 277-318.

Ott, J. (1991) *Analysis of Human Genetic Linkage*. Baltimore: Johns Hopkins University Press.

Owen, M. (1992) Will schizophrenia become a graveyard for molecular geneticists? (Editorial) *Psychological Medicine*, **22**, 289-293.

—— & McGuffin, P. (1992) The molecular genetics of schizophrenia (Editorial). *British Medical Journal*, **305**, 664-665.

Paterson, A. H., Lander, E. S., Hewitt, J. D., *et al* (1988) Resolution of quantitative traits into mendelian factors by using a complete linkage map of restriction fragment length polymorphisms. *Nature*, **335**, 721-726.

Plomin, R. (1990) The role of inheritance in behavior. *Science*, **248**, 183-188.

Risch, N. (1990) Linkage strategies for genetically complex traits. III: The effect of marker polymorphism analysis on affected relative pairs. *American Journal of Human Genetics*, **46**, 242-253.

Sobell, J. L., Heston, L. L. & Sommer, S. S. (1993) Novel association approach for determining the genetic predisposition to schizophrenia: case-control resource and testing of a candidate gene. *American Journal of Medical Genetics*, **48**, 28-35.

Strachan, T. (1992) *The Human Genome*. Oxford: BIOS Scientific.

Suarez, B. K., Rice, J. & Reich, T. (1978) The generalized sib pair IBD distribution: its use in the detection of linkage. *Annals of Human Genetics*, **42**, 87-94.

Weeks, D. R. & Lange, K. (1988) The affected pedigree member method of linkage analysis. *American Journal of Human Genetics*, **42**, 315-326.

Weissenbach, J., Gyapay, G., Dib, C., *et al* (1992) A second generation linkage map of the human genome. *Nature*, **359**, 794-801.

# 4   Mental retardation

---

*Idiopathic mental retardation • Single-gene defects • Chromosomal abnormalities • Autosomal anomalies • Sex chromosome anomalies . Other disorders • Conclusions*

---

Mental retardation is defined in ICD–10 as "a condition of arrested or incomplete development of the mind, which is especially characterized by impairment of skills ... which contribute to the overall level of intelligence" (World Health Organization, 1992). However, concepts and definitions of mental retardation and mental handicap vary widely.

Mental retardation can be subclassified in a variety of ways. For example, mental retardation is commonly separated on the basis of IQ test scores into mild (IQ 50–70) and severe mental retardation (IQ < 50). Mild mental retardation is strongly associated with psychosocial adversity and there is often no identifiable biological cause. On the other hand, severe mental retardation is commonly due to identifiable biological (infectious, traumatic, toxic and genetic) causes and is much less often attributable to psychosocial adversity.

Mild mental retardation can be thought of as representing the lower end of the normal distribution curve for intelligence in the general population or as a quantitative variation from the normal. Conversely, severe mental retardation could be regarded as differing qualitatively from the normal. This would explain the asymmetry at the lower end of the otherwise Gaussian (bell shaped) population distribution for IQ scores (see Fig. 4.1). There is some empirical support for this distinction, in that the recurrence risk in relatives of those with mild mental retardation is relatively high, whereas this does not hold for relatives of severely affected individuals except of course for those with Mendelian disorders.

However, mild and severe mental retardation are by no means aetiologically distinct categories. In a Swedish study of an unselected sample of adults with mild mental retardation, chromosomal aberrations were found in as many as 19% (Gostason *et al*, 1991). Similarly, not all severe mental retardation can be accounted for by discrete causes. Table 4.1 shows the main causes of mild and moderate mental retardation. It is apparent that mental retardation is a very heterogeneous set of conditions.

On an aetiological basis, mental retardation can be very broadly divided into two categories (see Fig. 4.1): idiopathic mental retardation; and mental retardation due to identifiable biological causes. Individuals with idiopathic

66

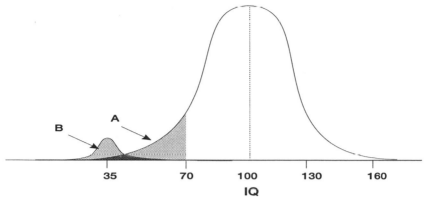

**Fig. 4.1** The 'two-group' approach to mental retardation. A, lower end of the Gaussian distribution or idiopathic mental retardation. B, People with mental retardation due to identifiable causes. (Modified from Zigler, 1967.)

**Table 4.1** Causes of mental retardation (figures in percentages)

|  | Mild retardation (Son Blomquist *et al*, 1981; Vasterbotten, Sweden, *n*=171; 4.2 per 1000) | Moderate retardation (Fryns *et al*, 1990; Belgian institution; *n*=262) |
|---|---|---|
| *Prenatal* | | |
| Genetic | | |
| chromosomal | 8 | 18 |
| Mendelian | 8 | 17 |
| dominant | | 6 |
| recessive | | 4 |
| X linked | | 7 |
| fragile X | | (11[1]) |
| 'multifactorial' | 15 | |
| | | |
| Others | 12 | 8 |
| (e.g. alcohol, infection, unknown) | | |
| | | |
| *Perinatal* | 7 | 14 |
| | | |
| *Postnatal* | 5 | 13 |
| | | |
| *'Psychosis'* | 2 | |
| | | |
| *Unknown* | 43 | 30 |

1. % of total males screened (103) .

mental retardation are often but not inevitably mildly affected. The second category consists of mental retardation due to identified genetic disorders and also environmental causes such as infection and birth injury. For the sake of clarification, in this chapter we will first discuss idiopathic mental retardation and then consider specific genetic syndromes associated with mental retardation.

## Idiopathic mental retardation

As mentioned above, individuals with idiopathic mental retardation are most commonly mildly affected. The number of individuals in this category (particularly those who are severely affected) is lessening as more identifiable causes, such as fragile X, are recognised. As this group is often considered to represent the lower end of the normal distribution of intelligence (i.e. about 2% of the general population), it would seem sensible first briefly to discuss the genetics of intelligence.

Family studies show increasing correlations for intelligence among biologically related individuals as a function of genetic relatedness; an average correlation of about 0.4 between first-degree relatives is reported (Plomin, 1990). Twin and adoption findings suggest that this familiality is largely a genetic effect with average correlations of about 0.86 for MZ twins and 0.61 for DZ twins (Bouchard & McGue, 1981). On the whole, adult MZ twins reared apart show similar correlations to those reared together. In adoption studies, although there appears to be some correlation between unrelated individuals at a young age, unrelated individuals become less similar as they grow older until average correlations approach zero (Loehlin *et al,* 1988).

Longitudinal studies have also shown that genetic influences become more important and shared family environmental effects decrease as individuals approach adulthood (Plomin & Rende, 1991).

On the basis of these studies, recent estimates of heritability for intelligence have been about 50%. However, adoption study findings have also shown the importance of environmental factors. In a study of French children born to socially disadvantaged parents and then reared in middle-class homes, the mean IQ of these children was appreciably higher than the IQ of their siblings raised in the disadvantaged circumstances (Schiff & Lewontin, 1986). Similarly, in a more recent cross-fostering study, both the biological parents' background and the adoptive socioeconomic status influenced the child's IQ (Capron & Duyme, 1989; McGue, 1989).

In conclusion, intelligence, like height, is not simply programmed genetically but is influenced considerably by environment. Genes determine a 'reaction range' but within that range environmental factors determine the level of intelligence (Gottesman, 1971; Turkheimer & Gottesman, 1991).

Unfortunately there are few family, twin and adoption studies of idiopathic mental retardation specifically, and it is difficult to know to what extent the results of genetic studies of normal intelligence can be directly extrapolated to this group. The rate of mental retardation among relatives of affected individuals has varied from study to study, and depends on the degree of mental retardation of the proband and on how the affected individual was identified (e.g. by IQ, special school). The reported rate has varied from 13% to 33% among first-degree relatives and from 5% to 9% among second-degree relatives (Reed & Reed, 1965; Nichols, 1984; Bundey *et al*, 1989).

There have been remarkably few twin studies. In an early twin study, concordance rates were 73% for monozygotic (MZ) twins and 29% for dizygotic (DZ) twins (Rosanoff *et al*, 1937). Higher concordance rates for MZ twins (100%) than for DZ twins (58%) were also found in another twin study (Juda, 1939, in Gottesman, 1971). However, these results should be interpreted with caution because of methodological problems, such as non-systematic ascertainment and the increased risk of obstetric complications among twins.

Overall, it seems that idiopathic mental retardation is familial. It is likely that both genetic and environmental influences contribute to this familiality, although it is more uncertain as to the relative contributions of genes and family environment. A polygenic/multifactorial model would fit most available data and explain transmission of idiopathic mental retardation. However, this type of model has been criticised by some (Akesson, 1986; Gostason *et al*, 1991), mainly because of studies showing a high rate of specific chromosomal aberrations among individuals with mild mental retardation. However, as mentioned earlier, even individuals with mild mental retardation are an aetiologically heterogeneous group. It seems most plausible that mental retardation, including mild mental retardation, is not a single condition but can be caused by single genetic aberrations in some cases, discrete environmental hazards in others and explained by polygenic/multifactorial influences in the remainder.

# Single-gene defects

In this section we review some of the commoner disorders which result from the action of single major genes. The number of recognised single-gene defects associated with mental retardation has been estimated as 210 (Gottesman *et al*, 1992). So far, 69 have been mapped to an autosome and 73 to the X chromosome (Wahlstrom, 1990). We have categorised the disorders according to the mode of inheritance, that is, autosomal dominant, autosomal recessive, and sex-linked disorders (including inborn errors of metabolism), with examples, in Tables 4.2–4.5.

**Autosomal disorders**

It is of note that although these disorders could be thought of as being more homogeneous than traditional psychiatric diagnoses, there are several clinical examples where despite apparent phenotypic homogeneity (either clinical or biochemical), genetic heterogeneity has been found. That is, several genes have been found to be associated with one disorder. Another point of note is that phenotypic heterogeneity is also not uncommon. That is, that one genetic defect has been shown to be associated with several clinical variants.

Advances in molecular genetic techniques have helped in localising many of the genes responsible for these disorders, as can be seen in Tables 4.2–4.5. Of course, a major advantage in identifying loci for many of these disorders is that there is a recognisable biochemical defect. As phenylketonuria is the best known and commonest inborn error of metabolism that is associated with mental retardation, we will consider this in some greater detail.

*Phenylketonuria*

Phenylketonuria (PKU) is an autosomal recessive disorder with an incidence of between 1 in 10 000 and 1 in 15 000 in Western Europe and

**Table 4.2** Autosomal dominant disorders

| Disorder | Clinical features | Chromosomal location |
|---|---|---|
| Tuberous sclerosis 1 per 10 000 | Variable mental handicap Epilepsy Facial rash (adenoma sebaceum) Cafe-au-lait spots, shagreen patches, sclerotic brain nodules, lung cysts, renal cysts and retinal lesions (variable expressivity) | Type 1 9q33–q34 Type 4 16p13 |
| Apert's syndrome | Mental handicap in some, 'tower skull', protuberant eyes, abnormalities of fingers and toes | – |
| Crouzon's syndrome | Mental handicap (~20%), 'tower skull', protuberant eyes | – |
| Mandibulofacial dysostosis (Berry Franceschetti or Treacher Collins) | Sheep like face, deafness, variable mental handicap in some, 'antimongoloid' slant of eyes | 5q31.3–q33.3 |

**Table 4.3** Autosomal recessive disorders

| Disorder | Clinical features | Chromosomal location |
|---|---|---|
| Ataxia telangiectasia (Louis Barr syndrome) | Mental deterioration after age 3–5, telangiectasia, cerebellar ataxia, extrapyramidal signs, immune deficiency, predisposition to malignancy | 11q22–q23 |
| Laurence Moon Biedl syndrome | Mental handicap, obesity hypogenitalism, pigmentary retinopathy, spastic paraplegia | – |
| Virchow Sekel dwarf | Short stature, facial abnormalities, mental handicap | – |
| Marinesco Sjogren syndrome | Mental handicap, cerebellar ataxia, cataracts, skeletal abnormalities | – |
| True microcephaly | Mental handicap, small cranial vault | – |

**Table 4.4** X-linked disorders

| Disorders | Clinical features | Chromosomal location |
|---|---|---|
| Nephrogenic diabetes insipidus | (Renal tubules not responsive to ADH) Polyuria, excessive thirst, vomiting, dehydration, convulsions. Mental handicap secondary to dehydration | Xq28 |
| Lesch Nyhan syndrome (hypoxanthine guanine phosphoribosyl transferase deficiency) | Spasticity, choreoathetosis, self-mutilation, severe mental handicap, hyperuricaemia | Xq26–q27.2 |
| Norrie's disease | Cataracts, blindness, epilepsy, hearing impairment | Xp11.4 |
| Lowe's syndrome | Vitamin D resistant rickets, cataracts, hypotonia, dome-shaped head, severe mental retardation | Xq26.1 |
| X-linked hydrocephalus (aqueductal stenosis) | Mental retardation, hydrocephalus, spastic paraplegia | Xq28 |
| Duchenne muscular dystrophy | Hypertrophic muscular dystrophy, mental handicap in some (1/3). Onset before the age of 6, usually chairbound by 12 years and death by 20 years | Xp21.2 |
| Aicardi syndrome | Mental retardation, agenesis of corpus callosum, choreoretinopathy, microphthalmia, seizures. X dominant, lethal in males | Xp22 |

**Table 4.5** Inborn errors of metabolism

| Disorder | Clinical features | Enzyme defect and chromosomal location |
|---|---|---|
| *Disorders of protein metabolism* | | |
| Phenylketonuria 1 per 10 000 | Mental handicap, retarded growth, microcephaly, epilepsy. Fair hair and skin, eczema, hyperactivity, autistic features | PAH deficiency 12q24.1 Dihydropteridine reductase deficiency 4p15.31 |
| Homocystinuria 1 per 300 000 | Mental handicap, ectopia lentis, skeletal abnormalities, fair, poor peripheral circulation, thromboembolic episodes, epilepsy, liver degeneration (B6 responsive and non-responsive variants) | Cystathionine beta synthetase deficiency 21q22.3 |
| Maple syrup urine disease 1 per 120 000–200 000 | Mental handicap, epilepsy, spasticity, characteristic odour to urine | 1.19q13.1–q13.2 2.1p31 3.6p22–p21 |
| Arginosuccinic aciduria | Dry brittle hair, epilepsy | Arginosuccinate lyase deficiency 7cen–q11.2 |
| *Renal (transport) aminoacidurias* | | |
| Hartnup disease 1 per 14 000 | Photosensitive skin, pellagra rash, cerebellar ataxia, mental deterioration | – |
| *Carbohydrate metabolism* | | |
| Galactosaemia 1 per 60 000 | Vomiting, lethargy, jaundice, hepatosplenomegaly, cataracts, mental handicap (many clinical variants) | Galactose-1-phosphate uridyl transferase deficiency 9p13 |

*Continued opposite*

the USA. The metabolic error consists of a defect in the enzyme phenylalanine hydroxylase (PAH), which catalyses the formation of tyrosine from phenylalanine. A few people can also show clinical features of the disorder if synthesis of the co-factor, tetrahydrobiopterin, which is involved in the enzymatic reaction, is defective.

Table 4.5 *Continued*

| Disorder | Clinical features | Enzyme defect and chromosomal location |
|---|---|---|
| *Lipid metabolism & connective tissue disorders* | | |
| Tay Sachs disease<br><br>1 per 2500<br>Ashkenazi<br>Jews | Mental handicap (early regression), 'cherry red spot' of macula, blindness, early death (High frequency among Ashkenazi Jews, several variants) | Type I<br>Hexosaminidase A deficiency<br>15q23–q24<br>Type AB<br>Hexosaminidase activator deficiency |
| Niemann Pick disease | Mental deterioration, hepatosplenomegaly, spasticity seizures, death in early life (Many clinical variants) | Sphingomyelinase deficiency<br>11p15.4–15.1 |
| Gaucher disease | Mental handicap, hypersplenism, bone lesions, skin pigmentation | Glucocerebrosidase deficiency 1q21 |
| Refsum disease | Mental deterioration, retinitis pigmentosa, polyneuritis, cerebellar signs, auditory loss in some | Phytanic acid oxidase deficiency |

*Mucopolysaccharidoses*

~ 1 per 10 000 for all mucopolysaccharidoses

| | | |
|---|---|---|
| Type I<br>Hurler's syndrome | Mental deterioration, gargoylism, corneal clouding, hepatosplenomegaly | α-l-iduronidase deficiency 4p16.3 |
| Type II<br>Hunter syndrome | Mental retardation, gargoylism, deafness, hepatosplenomegaly, X-linked disorder | Iduronate sulphatase deficiency<br>Xq28 |
| Type III<br>Sanfilippo | Severe mental retardation, mild physical signs | Four biochemical varieties<br>Type A-heparin sulphatase deficiency |
| Type IV | Normal intellect, corneal clouding, skeletal and aortic valve disorders | Type A galactosamine 6 sulphatase deficiency<br>Type B6 – galactoside deficiency<br>3p21-p14.2 |

It is thought that the resultant hyperphenylalanaemia and tyrosine deficiency are responsible for the characteristic clinical features of PKU (see Table 4.5). Like many other inherited disorders, affected individuals can present with a variety of clinical and biochemical phenotypes.

The gene for phenylalanine hydroxylase (PAH), which is the PKU locus, has been localised to chromosome 12q22–24.1 (the gene for dihydropteridine reductase, the deficiency of which has been associated with PKU, has been localised to chromosome 4p15.3) (Ledley *et al*, 1985; Lidsky *et al*, 1985). However, there is no single defect of the PAH locus responsible for PKU. By the beginning of 1992, 60 different mutations in the PAH gene resulting in disorders of PAH deficiency had been published (Konecki & Lichter-Konecki, 1991; Eisensmith & Woo, 1992). Different mutations in the PAH locus have been shown to be associated with classic PKU as well as milder variants.

So far most published work has been on mutations causing the most clinically and biochemically severe PAH deficiency. However, further mutations associated with a wider variety of biochemical phenotypes in populations throughout the world are being identified. This may well improve prediction of clinical outcome for those affected, allow more accurate prenatal screening, and even suggest new modes of treatment.

Of course, PKU is one of the best examples of a genetic disorder which can be treated by environmental manipulation and is often used as an example to counteract arguments that genetic aetiology means therapeutic pessimism. Screening in the UK, which occurs from day 6 to day 14 after birth, in conjunction with dietary treatment to lower blood phenylalanine levels, has been very successful. Current opinion, based on recent research, stresses the importance of maintaining the diet for as long as possible to prevent later intellectual and behavioural deterioration (*Lancet*, 1991).

## X-linked disorders

It has long been recognised that males with mental retardation outnumber females. These findings apply both in the general population as well as in institutions. This provided early, indirect evidence that sex linkage may account for a significant percentage of mental retardation. More recently, an increasing number of conditions have been shown to segregate in an X-linked fashion in families (Glass, 1991). Growing interest in X-linked mental retardation has been particularly encouraged by positive research findings for the fragile X syndrome and this interest is evident by the recent staging of the 5th International Workshop on the fragile X syndrome and X-linked mental retardation (Mandel *et al*, 1992). The commonest disorders and their regional assignment where known are listed in Table 4.4.

X-linked disorders seem to be especially important for the mild to moderate range of mental retardation. By 1993, 95 specifically X-linked phenotypic entities (excluding inborn errors of metabolism) associated with mental retardation had been recognised (Neri *et al*, 1992; Schwartz, 1993). However, many of these conditions are restricted to single families, and merging different family phenotypic data to delineate a definite syndrome is not safe. So far, a number of these X-linked syndromes (43 genes by 1993) have been broadly assigned to chromosome regions, and gene localisation of a mutant gene for fragile X is described below.

## Fragile X syndrome

Fragile X syndrome is the second most common known genetic cause of mental retardation after Down's syndrome. The estimated population prevalence rates are 1 in 1250 males and 1 in 2000 females. It accounts for about 7% of moderate and 4% of mild mental retardation of no obvious cause in males, and for approximately 2.5% of moderate and 3% of mild idiopathic retardation in females (Webb & Thake, 1991).

In simple terms, a fragile site is a non-staining gap on a chromosome. Fragile X syndrome is characterised by a fragile site located at the band location q27.3 on the X chromosome, which is only evident in certain culture mediums (Sutherland, 1977). The most characteristic clinical features are mental retardation, macroorchidism, large ears, macrocephaly, long face and wide jaw. Affected individuals may have abnormal speech and can show marked social fears (Brown *et al*, 1991). However, the fragile X phenotype is variable. A weak association between cytogenetic fragile X and autism has been seen in a few studies. Although some children with fragile X may show autistic-like features and even full-blown autism, other evidence suggests that the rate of fragile X is no higher among autistic children than in controls (Fisch, 1992). More recently, there has been some interest in the clinical manifestations of female carriers. Although 70% appear of normal intellect, it now appears that psychopathology among this group, notably lower IQ and schizotypal features, is related to the degree of cytogenetically evident fragility (Reiss *et al*, 1988; Freund *et al*, 1992).

### Mode of inheritance

Fragile X syndrome is not inherited in a straightforward X-linked fashion. Variable penetrance is suggested by the observations that it can be transmitted through non-retarded males and is relatively common among mentally retarded females. Some males who show neither the fragile site nor clinical symptoms have been shown to transmit the defect (normal transmitting males); their phenotypically normal daughters, without the fragile site, can then have affected male offspring.

Recent molecular findings have now provided an explanation for this otherwise puzzling mode of inheritance.

*Molecular genetics*

The current criterion for making a diagnosis of fragile X cytogenetically, is that 4% or more of lymphocytes should show the fragile site (Goodyear & Sonkson, 1990). The expression of fragile X sites is highly correlated with intelligence and, as described above, may be an indicator of psycho-pathology. However, as yet the clinical significance of lower rates of fragile X expression is still uncertain. Although it is of great importance that this fragile site appears to be tightly linked to the characteristic phenotype, its detection is not always a reliable indicator of carrier status. About half of the obligate female carriers show the fragile site but those who are not mentally retarded often do not (Wolff *et al*, 1988) and it is rarely expressed in carrier males.

Recent findings have been particularly exciting in that the interesting and unusual pattern of inheritance now appears to have a molecular basis. A gene (FMR-1), which may be involved in the clinical expression of the fragile X syndrome, and a mutation within this gene, which is highly associated with the fragile X phenotype, have actually been identified (Verkerk *et al*, 1991; Oberle *et al*, 1991; Yu *et al*, 1991).

The molecular basis of the disorder appears to be related to a heritable sequence of trinucleotide repeats (CGG). In normal individuals this sequence is repeated about 6 to 54 times, and in normal families the region is transmitted in a stable fashion. However, carrier females and normal transmitting males have a greater length of repeats than normal individuals, which is sometimes referred to as a 'premutation'. In affected individuals, this region consists of an even longer sequence of repeats and the length appears to be related to clinical severity.

When the fragile X chromosome is transmitted to offspring from the carrier mother, the sequence becomes longer and varies in length among the siblings. Interestingly, the sequence length usually appears unchanged when transmitted by an unaffected transmitting male which explains the unusual pattern of inheritance. Thus this heritable region in fragile X families is characterised by its instability and seems to become unstable when beyond a certain length (thought to be about 200 copies). The detection of this mutation has already enabled testing, with the use of the polymerase chain reaction (PCR: see Chapter 1), for both affected and carrier subjects (Pergolizzi *et al*, 1992).

The discovery of heritable unstable DNA not only explains the pattern of inheritance for fragile X syndrome but may well have implications in the transmission of other disorders (Sutherland *et al*, 1991). Hereditary unstable DNA may provide a molecular basis to previously unexplained genetic phenomena such as incomplete penetrance, imprinting (see Prader–Willi syndrome, p. 80) and anticipation (an increase in severity of the disorder and earlier age of onset in progressive generations). For example, a hereditary unstable sequence has also been identified as the basis for myotonic dystrophy, which explains the associated phenomenon of anticipation in this disorder (Harper *et al*, 1992).

# Chromosomal abnormalities

Chromosomal abnormalities are thought to account for up to 40% of severe mental retardation and as much as 10–20% of mild mental retardation (Hagberg & Hagberg, 1984; Gostason *et al*, 1991). Chromosomal abnormalities can be broadly categorised into two groups: those due to a change in the number of autosomal or sex chromosomes (aneuploidy); and those due to chromosome structural change, such as deletion and translocation (which usually results from breaks in the chromosome(s)). Many of these disorders are associated with increased maternal age. The commonest conditions associated with chromosomal abnormalities are summarised in Table 4.6 (p. 79) and disorders of particular interest will be discussed further.

# Autosomal anomalies

### Down's syndrome – trisomy 21

Down's syndrome is the commonest genetic cause of mental retardation. It occurs in about 1 in 1000 births and accounts for about 30% of severe mental retardation.

Most individuals (95%) affected with trisomy 21 have an extra chromosome in the chromosome 21 group because of non-disjunction. That is, at meiosis or mitosis, there is failure of separation of chromosomes which results in an extra chromosome in that gamete or embryo. However, about 2% of affected individuals show chromosomal translocations (the extra chromosome 21 is due to rearrangement of chromosomal material) and with this type of disorder the recurrence risk is much higher and is not associated with increased maternal age. An even smaller number show mosaicism, which means that some cells show the normal 46 chromosomes and others have an extra chromosome.

Although Down's syndrome is a genetic disorder, it is not heritable unless due to a translocation or parental mosaicism. The risk of recurrence of the prototypic trisomy varies with maternal age and is about 1 in 50 for women older than 45. Although the increase of risk with maternal age is well known and amniocentesis is widely available to women over the age of 35, most Down's babies are born to mothers under the age of 35.

Down's syndrome (historically mislabelled as 'mongolism') is characterised by well known phenotypic features, notably craniofacial abnormalities, mental retardation and cardiac defects. However, phenotypic expression can be variable and many structures can be affected (see Table 4.6). There has been particular interest in the Alzheimer-type lesions which have been found in the brains of relatively young affected individuals. By the age of 40, 95% of those with Down's syndrome show these changes. Moreover, the gene for the amyloid precursor protein, which has a derivative found in amyloid plaques and tangles involved in plaque formation, has been located on chromosome 21 (see Chapter 11). These findings have further fuelled interest in understanding the pathogenesis of the various phenotypic traits expressed in Down's syndrome (Serra & Neri, 1990).

Despite the characteristic phenotypic traits and the cytogenetically apparent trisomy 21, it is still not known whether all of the extra chromosome or only part of the chromosome (and if so which parts) is involved in producing the phenotype. Results of several studies have suggested that the q22 region on chromosome 21 may be a critical region in producing at least the most characteristic traits of mental handicap, heart anomalies and facial appearance (Korenberg *et al*, 1990; Serra & Neri, 1990); more detailed mapping of the whole chromosome and further localisation of genes is still very important.

In conclusion, although a cytogenetic abnormality is obvious, the path from genotype to phenotype in Down's syndrome still remains a question. However, the mapping of genes on chromosome 21 is progressing and holds hope for further understanding.

# Sex chromosome anomalies

The commonest syndromes and the usual clinical features are summarised in Table 4.6. In general, the more extra X chromosomes an individual has, the higher the chance of mental retardation, and in males, a greater number of X chromosomes can also be associated with a greater degree of physical abnormality. Non-disjunction accounts for most of these anomalies and although causative factors have not been identified, there does again appear to be an increased risk associated with higher maternal age.

These syndromes have been of particular interest to psychiatrists because of several reports of increased rates of mental disorder among affected individuals. However, these early studies were often biased in their sample selection, and the majority of individuals with a sex chromosome anomaly do not show signs of mental retardation, mental illness or personality disorder. It is also important to remember that most affected individuals remain unidentified.

We will now consider Klinefelter's syndrome (XXY) and the 'XYY syndrome' in further detail.

**Table 4.6** Chromosomal abnormalities

| Syndrome | Clinical features | Chromosomal abnormality |
|---|---|---|
| *Autosomal abnormalities* | | |
| Down's syndrome 1 per 1000 | Mental handicap, flat occiput, epicanthic folds, oval face, Brushfield spots, large tongue, hypotonia, clinodactyly, simian crease on palms. Increased rates of congenital heart defects, cataracts, hypothyroidism, respiratory infections, leukaemia | Trisomy 21 |
| Edward's syndrome 1 per 8000 | Mental handicap, low-set fawn-like ears, micrognathia, rocker bottom feet, cardiac abnormalities | Trisomy 18 |
| Patau's syndrome 1 per 4000–10 000 | Mental handicap, facial abnormalities, polydactyly | Trisomy 13 |
| Cri du chat 1 per 50 000 | Mental handicap, characteristic cry, facial abnormalities, spasticity | Deletion 5p |
| *Sex chromosome abnormalities* | | |
| Turner's syndrome 1 per 2500 females | Usually normal IQ, short stature, webbed neck, wide separation of nipples, cubitus valgus, lack of secondary sexual characteristics | 46X0 |
| Triple X syndrome 1 per 1000 females | No physical abnormalities, maybe mild mental handicap | 47XXX |
| Klinefelter's syndrome 1 per 1000 males | Phenotypically male, long limbs, small testes, gynaecomastia, lack of secondary sexual characteristics, maybe mild mental handicap | 47XXY |
| XYY syndrome 1 per 1000 males | Tall, maybe mild mental handicap | 47XYY |

## Klinefelter's syndrome (XXY)

Klinefelter's syndrome affects about 1 in 1000 males and the characteristic karyotype is XXY, although some individuals can show mosaicism or more rarely be 48 XXXY. About two-thirds of those with 47XXY are due to maternal non-disjunction. However, there are no known predisposing factors other than an association with slightly above average maternal age (Carothers & Filippi, 1988).

Affected individuals are phenotypically male but otherwise the phenotype can be very variable. The most characteristic clinical features are listed in Table 4.6. In early studies, there appeared to be a significant association between XXY and increased rates of psychiatric disorder, criminality and mental retardation. However, many of these studies used highly selected institutionalised samples. It now seems that the majority of XXY individuals are of normal intelligence and do not suffer from any psychiatric disorder.

Although global intelligence does not appear to be significantly different from the rest of the population, a number of studies of XXY individuals have shown significantly lower verbal scores on tests. It has also been noted that many XXY individuals show language delay and educational difficulties in childhood and poor verbalisation later (Mandoki *et al*, 1991). Similarly, in studies of children with language disorders, up to 5% have been found to have chromosomal anomalies, mostly XXY. Interestingly, individuals with Turner's syndrome ( X0 - see Table 4.6) show performance test (e.g. spatial ability) rather than verbal deficits. This has led to some speculation about the role of the X chromosome in specific cognitive and linguistic skills.

## XYY syndrome

In a study of the inmates of Carstairs, a hospital for mentally abnormal offenders, 3% of the men showed a 47XYY karyotype (Jacobs *et al*, 1968). These findings, in conjunction with results of other studies of similar institutions, suggested that 47XYY is not only associated with greater than average height and below average IQs, but also with criminality. A subsequent survey in Denmark of over 4000 tall men from military inductees revealed that of the 12 individuals (0.3%) with a 47XYY karyotype, 5 (42%) had a criminal record compared with only 9% of the normal XY males (Witkin *et al*, 1976). However, on closer examination the offences committed by XYY individuals were mostly non-aggressive in nature and included relatively minor crimes. Thus XYY syndrome is not associated with serious criminality or aggressiveness but more with milder social deviance.

# Other disorders

## Prader–Willi syndrome

Prader–Willi syndrome (PWS) is a disorder characterised by hypotonia, obesity, short stature, small hands and feet, almond-shaped eyes, strabismus and hypogenitalism. Affected individuals may well come to the attention of psychiatrists because of associated behaviour problems, notably temper outbursts, stubbornness, foraging for food and depression. Although some 40% show mental retardation, 60% of PWS individuals have normal or borderline IQ. The incidence has been estimated at about 1 in 25 000 live births. The majority of cases are sporadic and the recurrence risk in families is less than 1 in 1000 (Cassidy, 1987). Of reported cases, over a half show a *de novo* deletion at chromosome 15q12 which is of *paternal origin* (Knoll *et al*, 1989; Butler, 1990). This finding has provoked considerable interest, in that a similar deletion of chromosome 15 when of *maternal origin* is associated with Angelman syndrome (see below) (Knoll *et al*, 1989). Thus, the phenotypic manifestations of this lesion appear to depend on the parental origin of the chromosome. This differential expression of genes according to whether the origin is paternal or maternal is known as genomic imprinting. This interest in the role of imprinting has been further fuelled by reports of PWS occurring in individuals with uniparental disomy of chromosome 15 (Nichols *et al*, 1989) (i.e. both their chromosomes 15 are of *maternal origin*, so that effectively their paternal chromosome 15 has been 'deleted'). Similarly, in some cases uniparental disomy of *paternal origin* has been associated with Angelman syndrome (Malcolm *et al*, 1991).

The origin of the molecular abnormality is as yet unknown. Although it has been reported that paternal exposure to hydrocarbons is associated with a higher risk of PWS in offspring (Strakowski & Butler, 1987), this needs further study.

## Angelman syndrome ('Happy Puppet Syndrome')

Although the clinical manifestations of Angelman syndrome seem very different from those of Prader–Willi syndrome, for reasons described above it is appropriate to consider these two disorders together.

Affected individuals characteristically show a stiff, jerky gait, uplifted arms, frequent inappropriate laughter and severe mental retardation. The estimated incidence is approximately 1 in 20 000 (Clayton-Smith & Pembrey, 1992) and the majority of cases are sporadic.

Between 75% and 80% of affected individuals show molecular evidence of a deletion of maternally derived chromosome 15q11–13. Uniparental disomy of paternal origin accounts for a further 3% of cases (Clayton-Smith & Pembrey, 1992). Thus the absence of a *maternally* derived chromosome 15 region appears to be the critical defect.

It is hoped that the pathogenesis of PWS and Angelman syndrome will be better understood as the molecular structure of the affected region of chromosome 15 is further characterised. In addition, clinical studies continue to be important in elucidating the range of phenotypic manifestations and their correlation with abnormalities at a molecular level.

**Rett syndrome**

Rett syndrome is a progressive degenerative neurological disorder which only affects females. The incidence has been estimated at about 1 per 10 000 female live births. Affected individuals characteristically develop normally until 6–18 months, after which time there is gradual loss of motor, language and cognitive skills, deceleration of head growth, and stereotyped hand movements such as hand wringing.

There have been a few reports of familial cases and all known affected MZ twins (7 pairs) have been concordant for the disorder, whereas all known DZ twins (11) pairs have shown discordance (Ellison *et al*, 1992). However, most cases are sporadic and as yet little is known about underlying genetic mechanisms. Some studies have reported an increased rate of chromosomal breakages and specific associations with fragile Xp22 (Telvi *et al*, 1991) whereas others have found no evidence of chromosomal rearrangement (Martinho *et al*, 1990); these findings have not been widely replicated yet.

Currently an X-linked mutation would seem to be the most likely explanation. Exclusion mapping of the X chromosome may help focus the search for a causative gene at least to a specific region. However, it is possible that Rett's syndrome is transmitted autosomally but that being female is necessary for it to be expressed, that is, an extreme form of sex-limited expression.

# Conclusions

A major difficulty in considering the genetics of mental retardation is that it is clinically and aetiologically heterogeneous. There are a number of clearly genetic syndromes associated with mental retardation as well as a group of affected individuals where environmental hazards such as environmental toxins and infection have undoubtedly played an aetiological role. However, not all mental retardation can be attributed to a discrete cause and many affected individuals seem to be somewhere in between, with probably both environment (physical and psychosocial) and genes contributing.

New molecular genetic techniques have had considerable impact in understanding more about many of the genetic syndromes associated with mental retardation. An increasing number of disorders are being mapped to specific chromosomal locations and specific molecular abnormalities are being recognised. What is of particular interest is that there is evidence of genetic as well as clinical heterogeneity for many apparently homogeneous disorders. Even for a relatively straightforward disorder such as phenylketonuria, it is increasingly evident that there are a number of associated mutations. This has implications for genetic research into psychiatric disorders which are much more complex, at least phenotypically.

Although these exciting molecular findings are of great interest, it is important to remember that up to 70% of mental retardation is not attributable to a specific genetic anomaly. It is possible that among this group, some discrete genetic disorders may yet be identified. However, it is more than likely that a group of affected individuals about whom relatively little is understood will remain. It seems that for this group, there is still a need for the more traditional family, twin and adoption studies in order to clarify the aetiological role and interplay of both genetic and environmental factors. In addition, the success achieved in identifying trait loci for complex traits in plants and more recently in animals (see Chapter 3) has implications for the possibility of localising contributory loci for more complex human traits, including some types of mental retardation.

# References

Akesson, H. O. (1986) The biological origin of mild mental retardation. *Acta Psychiatrica Scandinavica*, **74**, 3-7.

Bouchard, T. J. & McGue, M. (1981) Familial studies of intelligence: a review. *Science*, **212**, 1055-1059.

Brown, W. T., Jenkins, E., Neri, G., *et al* (1991) Conference report: Fourth International Workshop on the fragile X and X-linked mental retardation. *American Journal of Medical Genetics*, **38**, 158-172.

Bundey, S., Thake, A. & Todd, J. (1989) The recurrence risks for mild idiopathic mental retardation. *Journal of Medical Genetics*, **26**, 260-266.

Butler, M. (1990) Prader-Willi syndrome: current understanding of cause and diagnosis. *American Journal of Medical Genetics*, **35**, 319-332.

Capron, C. & Duyme, M. (1989) Assessment of effects of socioeconomic status on I.Q. in a full cross-fostering study. *Nature*, **340**, 552-553.

Carothers A.D. & Filippi G. (1988) Klinefelter's syndrome in Sardinia and Scotland. *Human Genetics*, **81**, 71-75.

Cassidy, S.B. (1987) Recurrence risk in Prader-Willi syndrome. *American Journal of Medical Genetics*, **28**, 59-60.

Clayton-Smith, J. & Pembrey, M.E. (1992) Angelman syndrome. *Journal of Medical Genetics*, **29**, 412-415.

Eisensmith, R. C. & Woo, S. L. C. (1992) Molecular basis of phenylketonuria and related hyperphenylaninemias: mutations and polymorphisms in the human phenylalanine hydroxylase gene. *Human Mutation*, **1**, 13-23.

Ellison, K. A., Fill, C. P., Terwilliger, J., *et al* (1992) Examination of X chromosome markers in Rett syndrome: exclusion mapping with a novel variation on multilocus linkage analysis. *American Journal of Human Genetics*, **50**, 278-287.

Fisch, G.S. (1992) Is autism associated with the fragile X syndrome? *American Journal of Human Genetics*, **43**, 47-55.

Fryns, J. P., Volcke, P. H., Haspeslagh, M., *et al* (1990) A genetic diagnostic survey in an institutionalized population of 262 moderately mentally retarded patients: the Borgerstein experience. *Journal of Mental Deficiency Research*, **34**, 29-40.

Glass, I. (1991) X linked mental retardation. *Journal of Medical Genetics*, **28**, 361-371.

Goodyear, H. M. & Sonkson, P.M. (1990) Fragile X syndrome – an important cause of mental retardation. *Journal of the Royal Society of Medicine*, **83**, 1-2.

Gostason, R., Wahlstrom, J., *et al* (1991) Chromosomal aberrations in the mildly mentally retarded. *Journal of Mental Deficiency Research*, **35**, 240-246.

Gottesman, I. I. (1971) An introduction to behavioral genetics of mental retardation. In *Role of Genetics in Mental Retardation* (ed. R. M. Allen *et al*), pp. 49–69. Coral Gables: University of Miami.

——, Prescott, C. A. & Thompson, W. (1992) Personal communication.

Hagberg, B. & Hagberg, G. (1984) Aspects of prevention of pre-, peri- and postnatal brain pathology in severe and mild mental retardation. In *Scientific Studies in Mental Retardation* (eds J. Dobbing, A. D. B. Clarke, J. A. Corbett, *et al*), pp. 43-64. London/Basingstoke: Royal Society of Medicine/Macmillan.

Harper, P. S., Harley, H. G., Reardon, W., *et al* (1992) Anticipation in myotonic dystrophy: new light on an old problem. *American Journal of Human Genetics*, **51**, 10-16.

Jacobs, P. A., Price, W. H., Cower-Brown, W. M., *et al* (1968) Chromosome studies on men in maximum security hsopitals. *Annals of Human Genetics*, **31**, 339-358.

Knoll, J.H.M., Nicholls, R.D., *et al* (1989) Angelman and Prader-Willi syndrome share a common chromosome 15 deletion but differ in parental origin of the deletion. *American Journal of Human Genetics*, **32**, 285-290.

Konecki, D. S. & Lichter-Konecki, U. (1991) The phenylketonuria locus: current knowledge about alleles and mutations of the phenylalanine hydroxylase gene in various populations. *Human Genetics*, **87**, 377-388.

Korenberg, J., Kawashima, H., Pulst, S. M., *et al* (1990) Molecular definition of a region of chromosome 21 that causes features of the Down syndrome phenotype. *American Journal of Human Genetics*, **47**, 236-246.

Lancet (1991) Phenylketonuria grows up. *Lancet*, **337**, 1256-1257.

Ledley, F. D., Grenett, H. E., *et al* (1985) Gene transfer and expression of human phenylalanine hydroxylase. *Science*, **228**, 77-79.

Lidsky, A. S., Law, M. L., Morse, H. G., *et al* (1985) Regional mapping of the phenylalanine hydroxylase gene and the phenylketonuria locus in the human genome. *Proceedings of the National Academy of Sciences of the USA*, **82**, 6221-6225.

Loehlin, J. C., Willerman, L. & Horn, J.M. (1988) Human behavior genetics. *Annual Review of Psychology*, **39**, 101-133.

Malcolm, S., Clayton-Smith, J., Nichols, M., *et al* (1991) Uniparental disomy in Angelman syndrome. *Lancet*, **337**, 694-697.

Mandel, J. L., Hagerman, R., Froster, U., *et al* (1992) Fifth International Workshop on the Fragile X and X linked mental retardation. *American Journal of Medical Genetics*, **43**, 5-27.

Mandoki, M., Sumner, G. S., *et al* (1991) A review of Klinefelter's syndrome in children and adolescents. *Journal of the American Academy of Child and Adolescent Psychiatry*, **30**, 167-172.

Martinho, P. S., Otto, P. G., *et al* (1990) In search of a genetic basis for the Rett syndrome. *Human Genetics*, **86**, 131-134.

McGue, M. (1989) Nature - nurture and intelligence. *Nature*, **340**, 507-508.

Neri, G., Chiurazzi, P., Arena, F., *et al* (1992) XLMR genes: update, 1992. *American Journal of Medical Genetics*, **43**, 373-382.

Nicholls, R. D., Knoll, J. H. M., Butler, M. G., *et al* (1989) Genetic imprinting suggested by maternal heterodisomy in non–deletion Prader-Willi syndrome. *Nature*, **342**, 281-285.

Nichols, P. L. (1984) Familial mental retardation. *Behavior Genetics*, **14**, 161-170.

Oberle, I., Rousseau, F., Heitz, D., *et al* (1991) Instability of a 550 base pair DNA segment and abnormal methylation in fragile X syndrome. *Science*, **252**, 1097-1102.

Pergolizzi, R. G., Erster, S. H., Goonewardeena, P., *et al* (1992) Detection of full fragile X mutation. *Lancet*, **339**, 271-272.

Plomin, R. (1990) The role of inheritance in behaviour. *Science*, **248**, 183-188.

—— & Rende, R. (1991) Human behavioural genetics. *Annual Review of Psychology*, **42**, 161-190.

Reed, E. W. & Reed, S. C. (1965) *Mental Retardation: a Family Study*. Philadelphia: Saunders.

Reiss, A. L., Hagerman, R., Vinogradov, S., *et al* (1988) Psychiatric disorder in female carriers of the fragile X chromosome. *Archives of General Psychiatry*, **45**, 25-30.

Rosanoff, A. J., Handy, L. M. & Plesset, I. R. (1937) The etiology of mental deficiency with special reference to its occurence in twins. *Psychological Monograph*, **216**, 1-137.

Schiff, M. & Lewontin, R. (1986) *Education and Class: the Irrelevance of IQ Genetic Studies*. Oxford: Clarendon Press.

Schwartz, C. E. (1993) X–linked mental retardation: in pursuit of a gene map. (Invited editorial.) *American Journal of Human Genetics*, **52**, 1025–1031.

Serra, A. & Neri, G. (1990) Trisomy 21: Conference Report and 1990 update. *American Journal of Medical Genetics* (suppl. 7), 11-19.

Son Blomquist, H. K., Gustavson, K. H. & Holmgren, G. (1981) Mild mental retardation in children in a Northern Swedish county. *Journal of Mental Deficiency Research*, **25**, 169-186.

Strakowski, S. M. & Butler, M. G. (1987) Paternal hydrocarbon exposure in Prader-Willi syndrome. *Lancet, ii*, 1458.

Sutherland, G. R. (1977) Fragile sites on human chromosomes: demonstration of their dependence on the type of tissure culture medium. *Science*, **197**, 265-266.

——, Haan, E. A., Kremer, E., *et al* (1991) Hereditary unstable DNA: a new explanation for some old genetic questions? *Lancet*, **338**, 289-292.

Telvi, L., LeBoyer, M., *et al* (1991) *The Fragile Site Xp22 in Rett Syndrome as a Consequence of a 'Chromosome Breakage Syndrome'*. Second World Congress on Psychiatric Genetics.

Turkheimer, E. & Gottesman, I. I. (1991) Individual differences and the canalization of human behavior. *Developmental Psychology*, **27**, 18-22.

Verkerk, A. J., Pieretti, M., Sutcliffe, J. S., *et al* (1991) Identification of a gene (FMR-1) containing a CGG repeat coincident with a breakage point cluster region exhibiting length variation in fragile X syndrome. *Cell*, **65**, 905-914.

Wahlstrom, J. (1990) Gene map of mental retardation. *Journal of Mental Deficiency Research*, **34**, 11-27.

Webb, T. & Thake, A. (1991) Moderate and mild mental retardation in the Martin-Bell syndrome. *Journal of Mental Deficiency Research*, **35**, 521-528.

Witkin, H. A., Mednick, S. A. & Schulsinger, F. (1976) Criminality in XYY and XXY men. *Science*, **193**, 547- 555.

Wolff, P. H., Gardner, J., *et al* (1988) Variable expression of the fragile X syndrome in heterozygote females of normal intelligence. *American Journal of Medical Genetics*, **30**, 213-225.

World Health Organization (1992) *The ICD–10 Classification of Mental and Behavioural Disorders. Clinical Descriptions and Diagnostic Guidelines*. Geneva: WHO.

Yu, S., Pritchard, M., Kremer, E., *et al* (1991) Fragile X genotype characterised by an unstable region of DNA. *Science*, **252**, 1179-1181.

Zigler, E. (1967) Familial mental retardation: a continuing dilemma. *Science*, **155**, 292-298.

# 5  Schizophrenia

*Twin studies • Adoption studies • Defining the limits of schizophrenia •*
*Genetic marker studies • Candidate gene studies • Conclusions*

In Chapter 2, the assumptions, utility and limitations of classical genetic–epidemiological methods were discussed. However, before considering the applications of family, twin and adoption data in the refinement of phenotype, dissection of heterogeneity and the investigation of models of transmission, it is necessary to review the basic evidence that genes are in fact of major relevance to our understanding of schizophrenia.

Family studies provide the first clue. Although familial clustering of cases is not sufficient proof of genetic transmission, it is a prerequisite. Gottesman and Shields (Gottesman, 1991) have pooled about 40 family studies spanning seven decades of research in Western Europe (see Fig. 5.1). The data are presented in terms of lifetime morbid risk, with age correction of the sample. The general population risk is estimated to be about 1% worldwide. It is conspicuous that the relatives of affected individuals are at a higher risk for schizophrenia than the general population, and that the risk to a relative is a function of the degree of genetic relatedness to the proband. Thus, the highest morbid risks, of 46% and 48%, are found in the offspring of two schizophrenic parents and the co-twins of affected identical twins respectively, and this declines to a rate of 2% for third-degree relatives (e.g. cousins). This distribution of risks will be considered further in the discussion on the mode of inheritance.

An apparently anomalous observation is the low morbid risk in parents of schizophrenics compared with other first-degree relatives. The most likely explanation for this is that suffering from schizophrenia has a major impact on reducing an individual's marital and reproductive prospects and consequently in practice nearly all affected parents tend to produce their offspring before actually becoming psychotic. If this reduced period of risk is taken into account when calculating morbid risk, the result is a lifetime expectancy of 11% for the parents of schizophrenia probands, a rate comparable to other first-degree relatives (Essen-Möller, 1955). In addition, if a certain population sample consists exclusively of individuals who have had children, it is found that they have a lower risk for schizophrenia than the general population as a whole, at about 0.5%. Thus the increased risk in parents of an affected proband at 6% is roughly 10 times greater than the risk to parents in general and therefore comparable to that for other classes of first-degree relative.

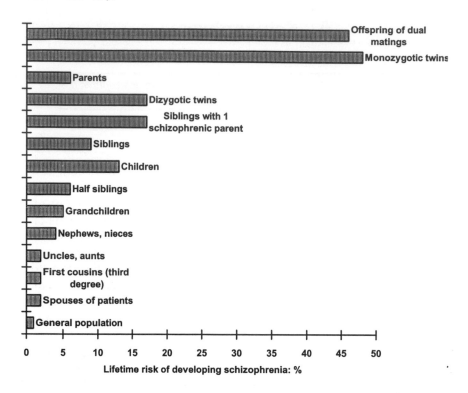

**Fig. 5.1**  Average risks for developing schizophrenia, compiled from European studies 1920–87 (from Gottesman, 1991)

Despite the wealth of data suggesting that schizophrenia is familial, this finding has been challenged in recent years by several authors who claimed to have failed to show elevated risks in first-degree relatives (Pope *et al*, 1982; Abrams & Taylor, 1983; Coryell & Zimmerman, 1988). However, these studies have a number of methodological shortcomings which reduce their credibility (Kendler, 1988). In particular, small numbers of subjects and unsatisfactory diagnostic methods have resulted in low power to detect differences between relatives and control populations. Fortunately, there are more satisfactory studies, which have used modern diagnostic criteria. These have confirmed the older observations that schizophrenia is a familial disorder (Baron *et al*, 1985; Cloninger *et al*, 1985; Frangos *et al*, 1985; Kendler *et al*, 1985). Of course, familial aggregation may be the result of factors which are other than genetic, and, historically, many family–environmental factors have been postulated, ranging from abnormal family dynamics engendered by 'schizophrenogenic' parents, to abnormal modes of communication to transmission of viruses. Therefore, evidence is required that the observed familiality is contributed to by shared genes and not just shared environment. For this we must turn to twin and adoption data.

## Twin studies

Early twin studies, for example those of Kallmann (1946) and Slater (1953), found concordance in monozygotic (MZ) twins to be in excess of 65%. These studies, however, might have suffered from the potential sources of bias discussed in Chapter 2. Methodologically more sophisticated investigations based upon systematic ascertainment of twin probands not restricted to long-stay hospitals find a lower rate of MZ concordance which is, nevertheless, much greater than is found in dizygotic (DZ) twins (see Table 5.1). Using these data, calculation of the broad heritability of schizophrenia (that is, the proportion of the variance in liability for the disorder accounted for by genes – see p. 41) results in an estimate of about 67% (McGuffin *et al*, 1984), which is in close agreement with the estimate produced by more complex methods (e.g. McGue *et al*, 1983).

It is worth noting that although all but one of the studies in Table 5.1 were performed before the introduction of current operational diagnostic criteria for schizophrenia, the Maudsley Twin Series of Gottesman & Shields have been reassessed using a variety of modern, reliable definitions (McGuffin *et al*, 1984; Farmer *et al*, 1987). In general, the results confirm substantially higher MZ than DZ concordance and in particular DSM–III criteria (American Psychiatric Association, 1980) gave a concordance of 48% in MZ twins versus 9.5% in DZ twins. The results of the only study so far that is 'purpose built' for the application of operational criteria (DSM–III–R) (Onstad *et al*, 1991) were, as we see from Table 5.1, similar.

**Table 5.1**  Concordance rates for schizophrenia in newer twin studies

|  | MZ pairs | | DZ pairs | |
| --- | --- | --- | --- | --- |
|  | Total no. of pairs | Probandwise rate (%) | Total no. of pairs | Probandwise rate (%) |
| Finland, 1963/71 | 17 | 35 | 20 | 13 |
| Norway, 1967 | 55 | 45 | 90 | 15 |
| Denmark, 1973 | 21 | 56 | 41 | 27 |
| UK, 1966/87 | 22 | 58 | 33 | 15 |
| Norway, 1991 | 31 | 48 | 28 | 4 |
| US, 1969, 1983 | 164 | 31 | 277 | 6 |

Psychodynamically based criticism of twin data has been advanced that MZ twins are likely to have higher rates of schizophrenia simply by virtue of being identical (Jackson, 1960). This, it is claimed, results in 'identity confusion' and 'dissolution of ego boundaries', making MZ twins more prone to psychosis. Perhaps more plausibly, birth trauma has been postulated to be of significance in the pathogenesis of schizophrenia (McNeill, 1987) and MZ twins are more likely to share exposure, since perinatal complications are more common in MZ than in DZ twins and considerably more common than in singletons. Against this, there does not appear to be any excess of schizophrenia among MZ twins as would be predicted by both the psychodynamic and birth trauma hypotheses (Gottesman & Shields, 1982). Although there are reports of an increased rate of obstetric complications in schizophrenic patients (O'Callaghan *et al*, 1992) the evidence is not unanimous (Done *et al*, 1991) and there do not seem to be the neuropathological changes in the brains of schizophrenics that would be expected to follow perinatal trauma (Roberts, 1991). A more cogent criticism of the twin method is that MZ and DZ twins may not share the same degree of environmental similarity; the assumption that underpins the twin study paradigm. However, the information, albeit sparse, that is available on twins reared apart confirms a high rate of MZ twin concordance of 58%, that is, 7 out of a total of 12 pairs taken from systematic studies (Gottesman & Shields, 1982). This supports the impression from studies of twins reared together that genes are the main contributors to familiality of schizophrenia, suggesting that family environment has, at most, a small role in schizophrenia as a whole.

# Adoption studies

The second important method of isolating genetic influences from the other causes of familial aggregation is by the use of adoption paradigms. Without exception (see Table 5.2) these studies have confirmed a genetic contribution to schizophrenia. In the studies of both Heston (1966) in the USA and Rosenthal *et al* (1968) in Denmark, the starting point was with schizophrenic parents who had given their offspring up for adoption. The rate of illness in the adoptees of these psychotic probands was compared to that in adoptees of non-psychiatric controls. The elevated rates of illness in the children of the schizophrenic probands is striking, and similar to the rates predicted from family studies, suggesting that perhaps all the familial transmission is under genetic rather than cultural influences.

A few further points arise from the Danish study. First, the majority of index adoptees were born before the onset of illness in the parent, and therefore the adoption agency, and subsequently the adoptive parents, could not have been aware of the diagnosis. Thus it cannot be said that the adoptees' illness resulted from the fulfilment of any negative

**Table 5.2** Principal findings from adoption studies – prevalence rates not age corrected

| Study | Type of study | Diagnosis | Genetic relatives of a schizophrenic | Not genetically related to a schizophrenic |
| --- | --- | --- | --- | --- |
| Heston (1966) | Adoptee | Schizophrenia | 10.6% of 47 adoptees who had a schizophrenic biological mother | 0% of 50 control adoptees |
| Rosenthal *et al* (1968) | Adoptee | Schizophrenia spectrum disorder | 18.8% of 69 children of schizophrenics raised by normals | 10.1% of 79 control adoptees |
| Wender *et al* (1974) | Cross-fostering | Schizophrenia spectrum disorder | 18.8% of 69 children of schizophrenics raised by normals | 10.7% of 28 children of controls raised by future schizophrenics |
| Kety (1983) Kety *et al* (1994) | Adoptee's family: national sample (47 chronic schizo-phrenic adoptees) | Chronic and latent (DSM–II) schizophrenics | 15.8% of 279 biological relatives of adopted-away schizophrenics | 18% of 228 adoptive relatives of schizophrenics and relatives of control adoptees |
| Kendler *et al* (1984, 1994) | Reassessment of of Kety's data (31 adoptees with spectrum disorder) | DSM-III schizo-phrenia plus schizotypal per-sonality disorder plus RDC schizo-affective disorder, mainly schizophrenic | 14.4% of 209 biological relatives of adopted-away schizophrenics (23.5% in 1st-degree relatives, 9.9% in 2nd-degree relatives) | 3% of 299 adoptive relatives of schizophrenics and relatives of control adoptees |
| Tienari (1991) | Adoptee (preliminary results) | Any form of psychosis | 9% of 138 adoptees who had a schizophrenic biological parent | 1.2% of 171 control adoptees |

expectations of the adoptive parents. Second, in many cases the affected parent was the father. This overcomes one of the criticisms of the Heston study, in which all of the schizophrenic parents were mothers and hence the role of intra-uterine environment could not be discounted. In the study of Rosenthal and colleagues the adopted-away offspring of schizophrenic fathers also had an elevated rate of schizophrenia spectrum disorder, suggesting that intra-uterine environmental factors were not the key aetiological factor. Third, an extension of the schizophrenia phenotype to include 'spectrum disorders', that is, borderline schizophrenia, schizoid personality and paranoid personality, seemed to have some justification, although spectrum diagnoses were not uncommon in control adoptees.

An alternative strategy allowed the effect of being raised by a psychotic adoptive parent to be investigated (Wender *et al*, 1974). In this *cross-fostering design*, a cohort of adoptees with schizophrenic biological parents raised by normal adoptive parents were compared with a group of adoptees born to normal parents but adopted by parents who subsequently became schizophrenic. While adoptees who had schizophrenic biological parents had high rates of spectrum disorder, those adoptees with normal biological parents but raised by schizophrenic adoptive parents did not.

The other variation of the adoption method is to select as probands adoptees who are schizophrenic and investigate the rate of illness in both their biological and adoptive relatives. With this adoptees' family design, Kety (1983) found that even half-siblings of schizophrenic probands sharing a common father had elevated rates of schizophrenia (13%) compared with the half-siblings of control adoptees (1%). Since these half-siblings have different mothers and hence were reared in different prenatal and perinatal environments, these can be excluded as potentially important confounding factors. Data from the national sample for 47 "chronic schizophrenic adoptees" are presented in Table 5.2 (Kety *et al*, 1994).

The adoptees' family study findings have been reanalysed using modern operational diagnostic criteria (Kendler *et al*, 1984, 1994). When diagnoses of schizophrenia, schizoaffective disorder – mainly schizophrenic, schizoid personality disorder and paranoid personality disorder were based upon DSM–III and RDC, the raw rates of illness in the biological relatives of adoptees fell. However, the magnitude of the difference of the apparent genetic effect was increased, with 23.5% of the biological relatives of the index adoptees receiving a spectrum disorder diagnosis compared with 3% of controls. To date, there have been no published studies which incorporated operational criteria from the beginning, but preliminary data from such a study currently underway in Finland (Tienari, 1991) appear to provide strong support for the importance of genetic factors.

We can conclude on the basis of family, twin and adoption study evidence that the hypothesis of a large genetic contribution to the aetiology of schizophrenia must be accepted. We now consider what it is that is inherited, and what, if any, natural divisions can be made in the phenotype.

# Defining the limits of schizophrenia

Some of the principles and problems surrounding psychiatric nosology and their implications for phenotype definition have been dealt with in Chapter 2 and elsewhere in this book. In this section we will consider only the attempts to refine the phenotype which Luxenburger (quoted in Jaspers, 1963) pointed to as merely a 'working hypothesis', for genetic research.

The most fundamental of the phenotypic delineations is the Kraepelinian dichotomy between schizophrenia and affective psychosis, but even this is the subject of debate (e.g. Crow, 1986). The least controversial finding from family, twin and adoption studies is the absence of overlap between schizophrenia and bipolar disorder. Both pre-modern (see Rieder & Gershon, 1978) and more recent family studies (e.g. Baron *et al*, 1985; Kendler *et al*, 1985; Gershon *et al*, 1988) have found that there is no excess of bipolar disorder in the relatives of schizophrenics and no excess of schizophrenia in the relatives of bipolar probands. Similarly, concordant MZ co-twins display a marked homotypia for these disorders, as do the biological relatives of probands in adoption paradigms. Less clear cut is the relationship between schizophrenia and both major depression and schizoaffective disorder.

Depression has been noted to be more common in the families of schizophrenics than schizophrenia itself (Slater, 1947); it must be borne in mind that depression is a ubiquitous, highly prevalent disorder and that the results of family studies are influenced by the stringency of definition (Gottesman, 1987). Of the three recent studies to have addressed this issue adequately, one (Kendler *et al*, 1985) found no difference in the rates of unipolar depression in the relatives of schizophrenic probands and controls, whereas the others (Gershon *et al*, 1988; Maier *et al*, 1990) report a two- to threefold increase in the relatives of probands. The different results obtained by these groups may be a consequence of the different diagnostic tools used. Kendler made diagnoses according to DSM–III, whereas the others used the Research Diagnostic Criteria (RDC) of Spitzer *et al* (1978). As the RDC have less stringent criteria for schizophrenia, it is possible that probands 'contaminated' with affective disorder were included, which might explain the elevated risks of affective disorder in these studies. Interestingly, a blind reassessment of the Gottesman & Shields (1972) Maudsley series revealed five pairs of MZ twins in whom one had schizophrenia and the other had affective disorder (Farmer *et al*, 1987*b*). In contrast, the reanalysis of the Danish adoption study of schizophrenia (Kendler & Gruenberg, 1984) did not find an elevation in the rates of affective disorder in the biological relatives of schizophrenic probands.

More controversy has surrounded the status of schizoaffective disorder, which, as the name implies, has symptoms which are a hybrid of the two major psychoses, though this does not imply that it is also a hybrid in aetiology. Whether the true status of schizoaffective disorder is that of an independent disorder, a subtype of either schizophrenia or affective disorder, the coincidental expression simultaneously of two diseases, or a mixture of all the above remains debated and family data do not allow firm conclusions. Baron *et al* (1982) found that schizoaffective disorder with mainly affective symptoms tended to cluster in families with affective disorder, whereas more schizophrenia-like schizoaffective disorder clustered with schizophrenia. Using different nomenclature, Rice *et al* (1987) reported schizophrenia to be more common in relatives of 'schizoaffective depressed' type probands, whereas bipolar disorder was elevated in the relatives of probands with 'schizoaffective bipolar disorder'. While agreeing on co-aggregation in families with schizophrenia, subtyping schizoaffective disorder has failed to achieve any degree of specificity in other studies (e.g. Gershon *et al*, 1988). The reasons for the different conclusions drawn from these studies are not clear, but may result from the small numbers in each category after the psychoses have been subdivided, together with a lack of consistency in diagnostic criteria.

To add to this uncertainty, it has been suggested that a number of other disorders may belong to an extended schizophrenia phenotype, including paranoia (delusional disorder), schizotypal and paranoid personality disorders, and atypical psychosis (Kendler *et al*, 1985).

Farmer *et al* (1987*b*) attempted to explore the boundaries by examining the effect of different extended phenotypes on the MZ/DZ concordance ratio with the general assumption (Farmer *et al*, 1990) that the higher the MZ/DZ ratio, the 'more genetic' is the phenotype. The 'optimum' MZ/DZ ratio was achieved by considering the co-twins to be 'affected' if they suffered from schizophrenia, schizotypal personality disorder, affective disorder with psychosis, or atypical psychosis (see Fig. 5.2). If, by contrast, any affective disorder was added, this lowered the ratio, which fell even further when *any* axis I diagnosis was included. Although the study cannot be regarded as conclusive, the implication is that it may be possible to 'improve' on narrow DSM–III schizophrenia by defining a phenotype which is somewhat, but not much, broader and is more genetically determined. Where the 'true' genetic boundaries lie will not become evident until a laboratory-based validating test of diagnosis is available, but in the meantime it seems sensible to collect data which allows a flexible polydiagnostic approach to hypothesis testing (Farmer *et al*, 1992).

In addition to the use of clinical features for phenotypic definition, several groups have attempted to define traits that may reflect liability to develop schizophrenia and which could then be used in genetic studies. Examples include abnormalities of smooth-pursuit eye tracking (Holzman *et al*, 1988; Clementz *et al*, 1992), attention/information processing deficits (Erlenmeyer-Kimling & Cornblatt, 1987), and deviance in a variety of measurements of the Minnesota Multiphasic Personality Inventory (Moldin *et al*, 1990). Currently it is premature to accept any of these as endophenotypes (Gottesman & Shields, 1972) or bona fide markers of a

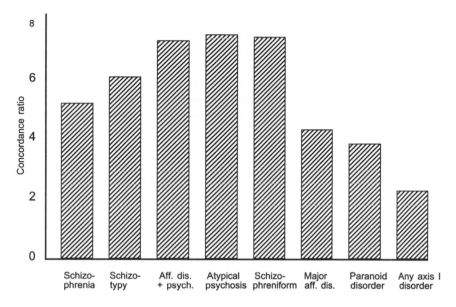

**Fig. 5.2**  Monzygotic/dizygotic concordance ratios for DSM–III schizophrenia and 'extended phenotypes' – cumulatively, from left to right, schizotypy, affective disorder with mood-incongruent psychosis, atypical psychosis, schizophreniform disorder, any major affective disorder, paranoid disorder, and any axis I disorder. (Data from Farmer *et al*, 1987*b*.)

genetic predisposition for schizophrenia, but the confirmation of any one would be a boon to future investigation.

## Heterogeneity

It seems intuitively likely to many clinicians that schizophrenia is a heterogeneous grouping of disorders since the clinical picture is so highly variable. The task of researchers is to discover whether aetiological heterogeneity underlies this variability. In contrast, pleiotropic effects may exist (i.e. a variety of phenotypes result from a single aetiology). Therefore we need to be aware when dealing with heterogeneity that purely phenotypic differences may provide "the most treacherous basis for decision" (McKusick, 1969).

The traditional classification of schizophrenia, following Bleuler (1911), is of paranoid, catatonic, hebephrenic and simple subtypes. More than 40 years ago it was shown that pairs of affected relatives tend toward homotypia, that is, they were more often of the same subtype than would be expected by chance (Slater, 1947), but modern studies have been more equivocal (see Kendler *et al*, 1986; McGuffin *et al*, 1987).

Another problem of the traditional subtypes is that they tend to be unstable over time; for example one study found at long-term follow-up a tendency for paranoid schizophrenic patients to progress to hebephrenic or undifferentiated types (Tsuang *et al*, 1990). In the fascinating case of the Genain identical quadruplets (Rosenthal, 1963), all of whom were schizophrenic, a variety of different Kraepelinian subtypes were observed in one 'clone', as well as acute and undifferentiated subtypes (Buchshaum, 1993).

Valuable insights into this issue may be provided by an examination of identical twins concordant for schizophrenia. Analysis of the Maudsley Twin Series, in which the assessment of both twins was made blindly, revealed marked but incomplete subtype concordance (McGuffin *et al*, 1987).

An alternative approach to subtyping has been taken by Crow (1980, 1985) in which schizophrenia may be divided into type I disorder with positive symptoms, good response to neuroleptics and absence of gross brain abnormalities, and type II disorder where negative symptoms predominate, the response to drug treatment is poor and computerised tomographic (CT) brain scan reveals dilated lateral cerebral ventricles. Once again this classification tends to show homotypia in twins, but the separation of subtypes is incomplete and a similar picture emerges for other reliable methods of subtyping (McGuffin *et al*, 1987).

If none of these methods generate genetically discrete subtypes, what is the explanation of the definite, but imperfect, tendency to homotypia in the twin studies? McGuffin *et al* (1987) conclude in favour of quantitative rather than qualitative differences between the various subtypes of schizophrenia, with, for example, nuclear (hebephrenic and catatonic) and peripheral (simple and paranoid) types being more and less severe forms of the disorder respectively. It is further postulated that they occupy different thresholds on a multiple-threshold liability continuum (see Chapter 2). Thus, the more severe nuclear disorders have greater familial loading, and greater twin concordance than the less severe, less genetic, peripheral disorders. The data from Kallmann's (1938) family study has been used to test this two-threshold hypothesis, and the correspondence between the actual frequency of disorder in relatives and that predicted by the model is good (McGuffin *et al*, 1987).

A more radical view has been forwarded (Murray *et al*, 1985) that schizophrenia can be divided into genetic and non-genetic forms and that a substantial portion of the cases without a family history have environmental causes. Since the majority of patients with schizophrenia, approximately 60%, have no history of the disorder in first- or second-degree relatives (Bleuler, 1978), it is argued that non-genetic 'phenocopies' constitute a substantial proportion of schizophrenia. It is further argued that the environmental agents result in a disruption of central nervous system development and that, as detected by brain imaging techniques or neuropathological investigation, this disruption will be more evident in schizophrenics with no family history.

It is therefore of interest that abnormalities such as enlarged lateral cerebral ventricles tend to be found in the affected, but not the unaffected members of discordant MZ twin pairs on CT (Reveley *et al*, 1982) or magnetic resonance imaging (MRI) (Suddath *et al*, 1990) brain scan. However, in general the evidence provided by neuroimaging does not suggest that the range of abnormalities detected in schizophrenia can be dichotomised by the presence or absence of family history (McGuffin *et al*, 1987; Jones & Murray, 1991) and there is no evidence of two discrete populations of schizophrenics on the basis of CT brain scan appearance (Harvey *et al*, 1990).

The hypothesis that a substantial proportion of cases of schizophrenia are caused exclusively by non-genetic factors can also be tested by studying the offspring of discordant MZ twins. If the hypothesis is correct, discordance will frequently be explained by the affected twin being a non-genetic phenocopy. Neither of the twins should then carry a genetic disposition for the disorder and the offspring of both twins will have a risk of schizophrenia no higher than that of the general population. Alternatively the affected twin's disorder may be caused by a factor that is familial but not genetic, in which case the offspring of the affected twin will carry a higher risk than those of the unaffected. However, if the hypothesis is not correct and all (or nearly all) cases of schizophrenia have a genetic component, then the offspring of both twins should have elevated risks and these will be comparable to the rates found in the offspring of schizophrenic parents in general.

A study examining these issues has been reported by Gottesman & Bertelsen (1989), following up and expanding upon the original Danish study of Fischer (1971). The data are summarised in Table 5.3. It is clear

**Table 5.3**  Schizophrenia and schizophrenia-like psychosis in offspring of schizoprenic twins

| | Index parents | | | |
| | Monozygotic | | Dizygotic | |
| | Schizo-phrenic twins (*n*=11) | 'Normal' co-twins (*n*=6) | Schizo-phrenic twins (*n*=10) | 'Normal' co-twins (*n*=20) |
|---|---|---|---|---|
| Number of offspring | 47 | 24 | 27 | 52 |
| Schizophrenia and schizophrenia-like | 6 | 4 | 4 | 1 |
| Morbid risk: % | 16.8 | 17.4 | 17.4 | 2.1 |

After Gottesman & Bertelsen (1989).

that the risk to the children of the normal MZ co-twin is the same as that to the affected twin. The risk to the children of the unaffected twin from discordant DZ pairs was similar to that found in the nephews and nieces of schizophrenics in family studies. Furthermore, out of the 47 children of schizophrenic MZ twins, 6 were affected, giving a risk of 13% (non-age-corrected). This is actually slightly lower than the risk in the offspring of the normal MZ co-twins (4/24 or 17%) and on age correction the risk to offspring of both the affected and unaffected MZ twins is almost identical.

These results agree with previous work showing little difference in the rates of schizophrenia in first-degree relatives in general of discordant versus concordant MZ twins (Luxenburger, 1928; Kringlen, 1967) and argue against the hypothesis that non-genetic phenocopies constitute a substantial proportion of those suffering from schizophrenia.

In conclusion, although aetiological heterogeneity must be strongly suspected, no genetically valid system of subclassifying schizophrenia has been developed to date. The most plausible interpretation of conventional subclassifications is that they define conditions which differ only quantitatively, being more or less severe forms of the same disorder.

## The mode of inheritance

The simplest hypothesis is that the resemblance between relatives in liability to schizophrenia is the result of a single major gene (see Chapter 2) but that penetrances differ from classical Mendelian values. A fully penetrant dominant gene can immediately be refuted by the lack of characteristic segregation patterns, as well as by the high rate of discordance in MZ twins. An alternative single-gene solution derived from family data is that all homozygotes are affected but less than 20% of heterozygotes express the disorder, with the number of sporadic cases being negligible (Slater & Cowie, 1971; Elston & Campbell, 1970). Unfortunately, the methods applied to arrive at these conclusions are misleading because they attempt a derivation of four unknowns (a gene frequency and three penetrances) from three parameters (estimates of the population frequency, the additive and the dominant variance). Mathematically this is not possible. Instead of providing a unique solution to these unknowns, the method can be modified to exclude those solutions which are biologically meaningless, that is, when penetrances or gene frequency are outside the range 0–1 (Suarez *et al*, 1976). When this method is applied, a single major locus seems mathematically (O'Rourke *et al*, 1982) and statistically incompatible (McGue *et al*, 1985) with the available data.

A polygenic liability threshold model, in which it is assumed that liability to develop schizophrenia is contributed many genes of small effect at different loci, was first suggested and explored by Gottesman & Shields (1967). Variants of this model are the multifactorial (polygenic plus environmental effect), the oligogenic (a few genes of moderate effect), and the 'mixed' model (a major locus with a multifactorial background). These are described in detail in Chapter 2. All of these models can explain how concordance in twins and the risk to first-degree relatives increase with the severity of the disorder in the proband, if severity is held to reflect greater genetic (or multifactorial) loading. Such models also account better than would a single gene for the persistence of schizophrenia in the population despite the low 'reproductive fitness' of schizophrenics (the finding that having offspring is unusual once someone is affected by the disorder).

Assuming that liability to develop schizophrenia is approximately normally distributed, it is possible, as outlined in Chapter 2 (p. 41), to estimate correlations in liability between twins and other pairs of relatives and then to apply path analysis to explore contributions of various factors to transmission of the disorder. For example, it may be possible to estimate heritability ($h^2$), the proportion of variance due to additive genetic effects, and common environment ($c^2$), the variance explained by any shared environment within families, as well as assortative mating and, in some models, gene–environment correlation. McGue *et al* (1985) have applied a path model to a compilation of European twin and family data and estimated that $h^2$ was 63%. In the full model $c^2$ was 29% but could be dropped without worsening the fit. Subsequently McGuffin *et al* (1994) have applied a simpler model to the twin data of Farmer *et al* (1987*b*) and Onstad *et al* (1991), where the diagnostic criteria were narrower, and estimated that $h^2$ was over 80%, with no evidence of any common environmental effect (i.e. $c^2 = 0$).

When it comes to resolving major gene effects and distinguishing between competing models of transmission, segregation analysis of whole pedigrees provides much more information than simple rates of disorder in various categories of relatives. Unfortunately, however, attempts at segregation analysis so far, taking a mixed-model approach, have yielded disappointing results, with low discriminating power between models (Vogler *et al*, 1991). The discriminatory power would be greatly enhanced by a reliable and valid method of quantifying schizotypy or 'schizophrenic traits' in subjects who are not overtly affected, but so far this has evaded the best endeavours of researchers (Gottesman, 1987; Claridge, 1994). A further problem with the models discussed is that they assume all contributing factors to be additive rather than multiplicative. It may be that multiple loci interact epistatically, with the final effect greater than the sum of the effects of the individual loci (Risch, 1990).

Another possible reason for the inconclusive results of model-fitting exercises to date is that they have sought a unitary explanation for the transmission of schizophrenia. As we have already discussed, it is plausible, indeed probable, that schizophrenia is genetically and aetiologically heterogeneous. If this is so, then there may be multiple modes of inheritance. A 'combined model' has been proposed (Gottesman & Shields,

1982) in which some cases are caused by mutations in a single gene, some by multiple genes, some by multifactorial transmission with or without major gene effects, and some by primarily environmental factors (see Chapter 2). The major gene effects can be further complicated by some operating dominantly with different penetrances, some recessively, and still others sex-linked. If this combined model is even partially correct, the application of even the most sophisticated quantitative methods will be uninformative for resolving major gene effects. It is with this background of uncertainty that we now turn to review genetic marker studies. Although ideally genetic linkage studies are most promising in disorders with known, simple modes of transmission, there are now good justifications for carrying out such studies in complex disorders where they may be supplemented by other methods such as association, with the aim also of detecting genes of smaller effect (Chapter 3).

# Genetic marker studies

Although the past decade has seen a shift from the use of classical markers to the generally more informative DNA polymorphisms, important lessons are to be learned from the earlier studies. Therefore, before discussing the modern generation of linkage and association studies, we will look first at their classical predecessors.

## Association studies using classical markers

Numerous investigators have sought possible association between schizophrenia and ABO blood groups. Mourant *et al* (1975) list no less than 48 such studies, although they suffer from the major drawback of an absence of standardised diagnostic criteria. This situation has been rectified in more recent studies, with no significant association between schizophrenia and ABO blood types being found (Rinieris *et al*, 1982; McGuffin & Sturt, 1986).

The HLA system has provided a rich source for detecting associations with common diseases of complex inheritance, for example insulin-dependent diabetes mellitus and ankylosing spondylitis. Taking encouragement from these examples, similar studies of HLA and schizophrenia have been undertaken (summarised by McGuffin & Sturt, 1986). The only replicated associations were between schizophrenia and both HLA A9 and B5, as well as a negative association with BW35.

A more consistent picture has been achieved by subdividing schizophrenia. Out of nine studies of paranoid schizophrenia, seven have found HLA A9 to be more common in patients compared with controls, and on pooling the data from all the centres this difference remains highly significant ($P = 0.003$), even after a rather stringent correction for the number of antigens tested (McGuffin & Sturt, 1986).

The same reviewers also pooled the data on three studies which had found HLA A1 to be more common in hebephrenic schizophrenics, but on this occasion statistical significance did not survive correction for multiple tests.

A subsequent study has failed to find any association between HLA A9 and paranoid schizophrenia (Alexander *et al*, 1990), which may mean that the HLA contribution is small rather than that it does not exist. McGuffin & Sturt (1986) calculated that, assuming a liability/threshold model, the A9 association accounts for only about 1% of the variation. Nevertheless, this serves to illustrate the potential power of the association strategy to detect even weak genetic effects.

## Linkage studies using classical markers

Linkage studies using classical markers have been much scarcer than association studies, and this probably reflects the greater difficulty both in design and analysis. An early study (Turner, 1979) using HLA markers examined 'multiplex' families (i.e. those with multiple affected members) and the broadly defined phenotype 'schizotaxia' (cf. Meehl, 1962). Suggestive, but not conclusive, evidence of linkage was found with a maximum lod score 2.57 at a recombination fraction of 0.15. Subsequently a number of studies (McGuffin *et al*, 1983; Chadda *et al*, 1986; Andrew *et al*, 1987; Goldin *et al*, 1987) not only failed to replicate this finding, but were able to exclude linkage up to a recombination factor of 0.25 (McGuffin, 1989). It should be noted that exclusion in these studies, as well as those we will discuss below and elsewhere in the book, requires that the model of transmission of the disorder (see Chapter 3) is approximately correct.

McGuffin (1989) also examined the possibility that the difference between positive and negative studies was a consequence of heterogeneity but was unable to detect this on formal testing. As should be evident, the interpretation of a positive result in a background of several negative findings is difficult. Without replication, positive findings should be treated as interesting but no more than preliminary.

Three of the studies quoted above (Turner, 1979; McGuffin *et al*, 1983; Andrew *et al*, 1987) also examined several other classical markers, none of which were linked to schizophrenia. It is worth noting that for the marker known as 'group specific component' (Gc), close linkage was rejected despite previous reported suggestions of linkage (Elston *et al*, 1973) and association (Lange, 1982).

Two pedigrees have now been reported in which albinism appears to co-segregate with schizophrenia (Baron, 1976; Clarke & Buckley, 1989). Since the tyrosinase gene is the site of mutation in some types of albinism and maps to 11q14–q21, it is of further interest that two other families have been independently found in which psychotic illness appears to assort with translocations involving a common region of chromosome 11 (Smith *et al*, 1989; St Clair *et al*, 1990). As the dopamine $D_2$ receptor gene also maps to this region (Grandy *et al*, 1989) these studies suggest that chromosome 11q21–22 might contain a gene or genes contributing to the aetiology of schizophrenia. Thus, this is one of the regions that has been a focus of DNA marker studies, as described in the next section.

## Linkage studies using DNA markers

As we have just mentioned, a number of lines of evidence have suggested that chromosome 11q21–22 is a potentially promising area. However, linkage specifically between schizophrenia and a polymorphism at the dopamine $D_2$ receptor has been excluded (Moises *et al*, 1991) and an extensive search through the 11q21–22 region has also proved negative (Gill *et al*, 1993).

A different clue for molecular genetic investigation of schizophrenia was provided by the observation that an Oriental family in Canada contained an uncle and a nephew pair similarly affected by both schizophrenia and a chromosomal translocation resulting in a partial trisomy of chromosome 5 (Bassett *et al*, 1988). Following up this lead, Sherrington *et al* (1988) reported linkage between schizophrenia and restriction fragment length polymorphism (RFLP) markers in the 5q11–13 region in several moderately large Icelandic and British pedigrees showing an autosomal-dominant-like pattern of transmission. However, other teams have now been unable to replicate this finding, in pedigrees from Sweden (Kennedy *et al*, 1989), Scotland (St Clair *et al*, 1989), North American (Detera-Wadleigh *et al*, 1989), the Republic of Ireland (Diehl *et al*, 1989), and Wales (McGuffin *et al*, 1990). McGuffin *et al* (1990) have also combined most of the published data and have rejected the hypothesis that a gene causing schizophrenia is located on chromosome 5q11–13, or that differences between studies simply resulted from genetic heterogeneity.

In contrast to studies focusing upon autosomes, Crow (1988) has postulated that a gene for schizophrenia is located in the 'pseudoautosomal' region of the sex chromosomes. The pseudoautosomal region is a small portion of the X and Y chromosomes between which recombination takes place in male meiosis. Genes so located are, therefore, not inherited in a classical sex-linked pattern. Instead, when transmission occurs from the paternal side, affected offspring will be the same sex more often than by chance. Thus if the schizophrenia allele resides upon the father's X chromosome, then the affected individuals are most likely to be female, if on his Y chromosome, schizophrenics would most likely be male. When transmission is through the mother then affected sibs are as likely to be mixed as same sexed. Crow *et al* (1989) have shown that such a pattern of inheritance does indeed occur in schizophrenia. Some support for the hypothesis has been provided by molecular studies, utilising DNA probes for the pseudoautosomal region (Collinge *et al*, 1991), in which affected sib pairs shared pseudoautosomal alleles more often than by chance. However, findings from other studies have been negative (Asherson *et al*, 1992).

If, as seems possible, all of the recently pursued clues as to 'favoured' regions of the genome to search for schizophrenia genes prove incorrect, then an alternative strategy is to mount a systematic search throughout the entire genome. This has in fact already been initiated, and large multicentre collaborative projects have begun in Europe and in North America. The aim is to collect a large sample of extended families who are multiply affected and to carry out linkage analysis with roughly evenly spaced markers at about 10 cM intervals (Leboyer & McGuffin, 1991). This approach is made feasible by recent advances in technology and the discovery of large numbers of single-sequence repeat polymorphisms (see Chapter 1) leading to the continuation of a 'second-generation' linkage map of the entire human genome (Weissenbach *et al*, 1992). It therefore seems likely that if major genes do exist they will be detected within a few years.

# Candidate gene studies

The 'candidate' gene approach provides a more targeted alternative to the 'shotgun' strategy of a whole genome search (see Chapter 1). The focus is on cloned genes coding for proteins which might plausibly be involved in the pathogenesis of the disorder. For example, in schizophrenia we might choose to focus on dopamine receptor genes or on genes encoding for enzymes involved in dopamine metabolism. Until fairly recently it was thought that there were just two dopamine receptor types, called $D_1$ and $D_2$, but molecular biological studies have revealed that there are at least five receptor types, some of which also have splicing variants.

As we have already mentioned, linkage studies with $D_2$ receptor polymorphisms have been negative, but there is much current interest in the other receptor types. So far, linkage seems unlikely with $D_1$ (Wildenaur *et al*, 1991) and $D_4$ (Shaikh *et al*, 1994) receptors and one group claims to have excluded linkage with all five dopamine receptor loci (Coon *et al*, 1993). However, two groups in France and in the UK have reported an association between schizophrenia and homozygosity at the $D_3$ receptor locus. Although not strong, $D_3$ homozygosity approximately doubles the risk of schizophrenia; this association is of considerable interest since the polymorphism is due to a variation in DNA which is actually in an exon (or coding region) of the gene (Crocq *et al*, 1992).

Associations, as previously pointed out, detect loci which may only account for a small proportion of variance. It is therefore clearly worth investigating other candidates in other neurotransmitter systems, and there is current interest in GABAergic, serotinergic and adrenergic receptors in particular, as well as in excitatory amino acid receptors. It seems increasingly likely that association studies in schizophrenia will focus on variations affecting protein structure or expression (VAPSE) in candidate genes (Sobell *et al*, 1992).

# Conclusions

Schizophrenia is a disorder or group of disorders with a strong genetic component, and this is by far the most important clue we have about its aetiology. The genetic evidence rests firmly on classic methods of study using families, twins and adoptees, but there is much current activity in attempting to apply molecular genetic methods. So far the results are contradictory and somewhat confusing, but this is to be expected in a disorder which clearly does not have a simple Mendelian mode of transmission. If genes of major effect exist in at least some families, these are likely to be detected and localised within the next few years. However, even if 'schizophrenia' proves to be entirely oligogenic or polygenic, molecular studies are likely to contribute to our understanding of the disorder in the foreseeable future.

# References

Abrams, R. & Taylor, M.A. (1983) The genetics of schizophrenia: a reassessment using modern criteria. *American Journal of Psychiatry*, **140**, 171-175.

Alexander, R. C., Coggiano, M., Daniel, D. G., *et al* (1990) HLA antigens in schizophrenia. *Psychiatry Research*, **31**, 221-233.

American Psychiatric Association (1980) *Diagnostic and Statistical Manual of Mental Disorders* (3rd edn) (DSM–III). Washington, DC: APA.

Andrew, B., Watt, D. C., Gillespie, C., *et al* (1987) A study of genetic linkage in schizophrenia. *Psychological Medicine*, **17**, 363-370.

Asherson, P., Parfitt, E., Sargeant, M., *et al* (1992) No evidence for a pseudoautosomal locus for schizophrenia. Linkage analysis of multiply affected families. *British Journal of Psychiatry*, **161**, 63-68.

——, Walsh, C., Williams, J., *et al* (1994) Imprinting and anticipation. Are they relevant to genetic studies of schizophrenia? *British Journal of Psychiatry*, **164**, 619-624.

Baron, M. (1976) Albinism and schizophreniform psychosis: a pedigree study. *American Journal of Psychiatry*, **133**, 1070-1073

——, Gruen, R., Asius, L., *et al* (1982) Schizoaffective illness, schizophrenia and affective disorders, morbidity risk and genetic transmission. *Acta Psychiatrica Scandinavica*, **65**, 253-262.

——, ——, Rainder, J. D., *et al* (1985) A family study of schizophrenic and normal control probands: implications for the spectrum concept of schizophrenia. *American Journal of Psychiatry*, **142**, 447-455.

Bassett, A. S., McGillivray, B. C., Jones, B. D., *et al* (1988) Partial trisomy chromosome 5 cosegregating with schizophrenia. *Lancet*, *i*, 799-801.

Bleuler, E. (1911) *Dementia Praecox or the Group of Schizophrenias* (trans. J. Zinkin (1950)). New York: International Universities Press.

Bleuler, M. (1978) *The Schizophrenia Disorders* (trans. S. Clemens). New Haven: Yale University Press.

Buchshaum, M. S. (1993) Brian imaging studies. In *Twins as a Tool of Behavioural Genetics* (eds Bouchard & Propping), pp. 257-271. New York: Wiley (in press)

Campion, D., Leboyer, M., Hillaire, D., *et al* (1992) Relationship of HLA to schizophrenia not supported in multiplex families. *Psychiatry Research*, **41**, 99-105

Chadda, R., Kulhara, P., Singh, T., *et al* (1986) HLA antigens in schizophrenia: a family study. *British Journal of Psychiatry*, **149**, 612-615.

Claridge, G. (1994) A single indicator of risk for schizophrenia: probable fact or likely myth? *Schizophrenia Bulletin* (in press).

Clarke, D. J. & Buckley, M. E. (1989) Familial association of albinism and schizophrenia. *British Journal of Psychiatry*, **155**, 551-553.

Clementz, B. A., Grove, W. M., Iacono, W. G., *et al* (1992) Smooth-pursuit eye movement dysfunction and liability for schizophrenia: implications for genetic modelling. *Journal of Abnormal Psychology*, **101**, 117-129.

Cloninger, C. R., Martin, R. L., Guze, S. B., *et al* (1985) Diagnosis and prognosis in schizophrenia. *Archives of General Psychiatry*, **42**, 15-25.

Collinge, J., DeLisi, L. E., Boceio, E., *et al* (1991) Evidence for a pseudo-autosomal locus for schizophrenia using the methods of affected sibling pairs. *British Journal of Psychiatry*, **158**, 624-629.

Coon, H., Byerley, W., Holik, J., *et al* (1993) Linkage analysis of schizophrenia with five dopamine receptor genes in nine pedigrees. *American Journal of Human Genetics*, **52**, 327-334.

Coryell, W. & Zimmerman, M. (1988) The heritability of schizoaffective disorder. *Archives of General Psychiatry*, **45**, 223-327.

Crocq, M. A., Mant, R., Asherson, P., *et al* (1992) Association between schizophrenia and homozygosity at the dopamine D3 receptor gene. *Journal of Medical Genetics*, **29**, 858-860.

Crow, T. J. (1980) The molecular pathology of schizophrenia: more than one disease process. *British Medical Journal*, **280**, 66-68.

—— (1985) The two syndrome concept: origins and current states. *Schizophrenia Bulletin*, **11**, 471-486.

—— (1986) Left brain, retrotransposons and schizophrenia. *British Medical Journal*, **293**, 3-4.

—— (1986) The continuum of psychosis and its implication for the structure of the gene. *British Journal of Psychiatry*, **149**, 419-429.

—— (1988) Sex chromosomes and psychosis. *British Journal of Psychiatry*, **153**, 675-683.

—— & Johnstone, E. C. (1980) Dementia praecox and schizophrenia: was Bleuler wrong? *Journal of the Royal College of Surgeons*, **14**, 238-240.

——, DeLisi, L. E. & Johnstone, E. C. (1989) Concordance by sex in sibling pairs with schizophrenia is paternally inherited. Evidence for a pseudoautosomal locus. *British Journal of Psychiatry*, **155**, 92-97.

Detera-Wadleigh, S. D., Goldin, I. R., Sherrington, R., *et al* (1989) Exclusion of linkage to 5q11-13 in families with schizophrenia and other psychiatric disorders. *Nature*, **339**, 391-393.

Diehl, S. R. & Kendler, K. S. (1989) Strategies for linkage studies of schizophrenia: pedigrees, DNA markers and statistical analyses. *Schizophrenia Bulletin*, **15**, 403-419.

Done, D. J., Johnstone, E. C., Frith, C. D., *et al* (1991) Complications of pregnancy and delivery in relation to psychosis in adult life: a study using the British perinatal mortality survey. *British Medical Journal*, **302**, 1576-1580

Elston, R. C. & Campbell, A. A. (1970) Schizophrenia, evidence for a major gene hypothesis. *Behaviour Genetics*, **1**, 101-106.

——, Kringlen, E. & Namboodri, K. K. (1973) Possible linkage relationship between certain blood groups and schizophrenia or other psychosis. *Behaviour Genetics*, **3**, 101-106.

Erlenmeyer-Kimling, L. & Cornblatt, B. (1987) High risk research in schizophrenia: a summary of what had been learned. *Journal of Psychiatric Research*, **21**, 401-411.

Essen-Möller, E. (1955) The calculation of morbid risk in parents of index cases, as applied to a family sample of schizophrenics. *Acta Genetica*, **5**, 334-342.

Farmer, A. E., McGuffin, P. & Gottesman, I. I. (1984) Searching for a split in schizophrenia: a twin study perspective. *Psychiatry Research*, **13**, 109-118.

——, Jackson, R., McGuffin, P., *et al* (1987*a*) Cerebral ventricular enlargement in schizophrenia: consistencies and contradictions. *British Journal of Psychiatry*, **150**, 324-330.

——, McGuffin, P. & Gottesman, I. I. (1987*b*) Twin concordance for DSM–III schizophrenia: scrutinising the validity of the definition. *Archives of General Psychiatry*, **44**, 634-641.

——, —— & —— (1990) The problems and pitfalls of family history of positive and negative dichotomy in classifying schizophrenia. *Schizophrenia Bulletin*, **26**, 367-370.

——, Wessely, S., Castle, D., *et al* (1992) Methodological issues in using a poly-diagnostic approach to define psychotic illness. *British Journal of Psychiatry*, **161**, 824-830.

Fischer, M. (1971) Psychoses in the offspring of schizophrenic monozygotic twins and their normal co-twins. *British Journal of Psychiatry*, **115**, 981-990.

Frangos, E., Athanassesnas, G., Tsitourides, S., *et al* (1985) Prevalence of DSM–III schizophrenia among the first-degree relatives of schizophrenic probands. *Acta Psychiatrica Scandinavica*, **72**, 382-386

Gershon, E. S., Delisi, L. E., Hamovit, J. A., *et al* (1988) A controlled family study of chronic psychoses. Schizophrenia and schizoaffective disorder. *Archives of General Psychiatry*, **45**, 328-336.

Gill, M., McGuffin, P., Parfitt, E., *et al* (1993) A linkage study of schizophrenia with DNA markers from the long arm of chromosome 11. *Psychological Medicine* (in press).

Goldin, L. R., DeLisi, L. E. & Gershon, E. S. (1987) The relationship of HLA to schizophrenia in 10 nuclear families. *Psychiatry Research*, **20**, 69-78.

Gottesman, I. I. (1987) The psychotic hinterlands or the fringes of lunacy. *British Medical Bulletin*, **43**, 557-569.

—— (1991) *Schizophrenia Genesis*. New York: W. H. Freeman.

—— & Shields, J. (1967) A polygenic theory of schizophrenia. *Proceedings of the National Academy of Sciences of the USA*, **58**, 199-205.

—— & —— (1972) A polygenic theory of schizophrenia. *International Journal of Mental Health*, **1**, 107-115.

—— & —— (1982) *Schizophrenia, the Epigenetic Puzzle*. Cambridge: CUP.

—— & Bertelsen, A. (1989) Confirming unexpressed genotypes for schizophrenia. Risks in the offspring of Fischer's Danish identical and fraternal discordant twins. *Archives of General Psychiatry*, **46**, 867-872.

Grandy, K. D., Litt, M., Allen, N., *et al* (1989) The human dopamine D2 receptor gene is located on chromosome 11 at q22-23 and identifies a Taq 1 RFLP. *American Journal of Human Genetics*, **45**, 778-785.

Harvey, I., McGuffin, P., Williams, M., *et al* (1990) The ventricular brain ratio (VBR) in functional psychoses I. An admixture analysis. *Psychiatry Research, Neuro-imaging*, **35**, 61-69.

Heston, L. L. (1966) Psychiatric disorders in foster home reared children of schizophrenic mothers. *British Journal of Psychiatry*, **112**, 819-825.

Holzman, P. S., Kringlen, E., Matthysse, S., *et al* (1988) A single dominant gene can account for eye tracking dysfunctions and schizophrenia in offspring of discordant twins. *Archives of General Psychiatry*, **45**, 641-647.

Jackson, D. D. (1960) A critique of the literature on the genetics of schizophrenia. In *The Etiology of Schizophrenia* (ed. D. D. Jackson). New York: Basic Books.

Jaspers, K. (1963) *General Psychopathology* (transl. M. W. Hamilton & J. Hoeing). Manchester: Manchester University Press.

Jones, P. B. & Murray, R. M. (1991) Aberrant neurodevelopment as the expression of schizophrenia genotype. In *The New Genetics of Mental Illness* (eds P. McGuffin & R. Murray), pp. 112-129. Oxford: Butterworth-Heinemann.

Kallmann, F. (1938) *The Genetics of Schizophrenia.* New York: Augustinin.

—— (1946) The genetic theory of schizophrenia. *American Journal of Psychiatry*, **103**, 309-322.

Kendler, K. S. (1988) Familial aggregation of schizophrenia and schizophrenia spectrum disorder. *Archives of General Psychiatry*, **45**, 377-383.

—— & Gruenberg, A. M. (1984) An independent analysis of the Danish adoption study of schizophrenia VI. The patterns of psychiatric illness as defined by DSM III in adoptees and relatives. *Archives of General Psychiatry*, **41**, 555-564.

——, —— & Tsuang, M. T. (1985) Psychiatric illness in first-degree relatives of schizophrenia and surgical control patients. *Archives of General Psychiatry*, **42**, 770-779.

——, Heath, A., Martin, N. G., *et al* (1986) Symptoms of anxiety and depression in a volunteer twin population. The etiologic role of genetic and environmental factors. *Archives of General Psychiatry*, **43**, 213-221.

——, Gruenberg, A. M. & Kinney, D. K. (1994) Independent diagnoses of adoptees and relatives, using DSM–III criteria, in the provincial and national samples of the Danish adoption study of schizophrenia. *Archives of General Psychiatry* (in press).

Kennedy, J. L., Giuffra, L.A., Moises, H. W., *et al* (1989) Molecular genetic studies in schizophrenia. *Schizophrenia Bulletin*, **15**, 383-391.

——, Hallmayer, J., Wetterberg, L., *et al* (1992) Exclusion of linkage between the serotonin 2 receptor and schizophrenia in a large Swedish kindred. *Archives of General Psychiatry*, **49**, 216-219.

Kety, S. S. (1983) Mental illness in the biological and adoptive relatives of schizophrenic adoptees, findings relevant to genetic and environmental factors in etiology. *American Journal of Psychiatry*, **140**, 720-727.

——, Wender, P. H., Jacobsen, B., *et al* (1994) Mental illness in the biological and adoptive relatives of schizophrenic adoptees: replication of the Copenhagen study in the rest of Denmark. *Archives of General Psychiatry* (in press).

Kringlen, E. (1967) *Heredity and Environment in the Functional Psychoses.* London: Heinemann.

Lange, V. (1982) Genetic markers for schizophrenic subgroups. *Psychiatria Clinica*, **15**, 133-144.

Leboyer, M. & McGuffin, P. (1991) Collaborative strategies in the molecular genetics of the major psychoses. *British Journal of Psychiatry*, **158**, 605-610.

Luxenburger, H. (1928) Vorlaufizer Bericht uber Psychiatrische Serien Untersuchungen an Zwillinger. *Zeitschift fur gesamte Neurologie und Psychiatrie*, **116**, 297-326.

Maier, W., Hallmayer, J., Minges, J., *et al* (1990) Morbid risks in relatives of affective, schizoaffective and schizophrenic patients – results of a family study. In *Affective and Schizoaffective Disorders* (eds M. T. Tsuang & A. Marneros). Berlin: Springer.

——, Franke, P., Hain, C., *et al* (1992) Neuropsychological indicators of the vulnerability to schizophrenia. *Progress in Neuro-Psychopharmacology and Biological Psychiatry*, **16**, 703-715.

McGue, M., Gottesman, I. I. & Rao, D. C. (1983) The transmission of schizophrenia under a multifactorial threshold model. *American Journal of Human Genetics*, **35**, 1161-1178.

——, —— & —— (1985) Resolving genetic models for the transmission of schizophrenia. *Genetic Epidemiology*, **2**, 99-110.

—— & —— (1989) Genetic linkage in schizophrenia, perspectives from genetic epidemiology. *Schizophrenia Bulletin*, **15**, 453-464.

McGuffin, P. (1989) Genetic markers: an overview and future persectives. In *A Genetic Perspective for Schizophrenic and Related Disorders* (eds E. Smeraldi & L. Belloni). Milan: Edi-Ermes.

——, Festenstein, H. & Murray, R. M. (1983) A family study of HLA antigens and other genetic markers in schizophrenia. *Psychological Medicine*, **13**, 31-43.

——, Farmer, A. E., Gottesman, I. I., *et al* (1984) Twin concordance for operationally defined schizophrenia. *Archives of General Psychiatry*, **41**, 541-555.

—— & Sturt, E. (1986) Genetic markers in schizophrenia. *Human Heredity*, **16**, 461-465.

——, Farmer, A. E. & Gottesman, I. I. (1987) Is there really a split in schizophrenia? The genetic evidence. *British Journal of Psychiatry*, **150**, 581-592.

——, Sargeant, M., Hett, G., *et al* (1990) Exclusion of a schizophrenia susceptibility gene from the chromosome 5q11-q13 region. New data and a reanalysis of previous reports. *American Journal of Human Genetics*, **47**, 524-535.

——, Asherson, P., Owen, M., *et al* (1994) The strength of the genetic effect – is there room for an environmental influence in the aetiology of schizophrenia? *British Journal of Psychiatry*, **164**, 593-599.

McKusick, V. A. (1969) On lumpers and splitters, or the nosology of genetic disease. *Perspectives on Biology and Medicine*, **12**, 298-312.

McNeil, T. F. (1987) Perinatal influences in the development of schizophrenia. In *Biological Perspectives of Schizophrenia* (eds H. Helmchen & F. A. Henn), pp. 125–138. Chichester: Wiley.

Meehl, P. E. (1962) Schizotaxia, schizotypy, schizophrenia. *American Psychologist*, **17**, 827-838.

Moises, H. W., Gelertner, J., Giuffra, L., *et al* (1991) No linkage between D2 dopamine receptor gene region and schizophrenia. *Archives of General Psychiatry*, **48**, 643-647.

Moldin, S. O., Rice, J. P., Gottesman, I. I., *et al* (1990) Transmission of a psychometric indicator for liability to schizophrenia in normal families. *General Epidemiology*, **7**, 163-176.

Mourant, A. E., Kope, A. C. & Domanieska, S. K. (1975) *Blood Groups and Diseases*. Oxford: Oxford University Press.

Murray, R. M., Lewis, S. W. & Reveley, A. M. (1985) Towards and aetiological classification of schizophrenia. *Lancet*, **i**, 1023-1026.

O'Callaghan, E., Gibson, T., Colohan, H. A., *et al* (1992) Risk of schizophrenia in adults born after obstetric complications and their association with early onset of illness, a controlled study. *British Medical Journal*, **305**, 1256-1259.

Onstad, S., Skre, I., Torgersen, S., *et al* (1991) Twin concordance for DSM-III-R schizophrenia. *Acta Psychiatria Scandinavica*, **83**, 395-401.

O'Rourke, D. H., Gottesman, I. I., Suarez, B. K., *et al* (1982) Refutation of the single locus model in the aetiology of schizophrenia. *American Journal of Human Genetics*, **33**, 630-649.

Pope, H. G., Jones, J. M., Cohen, B. M., *et al* (1982) Failure to find evidence of schizophrenia in first-degree relatives of schizophrenic probands. *American Journal of Psychiatry*, **139**, 826-828.

Reveley, A. M., Reveley, M. A., Clifford, C. A., *et al* (1982) Cerebral ventricular size in twins discordant for schizophrenia. *Lancet*, **i**, 540-541.

Rice, J., Reich, T., Andreasen, N. C., *et al* (1987) The familial transmission of bipolar illness. *Archives of General Psychiatry*, **44**, 441-447.

Rieder, R. O. & Gershon, E. S. (1978) Genetic strategies in biological psychiatry. *Archives of General Psychiatry*, **35**, 866-873.

Rinieris, P., Stefanis, C., *et al* (1982) Subtypes of schizophrenia and ABO blood types. *Neuropsychobiology*, **8**, 57-59.

Risch, N. (1990) Linkage strategies for genetically complex traits. III, The effect of marker polymorphism analysis on affected relative pairs. *American Journal of Human Genetics*, **46**, 242-253.

Roberts, G. W. (1991) Schizophrenia, a neuropathological perspective. *British Journal of Psychiatry*, **158**, 8-17.

Rosenthal, D. (1963) *The Genain Quadruplets*. New York: Basic Books.

——, Wender, P. H., Kety, S. S., *et al* (1968) Schizophrenics' offspring reared in adoptive homes. In *The Transmission of Schizophrenia* (eds D. Rosenthal & S. S. Kety). Oxford: Pergamon Press.

Shaikh, S., Gill, M., Owen, M., *et al* (1994) Failure to find linkage between a functional polymorphism in the dopamine D4 receptor gene and schizophrenia. *American Journal of Medical Genetics: Neuropsychiatric Genetics* (submitted).

Sherrington, R., Brynjolfsson, J., Petursson, H., *et al* (1988) Localization of a susceptibility locus for schizophrenia on chromosome 5. *Nature*, **336**, 164-167.

Slater, E. (1947) Genetical causes of schizophrenia symptoms. *Monatsschrift fur Psychiatrie und Neurologie*, **113**, 50-58.

—— (1953) *Psychotic and Neurotic Illness in Twins*. London: HMSO.

—— & Cowie, V. (1971) *The Genetics of Mental Disorder*. Oxford: OUP.

Smith, M., Wasmuth, J., McPherson, J. D., *et al* (1989) Cosegregation of an 11q22-9p22 translocation with affective disorder, proximity of the dopamine D2 receptor gene relative to the translocation breakpoint. *American Journal of Human Genetics*, **45**, A220.

Sobell, J. L., Heston, L. L. & Sommer, S. S. (1992) Delineation of genetic predisposition to multifactorial disease: a general approach on the threshold of feasibility. *Genomics*, **12**, 1-6.

Spitzer, R. L., Endicott, J. & Robins, E. (1978) Research diagnostic criteria, rationale and reliability. *Archives of General Psychiatry*, **35**, 773-782.

St Clair, D., Blackwood, D., Muir, W., *et al* (1989) Absence of linkage of chromosome 5q11-q13 markers to schizophrenia in Scottish families. *Nature*, **339**, 305-309.

——, Blackwood, D., Muir, W., *et al* (1990) Association within a family of balanced autosomal translocation with major mental illness. *Lancet*, **336**, 13-16.

Suarez, B. K., Reich, T. & Trost, J. (1976) Limits of the general two-allele single locus models with incomplete penetrance. *Annals of Human Genetics*, **40**, 231-244.

Suddath, R. L., Christison, G. W., Torrey, F., *et al* (1990) Anatomic abnormalities in the brains of monozygotic twins discordant for schizophrenia. *New England Journal of Medicine*, **322**, 789-794.

Tienari, F. (1991) Gene–environment interaction in adoptive families. In *Search for the Causes of Schizophrenia*, Vol. II (eds H. Hafner & W. F. Gattaz), pp. 126-143. Berlin Heidelberg: Springer.

Tsuang, M. T. & Winokur, G. (1974) Criteria for sub-typing schizophrenia. *Archives of General Psychiatry*, **31**, 43-47.

——, Lyons, M. J. & Faraone, S. V. (1990) Heterogeneity of schizophrenia. Conceptual models and analytic strategies. *British Journal of Psychiatry*, **156**, 17-26.

Turner, W. J. (1979) Genetic markers for schizophrenia. *Biological Psychiatry*, **14**, 177-205.

Vogler, G. P., Gottesman, I. I., McGue, M. K., *et al* (1991) Mixed model segregation analysis of schizophrenia in the Lindelius Swedish pedigrees. *Behaviour Genetics*, **20**, 461-472.

Weissenbach, J., Gyapay, G., Dib, C., *et al* (1992) A second generation linkage map of the human genome. *Nature*, **359**, 794-801.

Wender, P. H., Rosenthal, D., Kety, S. S., *et al* (1974) Cross-fostering. A research strategy for clarifying the role of genetic and experimental factors in the etiology of schizophrenia. *Archives of General Psychiatry*, **30**, 121.

Wildenaur, D. B., Schwab, S., Wurl, D., *et al* (1991) Linkage analysis in schizophrenia, exclusion of 5q11-q13, 5q34-qter, 11q22, 23, Xpter and chromosome 19 in 15 systematically ascertained European families. *American Journal of Human Genetics*, **49** (suppl.), 363.

# 6 Affective disorders

Family studies • Twin studies • Adoption studies • Modes of
transmission • Other forms of depression • Adversity, heredity and
depression • Sex differences • Linkage, association and molecular
biology

One of the major problems in reviewing genetic studies from a variety of sources is that the term 'affective disorder' is used to embrace a broad spectrum of diagnostic categories, ranging from full-blown acute psychosis at one extreme, to understandable adversity-related distress at the other. Traditional terminology is confusing and unsatisfactory (Kendell, 1976) and the recent introduction of operational diagnostic criteria, while improving reliability, has not entirely resolved the difficulties (Farmer & McGuffin, 1989).

Most genetic studies have attempted to focus on 'endogenous' or typical forms of affective disorder, and all are agreed that this includes mania. However, when it comes to depression, Anglo-European psychiatrists have tended to emphasise biological or psychotic features, whereas in North American classifications such as DSM–III–R the recent emphasis has been on severity, duration and number of symptoms (American Psychiatric Association, 1987). The recently published ICD–10 classification (World Health Organization, 1992) shows some convergence with DSM–III–R and the soon to be published DSM–IV in that severity has become the main way of distinguishing between categories of depression, although the ability to distinguish certain symptom profiles has been retained. For the time being, however, we will sidestep diagnostic complexity and review the genetic evidence from family, twin and adoption studies, mainly concerning ourselves with studies where the authors have focused on severe or hospital-treated forms of disorder.

## Family studies

There is no doubt that affective disorder tends to run in families. Among the first to remark on this was Kraepelin (1922), who noted that 'hereditary taint' was apparent in 80% of his patients suffering from manic–depressive illness. Subsequent studies lumping all of severe affective disorder together in this category have consistently confirmed that manic depression was more common in the relatives of index cases than in the general population (Slater & Cowie, 1971). However, in more recent years it has become the rule in family studies to follow the suggestion of Leonhard (1959), who divided the Kraepelinian entity, manic depressive disorder, into two types: bipolar (BP) disorder, in which there are episodes of mania *and* depression (or less commonly mania alone); and unipolar (UP) disorder, where there are attacks only of depression. This distinction was first used in family studies by Angst (1966), a Swiss psychiatrist, and independently, in the same year, by Perris (1966) in Sweden. Perris found that there was a striking degree of homotypia, that is, a tendency for relatives of UP and BP probands to 'breed true' and exhibit the same type of disorder. However, the findings of Angst were more complex. Among the relatives of probands with UP disorder there was an increase only of UP illness, but among the relatives of BP probands there was an excess of both UP and BP disorder, thereby supporting the existence of 'pseudo-unipolars' who do not have the opportunity to express their BP predisposition.

Most subsequent studies have conformed to the pattern found by Angst. McGuffin & Katz (1986) reviewed 12 studies in which the UP/BP distinction was made, and calculated that the weighted average morbid risk of severe affective disorder was 19.2% (7.8% BP + 11.4% UP) in the first-degree relatives of BP probands (Table 6.1). The range of morbid risks reported in the various studies was very broad. Although this may reflect real differences between the centres, it may also be attributable to differing diagnostic criteria. Nevertheless, the fairly consistent result is one of more relatives affected in the families of BP than UP probands, and the average risk of both BP disorder and UP disorder is increased in the relatives of BP probands compared with a population risk of severe affective illness requiring in-patient treatment of about 3% for UP disorder (Sturt *et al*, 1984) and under 1% for BP disorder (Reich *et al*, 1982). By contrast the first-degree relatives of UP probands have a higher rate only of UP disorder.

**Table 6.1**   Affective illness in the first-degree relatives of unipolar (UP) and bipolar (BP) probands

| Proband type | No. of studies | Relatives | | |
|---|---|---|---|---|
| | | Age-corrected[1] *n* at risk | Morbid risk[2] (range): % BP | UP |
| BP | 12 | 3710 | 7.8 (1.5–17.9) | – |
| | | 3648 | – | 11.4 (0.5-22.4) |
| UP | 7 | 2319 | 0.6 (0.3–2.1) | 9.1 (5.9–18.4) |

1. Corrected denominator (*Bezugsziffer*) to allow for relatives who have not lived through the period of risk.
2. Weighted means.
Data from studies reviewed by McGuffin & Katz (1986).

**Table 6.2** Twin concordance for disorders of mood (including unipolar and bipolar)

| Authors | MZ | | DZ | |
|---------|-----|-----------|-----|-----------|
| | *n* | Concord-ance: % | *n* | Concord-ance: % |
| Gershon *et al* (1975)[1] | 91 | 69 | 226 | 13 |
| Bertelsen *et al* (1977)[2] | 69 | 67 | 54 | 20 |
| Torgersen (1986)[2] | 37 | 51 | 65 | 20 |
| McGuffin *et al* (1991)[2] | 62 | 53 | 79 | 28 |

MZ, monozygotic; DZ, dizygotic.
1. Combined figures from six earlier studies reporting pairwise concordance.
2. Systematic register-based studies reporting probandwise concordance.

Although the majority of studies concur in finding that the total risk of affective disorder is higher than in the families of BP than of UP probands, two investigations (Tsuang *et al*, 1980; Rice *et al*, 1987) did not find this effect. Although it is not certain why this is so, the large sample size in the study of Rice *et al* makes sampling error an unlikely explanation. Nevertheless, their method of relying on a lifetime interview and including subjects in the BP category who gave retrospective accounts of untreated mania, so-called bipolar II disorder, probably broadens the definition considerably beyond that used by many researchers outside North America.

There are comparatively few data on the unusual situation where both parents were manic depressive. However, this does seem to confer a very high risk of affective disorder in the offspring. Gottesman & Bertelsen (1989) found that the morbid risk of definite plus probable manic depressive psychosis was 63%. In addition, there was an 8% risk of other forms of disorder including schizoaffective disorder, schizophrenia, and reactive psychosis.

# Twin studies

As emphasised throughout this book, familial aggregation does not necessarily compel the inference that a disorder is genetically determined. Studies of monozygotic (MZ) and dizygotic (DZ) twins provide a means of assessing the relative contribution of genes and shared environment. Another advantage of twin studies, given the classificatory problems in affective disorder, is that if we merely want to assess whether genetic influences are present, there is no necessary recourse to population figures. Whatever the definition, a higher concordance rate in MZ than DZ twins is in itself suggestive of genetic effects. Four published sets of results based

**Table 6.3** Probandwise concordance for unipolar (UP) and bipolar (BP) affective disorder in twins

|  | Proband | n | UP | BP | Affective disorder: % |
|---|---|---|---|---|---|
|  |  |  | Co-twin |  |  |
| MZ | UP | 35 | 15 | 3 | 64 |
|  | BP | 34 | 6 | 21 | 79 |
| DZ | UP | 17 | 3 | 1 | 24 |
|  | BP | 37 | 4 | 3 | 19 |

Data from Bertelsen *et al* (1977).

on twin series where at least one of each pair received hospital treatment for affective disorder are summarised in Table 6.2. The data are consistent in showing MZ concordances significantly higher than DZ concordances but the size of the MZ/DZ concordance ratio ranges from just under 2 to over 5. The data reported by Gershon *et al* (1976) were derived from a compilation of older studies where the investigators mainly had not distinguished between UP and BP disorder. However, here and in later studies overall, the results strongly suggest an important genetic contribution.

Zerbin-Rudin (1969) has reviewed older studies from the viewpoint of BP/UP subtypes and found a strong tendency for twin pairs concordant for affective illness to be concordant also for subtypes. This was confirmed in the study by Bertelsen *et al* (1977) based on the Danish National Psychiatric Twin Register, the results of which are shown in more detail in Table 6.3. Here it is important to note that even in genetically identical individuals, MZ twins, homotypia was incomplete. Thus in 9 out of 45 pairs concordant for affective illness, the proband showed one subtype of disorder while the co-twin showed the other. Moreover, there is a suggestion of stronger genetic influences on BP disorder, where the MZ/DZ concordance ratio for any affective illness in the co-twin is greater than 4, compared with a ratio of less than 3 where the proband has UP disorder. The results therefore tend to support the impression from family studies that UP and BP disorder differ quantitatively rather than being qualitatively distinct conditions.

Another interesting finding in the Danish twins was that the offspring of normal MZ co-twins had a risk of affective disorder of 25%, which was therefore very similar to the 21% risk in the offspring of the affected probands (Bertelsen & Gottesman, 1986). The results therefore favour the hypothesis that the unaffected MZ co-twins of manic depressives have an unexpressed genotype rather than the alternative explanation that the probands simply have a 'sporadic' (non-genetic) form of the disorder. (See Chapter 5 for a description of a similar analysis in schizophrenia.)

Data on twins reared apart need to be interpreted cautiously because of the inevitable sampling difficulties, idiosyncratic circumstances (e.g. adoption, illegitimacy), and small numbers involved. However, Bertelsen (1985) reviewed the world literature and reported that there were 12 such pairs in which at least one had affective illness. Eight of these proved to be concordant (67%), a rate strikingly similar to that in the older studies for MZ twins reared together.

The two more recent studies in Table 6.2, by Torgersen (1986) and McGuffin *et al* (1991), both focused on unipolar disorder and found somewhat lower MZ concordances. Nevertheless, both studies suggest a substantially heritable condition. McGuffin *et al* (1991) carried out formal biometric model fitting (see Chapter 2), the results of which suggested that both additive ($h^2$) genetic and common environmental ($c^2$) factors were both necessary to explain the transmission of UP disorder.

The only other example of model fitting is in a report by Kendler *et al* (1992), who studied a large volunteer, population sample of ostensibly normal female twins who were examined with standardised psychiatric interviews by lay interviewers. A very high lifetime prevalence of DSM–III–R major depression, of over 30%, was reported. A variety of other definitions of depressive disorder were explored, but all resulted in similarly high lifetime prevalences, perhaps surprising in an apparently 'normal' population. Nevertheless, the correlations in liability for all definitions were higher for MZ than DZ twins. The most satisfactory biometric models in terms of parsimony and goodness of fit gave heritabilities ($h^2$) ranging from 24% to 45%, with no evidence of a shared familial environmental contribution to liability ($c^2$).

A reanalysis of their data by McGuffin *et al* (1993) also failed to find evidence of a common environmental contribution, but found a heritability of close to 80%. However, the criteria were applied in a much more restricted way, corresponding to a population lifetime risk of major depression of around 4%.

The very large difference in the population estimates for major depression in the two studies demonstrate how elastic is the concept of major depression, even when DSM–III–R is applied. Nevertheless, both studies appear internally consistent, and it is somewhat reassuring that despite the marked differences in the interpretation of the diagnostic criteria, the overall pattern of results is broadly similar.

# Adoption studies

It is perhaps surprising that adoption studies have received less emphasis in affective disorder than in schizophrenia, and it is tempting to propose that this is so because the genetic basis for affective illness is a less controversial topic. Among the more clear-cut results are those of Mendlewicz & Rainer (1977), who showed that 28% of the biological parents of BP adoptees had affective illness compared with 12% of their adopting parents. The rate of affective illness in the biological parents of adoptees did not differ significantly from that in the parents of BP non-adoptees, of whom 26% were affected. Again, there was a suggestion that the two subtypes of affective disorder are not distinct entities, as a majority of affectively ill, biological parents of BP probands had UP rather than BP disorder.

A smaller and less detailed study dealt mainly with UP illness and this time concentrated on the offspring of patients with affective disorder (Cadoret, 1978). Adopted-away offspring of patients with affective illness had higher rates of affective disorder than those adoptees whose natural parents were psychiatrically well.

Based mainly on health insurance records, a Swedish adoption study carried out by Von Knorring *et al* (1983) unexpectedly found little evidence of a genetic or family environmental component in affective illness. However, a more recent report of Scandinavian data from Denmark (Wender *et al*, 1986) found marked evidence of a genetic contribution to affective disorder. Assessments were made of hospital records of the biological relatives of adoptees with affective illness compared with the adoptive relatives and relatives of matched control adoptees. These were carried out blind to the status of the adoptee and showed an eightfold increase in UP depression in the biological relatives of adoptees with affective illness compared with the other categories of relatives, as well as a 15-fold increase in the rate of suicide.

## Modes of transmission

We can therefore conclude that, despite problems of diagnosis and definition, family, twin and adoption evidence consistently favours an important genetic contribution to BP disorder and the more severe, typical or 'major' forms of UP disorder. Before going on to discuss other forms of depression we will consider the possible modes of transmission of severe affective disorder.

As with nearly all the other disorders discussed in this book, the issue of mode of transmission of affective disorders is complicated. Although 'loaded' pedigrees are sometimes encountered, where there appears to be a dominant-like pattern of transmission, a broader outlook compels the conclusion that we are not dealing with a simple Mendelian disease.

Liability/threshold models again provide us with the best conceptual framework for understanding the transmission of affective disorders (Chapter 2). It is assumed that a variable termed 'liability to develop the disorder' is continuously distributed in the population, such that only those whose liability at some time exceeds a certain threshold manifest the disorder. In general, statistical analyses have one or two possible aims. The first, already touched upon in the discussion of twin studies, is to quantify genetic and environmental effects, and the second is to detect evidence of major genes even when a *single* major locus model, as in Huntington's disease, is not credible.

The biometric analysis of twin studies mentioned earlier (McGuffin *et al*, 1991; Kendler *et al*, 1992) agree that additive genetic affects are essential in explaining the transmission of UP disorder, although there is a considerable discrepancy in the estimated heritabilities, which probably reflects differences in definition. Previously, on applying a liability/threshold model to the twin data of Bertelsen *et al*, McGuffin & Katz (1986) estimated a heritability in excess of 80%, with a negligible contribution from shared environment. By contrast, their reanalysis of the twin study results of Torgersen (1986) suggested that 'neurotic depression' aggregates in families largely because of shared environment. In all of these analyses it was assumed that liability is normally distributed (or can be readily transformed to normality) and that it results from the additive combination of multiple genetic and environmental affects. However, given the very high heritability estimate from the analysis of those twin study data which include BP disorder, it is reasonable to speculate that a substantial contribution comes from one or a few major genes which may or may not be modified by multiple genes of smaller effect (polygenes) plus environmental factors.

## Model analysis

The broad principles of segregation analysis have been discussed in Chapter 2. Most modern studies are based on the concept of 'mixed' model analysis (Morton & McLean, 1974), where a full model of a major gene plus multifactorial background is compared with reduced models in which either major gene effects or multifactorial effects are excluded. Alternatively, a test is carried out for the probability of transmission of a major gene conforming to Mendelian expectations (but allowing for variable penetrances) (Elston & Stewart, 1971). Most sophisticated of all, the mixed-model concept and the notion of transmission probabilities are combined together in a 'unified' model (Lalouel *et al*, 1983).

Applying the Elston & Stewart approach, Bucher *et al* (1981) claimed to have rejected major gene effects in families ascertained via BP probands. However, using data that partially overlapped with that of Bucher *et al*, O'Rourke *et al* (1983) found that a major gene, with or without a multifactorial background, provided a satisfactory explanation of the transmission of affective disorder. Similarly, using a larger sample of families, Rice *et al* (1987) applied a mixed-model approach and found evidence for a major locus when they controlled for other possible confounding variables such as birth cohort effects and age of onset. On applying a more stringent test, however, they found that the major gene model compared unfavourably with the more general, vertical transmission model. That is, when probabilities of transmission of the major gene were constrained to Mendelian values, a significant improvement in model fit was found. Other studies have explored the idea that X-linked genes are involved in the transmission of BP disorder, with mixed results which we will consider later.

## Summary

Analyses based on large or reasonably large samples give at best only partial support for the hypothesis of major gene effects in BP disorder. However, most of these analyses have assumed that the disorder is mainly homogeneous and therefore cannot be taken as conclusively ruling out major genes in some forms of disorder. One of the particular problems is that all researchers are agreed that relatives of BP probands who have BP disorder should be classed as 'affected', but most are less certain about whether all relatives with UP disorder, including milder forms, should be similarly classified. We therefore need to consider the difficult area of the role of genes in 'neurotic', 'non-endogenous' or other forms of depression.

# Other forms of depression

As we noted at the beginning of this chapter, the classification of depression and our confidence in defining the phenotype become less certain as we move closer to the borderlines between clinical depression and common distress. The subdivision of depression into endogenous and neurotic types has enjoyed greater popularity in Britain and Europe than in North America.

A multicentre collaborative study in the USA found no difference in the frequency of depressive illness between the relatives of neurotically and endogenously depressed probands (Andreasen *et al*, 1986). This is in marked contrast with earlier Swedish studies of Stenstedt (1952, 1966), which demonstrated high risks of depression in the relatives of typical endogenous probands but a risk of depression of only 5.4% in the relatives of neurotically depressed probands. This compares with an estimated risk in the general population of about 3% (Stenstedt, 1966). A subsequent uncontrolled Scandinavian study reported a morbid risk of 9% among first-degree relatives of neurotic depressives, which the authors interpreted as showing a probable, but small, genetic effect (Perris *et al*, 1982).

It could be argued that the Swedish studies deserve less emphasis than the American collaborative study because of small samples and less satisfactory methods. However, it could also be that the apparent differences in the findings simply reflect differences in the definition of the disorder. We have already seen how with recent twin-study results ostensibly the same DSM–III–R category of major depression can be

**Table 6.4**  Frequency (%) of depression in the first-degree
relatives of probands with neurotic or endogenous depression

|  | Proband type | | General |
|  | neurotic | endogenous | population |
| --- | --- | --- | --- |
| Prevalence of current 'cases' | 23.5 | 12.7 | 11.1[1] |
| Morbid risk of moderate | | | |
|   plus severe depression | 23.7 | 25.7 | 8.9[2] |
| Morbid risk of severe depression | 7.9 | 14.7 | 2.6[2] |

From McGuffin *et al* (1987).
1. From Bebbington *et al* (1981).
2. From Sturt *et al* (1984).

interpreted differently by two groups of researchers, resulting in wide
differences in prevalence rates.

A demonstration of how the pattern of results is depends on the breadth
of diagnostic criteria was provided by a British study in which all available
first-degree relatives of 83 depressed probands were interviewed (McGuffin
*et al*, 1987). Some of the findings are summarised in Table 6.4. There were
actually more currently ill relatives in the families of neurotic than
endogenous probands when the definition of current illness was a broad
one based upon PSE-CATEGO criteria (Wing & Sturt, 1978). Regarding
lifetime risk, there was no difference in the rate of moderate-plus-severe
depression between the first-degree relatives of neurotically and
endogenously depressed probands. However, when consideration was
restricted to severe depression, the rate in first-degree relatives of the
endogenous group of probands was 14.7%, nearly twice that in the relatives
of neurotic probands. Thus the results suggest that neurotic depression
may be less familial than endogenous depression, but only when severe
depression in relatives is taken as the relevant phenotype.

Some support for the general impression that neurotic disorder is less
genetically influenced than endogenous depression comes from twin
studies. Once again the results are partially dependent on the choice of
diagnostic criteria. Data from three published studies and preliminary
results from a fourth are summarised in Table 6.5. Slater & Shields (1969)
found zero concordance for narrowly defined depression in the co-twins
of neurotically depressed probands and, like Torgersen (1986), found little
difference between MZ and DZ concordances even after taking a broader
diagnostic perspective. By contrast, Shapiro (1971) found evidence of a
substantial genetic contribution to 'non-endogenous' depression in psychiatrically hospitalised Danish twins. There were higher concordances for
depression whether narrowly or broadly defined in MZ than in DZ twins,
but it is probable that the probands in Shapiro's series were more severely
ill than in the Slater & Shields or Torgersen studies because all probands

**Table 6.5** Twin studies of neurotic or non-endogenous depression

| Authors | Monozygotic | | Dizygotic | |
|---|---|---|---|---|
| | No. of probands | Probandwise concordance (narrow based): % | No. of probands | Probandwise concordance (narrow based): % |
| Slater & Shields (1969)[1] | 8 | 0–38 | 16 | 0–25 |
| Shapiro (1970)[2] | 18 | 22–55 | 14 | 0–14 |
| Torgersen (1986)[1] | 17 | 36–53 | 33 | 33–45 |
| McGuffin & Katz (unpublished)[3] | 27 | 33–48 | 36 | 22–39 |

1. Narrow concordance = depression in co-twin; broad concordance = any psychiatric disorder.
2. Narrow concordance = co-twin hospitalised with depression; broad concordance = any form of treated depression in co-twin.
3. Narrow concordance = DSM–III–R major depression; broad concordance = any form of treated depression.

had been treated as in-patients. In addition, different use of terminologies may be important. The fourth study however (McGuffin & Katz, unpublished) found no significant difference between MZ and DZ concordance whether broad or narrow definitions of depression in co-twins applied. The probands here all fulfilled the criteria for DSM–III–R major depression but were classified using ICD–9 criteria as having a neurotic symptom pattern. These results suggest that the genetic contribution to neurotic depression is probably small, at most accounting for about 20% of the variance in liability using the broad definition.

Taken together, these data are complex and do not lend themselves to a simple interpretation. It is reasonable perhaps to conclude that even the lesser forms of depression show a tendency to aggregate in families and it is possible that both genes and environment contribute to the aetiology. Thus we are compelled to pursue the problem by examining ways in which genetic and environmental contributions can be quantified and in which familial and environmental factors can be examined simultaneously.

# Adversity, heredity and depression

We have already discussed how estimates of the variance in liability due to additive genetic affects, or heritability ($h^2$), and that due to common (shared familial) environment ($c^2$) have been derived from twin studies. These provide a useful starting point for considering the ways in which genes and environment may co-act to produce a depressive phenotype. However, biometric model fitting should not be seen as an end in itself.

As outlined in Chapter 2, estimates of the size of environmental contributions can be made without any direct attempts to measure environmental influences. It is now well established that certain forms of adversity, such as life events that carry a severe or moderately severe threat, have a strong association with the onset of depression (Brown & Harris, 1978; Bebbington, 1985). Unfortunately, there have been few attempts to study environmental stress and familial/genetic factors in the same sample at the same time.

One of the first attempts to include environmental components in a family study of depression was by Pollitt (1972). He found that the morbid risk of depression among relatives of depressed probands whose illness arose 'out of the blue' was higher, at about 21%, than when the proband's illness was justifiable (e.g. following severe physical stress or psychological trauma), where only 6–12% of relatives were affected.

More sophisticated methods are now available for studying 'stress' in relation to mental disorder (Brown & Harris, 1978; Paykel, 1978; Bebbington, 1985). In a collaborative study between social and genetic sections of the Institute of Psychiatry, London, 83 families were identified via depressed probands who had recent onsets of depression (Bebbington *et al*, 1988). A number of unexpected findings emerged. Depression was no more common among the relatives of probands whose illness was not in any discernible way 'reactive' than among the relatives of probands whose depression followed adversity (McGuffin *et al*, 1988*a*). Furthermore, the frequency of reported life events showed a highly significant increase among the relatives of depressives compared with a sample from the general population (McGuffin *et al*, 1988*b*). This finding held even when proband-associated events were discounted. Within families, exposure to life events showed only a weak and non-significant association with depression. This finding suggests the possibility that event-associated depression is something which occurs in hazard-prone rather than just stress-susceptible individuals. Furthermore, the authors suggested that part of the association between life events and depression, which has consistently been shown in previous studies, may be due to the fact that both show familial aggregation (McGuffin *et al*, 1988*b*).

Support for the surprising idea that experiencing (or reporting) life events is a familial trait has come from twin studies, two of which have found positive correlations for life events (Plomin, 1990; Kendler *et al*, 1993) and a third has also found positive correlations for a simple measure of subjective distress following life events (McGuffin & Katz, 1993). The first two studies included a differentiation between life events which may have been influenced by the subject's own actions ('controllable') and events which were not conceivably influenced by the subject ('uncontrollable'). Only controllable events, which by implication might be related to the subject's personality or mood state, appeared to have a genetic component.

Taken together, these family and twin-study data suggest that the relationship between life stress and genetic diathesis to depression may be more complex than was previously thought. It has been suggested (McGuffin *et al*, 1988*b*) that a better understanding of underlying personality variables is required. Unfortunately, personality measures tend to be confounded by abnormal mood states. For example, Katz & McGuffin (1987) found that the neuroticism scores were highest in family members who were currently depressed, lowest in those who had never suffered from depression, and intermediate in those who had been depressed in the past but on current examination were well.

Another piece in this still incomplete jigsaw puzzle is provided by the results of population-based studies of twins by Kendler *et al* (1986, 1992). They found strong evidence that probably the same genetic factors contribute to symptoms of both anxiety and depression, that is, multivariate analyses suggested that genes act in a fairly general way, with no evidence of a specific influence on either type of symptom. However, non-familial environmental factors differed, suggesting that some such factors influence symptoms of anxiety but have little impact on depression, and vice versa (see also Chapter 7).

# Sex differences

It is not possible to give an adequate account of the complex relationship between genes and the environment in the aetiology of depression without taking sex differences into consideration. Virtually all family studies have agreed with epidemiological studies in finding more women than men affected by depression (Reich *et al*, 1982). The excess of women is minimal, however, or even absent in studies of BP disorder.

Two types of explanation have been offered for sex differences in the frequency of depression, which can be broadly classified as biological and environmental. The most provocative biological theory is that X-linked dominant genes might explain the higher risk in women. However, as we will discuss later, genetic marker studies suggest that linkage can, at best, account for only a small proportion of cases of familial affective disorder, mainly where the probands have BP illness. A different approach was adopted by Rice *et al* (1984) in their analysis of data from a multicentre collaborative study of depression in the USA. Applying a liability/threshold model of sex differences, it was found that the data were compatible with a higher mean liability towards depression for women than men. This appeared to be due to systematic differences which were not familial but which may have had a biological or cultural explanation. The results were incompatible with the hypothesis that women simply have a lower threshold for reporting depressive symptoms. Furthermore a 'cohort effect' was observed, so that the sex ratio was close to unity among younger but not among older age groups. Other recent American family studies concur in finding only a modest sex difference in the frequency of affective disorder within families (Gershon *et al*, 1982; Weissman *et al*, 1984).

Again, conclusions about sex differences are influenced by methods of classification. The importance of the way that the phenotype is defined is shown in the results of the British study referred to earlier (Bebbington *et al*, 1988; McGuffin *et al*, 1988*a*). Here it was found that there were significantly higher rates of depression among female than male first-degree relatives of depressed patients when broader definitions were used. However, there was a small and non-significant excess of men among the relatives who had received in-patient treatment for depression (McGuffin *et al*, 1988*a*). This reduction in the sex difference for rates of depression in more severe forms of the disorder is a frequent finding (Bebbington, 1987).

The observed discrepancy in female preponderance in depression when self-report is compared with some less subjective criteria (e.g. referral to hospital) raises some intriguing questions. Do women have a tendency to volunteer more symptoms, despite the suggestions to the contrary by Rice *et al* (1984)? Conversely, do men have a tendency to under-report or tone down past or present feelings of depression? If this is the case, it appears that primary care doctors, at least in the UK, compensate by adopting a lower threshold for psychiatric referral when faced with depressive symptoms in a man (Farmer & Griffiths, 1992).

Overall, the family study findings, taken together with evidence of possible secular changes (Klerman *et al*, 1985), of less marked sex differences in developing countries (e.g. Orley & Wing, 1979), and of minimal difference in the prevalence of symptoms once employment status and other social factors are taken into account (Jenkins, 1985) suggest that most of the sex differences in the prevalence of depression are due to environmental factors.

## Linkage, association and molecular biology

Having surveyed the interface between environmental and genetic factors in affective disorders we will conclude this chapter by moving, as it were, to the other extreme of genetic research, the attempts to find the molecular basis of mood disturbance. As with other disorders, the starting place is to perform linkage or association studies with the genetic markers. As outlined elsewhere in this book (see especially Chapters 1 and 3), this general approach holds much promise in the study of psychiatric disorders. The results so far have been disappointingly negative. We will therefore focus only on the areas which have produced most interest and controversy (but for more extensive reviews see Tsuang & Faraone (1990) and McGuffin & Sargeant (1991)).

One of the most enduring controversies in psychiatric genetics has concerned the hypothesis (generated by the alleged female excess) that there may be some forms of affective disorder that are transmitted on the X chromosome. The first tangible evidence of an X-linked gene was in a report of two large pedigrees where the disorder appeared to be co-inherited with colour blindness, a character now known to be on the long arm of the X chromosome (Reich *et al*, 1969). However, the existence of many families showing father–son transmission, together with the results of segregation analysis (Bucher *et al*, 1981), suggest that X linkage can at best account for a minority of cases. A collaborative study combining data from one American and three European centres failed to confirm X linkage using colour blindness as a marker (Gershon *et al*, 1980). However, further support for the hypothesis came from two further studies, one of which strongly suggested linkage between manic depression and a polymorphic DNA marker on the long arm of the X chromosome using a probe for the gene encoding for blood clotting factor IX (Mendlewicz *et al*, 1987), and the other showing positive linkage again with colour blindness or with presence or absence of glucose-6-phosphate dehydrogenase (G6PD) deficiency (Baron *et al*, 1987). Although these results appeared at first to be mutually supportive, it is now known that the distance between the factor IX and the colour blindness loci is large so that it is unlikely that the same manic depression gene would be linked to both loci. A subsequent report (Baron *et al*, 1993) exploring the same region of the X chromosome with DNA markers makes X linkage look even less likely. This, together with a critical analysis pointing to the lack of formal evidence for X-linked inheritance even in those families included in positive linkage studies, suggests that the long debate is close to reaching a definite negative conclusion (Hebebrand, 1992).

Among studies of classical autosomal markers, greatest attention has focused on the HLA system (Weitkamp *et al*, 1981; Suarez & Croughan, 1982), with its rich and measurable polymorphisms. However, a reanalysis of original data suggestive of linkage, together with other published and unpublished results, effectively ruled out linkage between HLA and a major gene for manic depression (Price, 1989). More recently, a considerable flurry of media attention resulted from the report of linkage between manic depression and markers on the short arm of chromosome 11 in a large family multiply affected with the disorder and coming from a genetically isolated religious community, the Old Order Amish in Pennsylvania, USA. However, other studies exploring the same region proved to be negative (reviewed by McGuffin & Sargeant, 1991), as also did an extended follow-up investigation of the original large Amish pedigree (Kelsoe *et al*, 1989).

Subsequently other workers have attempted to detect association with polymorphisms near a 'candidate' gene for tyrosine hydroxylase (TH), which is in the same region on the short arm of chromosome 11. As outlined in Chapter 3, one of the attractions of association studies is that they require no prior knowledge of the mode of transmission of the disorder and can detect susceptibility loci or genes of comparatively small effect. One study has suggested an association between bipolar disorder and TH polymorphisms (Leboyer *et al*, 1990), but this has so far not been confirmed elsewhere (Gill *et al*, 1991).

Currently two main strategies are being pursued in the studies of affective disorder, particularly of the BP type. First there are studies with 'candidate' genes using both linkage analysis in multiply affected families and analyses using unrelated patient and control samples to detect association. The second approach is to perform a systematic search throughout the entire genome aiming to detect genes of major affect by linkage analysis. Collaborative projects are underway in Europe, under the auspices of the European Science Foundation, and in the USA, funded by the National Institute of Mental Health. Together these ambitious projects aim to collect a large number of multiply affected families from different centres. As we have seen, the evidence for a genetic contribution to affective disorder is strong, and genetic factors are particularly important in the aetiology of BP disorder. However, the mode or modes of transmission remain unknown. Despite this, we can be confident that major genes exist (and not just polygenes each of small effect). They will be detected and localised by collaborative systematic mapping programmes within the next few years.

# References

American Psychiatric Association (1987) *Diagnostic and Statistical Manual of Mental Disorders* (3rd end, revised) (DSM–III–R). Washington, DC: APA.

Andreasen, N. C., Rice, J., Endicott, J., *et al* (1986) The family history approach to diagnosis. *Archives of General Psychiatry*, **43**, 421-429.

Angst, J. (1966) Zur Atiologie und Nosologie endogener depressiver Psychosen. *Monographen ans der Neurologie und Psychiatrie No. 112*. Berlin: Springer..

Baron, M., Freimer, N. F., Risch, N., *et al* (1993) Diminished support for linkage between manic depressive illness and X-chromosome markers in three Israeli pedigrees. *Nature Genetics*, **3**, 49-55 .

Bebbington, P. (1985) Psychosocial etiology of schizophrenia and affective disorders. In *Psychiatry* (ed. R. Michels). Philadelphia: Lippincott.

——— (1987) The social epidemiology of clinical depression. In *Handbook of Studies on Social Psychiatry* (eds A. S. Henderson & G. Burrows). Amsterdam: Elsevier.

———, Tennant, C. & Hurry, J. (1981) The epidemiology of mental disorders in Camberwell. *Psychological Medicine*, **11**, 561-580.

———, Brugha, T., MacCarthy, B., *et al* (1988) The Camberwell Collaborative Depression Study. I. Depressed probands: adversity and the form of depression. *British Journal of Psychiatry*, **152**, 754-765.

Bertelsen, A. (1985) Controversies and consistencies in psychiatric genetics. *Acta Psychiatrica Scandinavica*, **71**, 61-75.

———, Harvald, B. & Gauge, M. (1977) A Danish twin study of manic-depressive disorders. *British Journal of Psychiatry*, **130**, 330-351.

——— & Gottesman, I. I. (1986) Offspring of twin pairs discordant for psychiatric illness. *Acta Geneticae Medicae et Gemellogiae*, **35**, 310 (abstract).

Brown, G. W. & Harris, T. (1978) *The Social Origins of Depression.* London: Tavistock.

Bucher, K. D., Elston, R. C., Green, R., *et al* (1981) The transmission of manic depressive illness - II. Segregation analysis of three sets of family data. *Journal of Psychiatric Research*, **16**, 65-78.

Cadoret, R. (1978) Evidence of genetic inheritance of primary affective disorder in adoptees. *American Journal of Psychiatry*, **133**, 463-466.

Elston, R. L. & Stewart, J. (1971) A general model for genetic analysis of pedigree data. *Human Heredity*, **21**, 523-542.

Farmer, A. E. & McGuffin, P. (1989) Classification of the depressions: contemporary confusion revisited. *British Journal of Psychiatry*, **155**, 437-443.

—— & Griffiths, H. (1992) Labelling and illness in primary care: comparing factors influencing general practitioners' and psychiatrists' decisions regarding patient referral to mental illness services. *Psychological Medicine*, **22**, 717-723.

Gershon, E. S., Bunney, W. F., Leckman, J. F., *et al* (1976) The inheritance of affective disorders: a review of data and hypotheses. *Behavior Genetics*, **6**, 227-261.

——, Mendlwicz, J., Gastpar, M., *et al* (1980) A collaborative study of genetic linkage of bipolar manic depressive illness and red/green colour blindness. *Acta Psychiatrica Scandinavica*, **61**, 319-338.

——, Hamovit, J., Guroff, J. J., *et al* (1982) A family study of schizo-affective bipolar I, bipolar II, unipolar and normal control probands. *Archives of General Psychiatry*, **39**, 1157-1167.

Gill, M., Castle, D., Hunt, N., *et al* (1991) Tyrosine hydroxylase polymorphisms and bipolar affective disorder. *Journal of Psychiatry Research*, **25**, 179-184.

Gottesman, I. I. & Bertelsen, A. (1989) Dual mating studies in psychiatry. *International Review of Psychiatry*, **1**, 287-296.

Hebebrand, J. (1992) A critical appraisal of X-linked bipolar illness. Evidence for the assumed mode of inheritance is lacking. *British Journal of Psychiatry*, **160**, 7-11.

Jenkins, R. (1985) Sex differences in minor psychiatric morbidity. *Psychological Medicine* (monograph, suppl. 7).

Katz, R. & McGuffin, P. (1987) Neuroticism in familial depression. *Psychological Medicine*, **17**, 155-161.

Kelsoe, J. R., Ginns, E. I., Egeland, J. A., *et al* (1989) A re-evaluation of the linkage relationship between chromosome 11q loci and the gene for bipolar affective disorder in the Old Order Amish. *Nature*, **325**, 238-243.

Kendell, R. E. (1976) The classification of depression: a review of contemporary confusion. *British Journal of Psychiatry*, **129**, 15-28.

Kendler, K. S., Heath, A. C., Martin, N. G., *et al* (1986) Symptoms of anxiety and symptoms of depression. *Archives of General Psychiatry*, **44**, 451-457.

——, Neale, M. C., Kessler, R. C., *et al* (1992) A population based twin study of major depression in women: the impact of varying definitions of illness. *Archives of General Psychiatry*, **49**, 273-281.

——, ——, ——, *et al* (1993) A twin study of recent life events and difficulties. *Archives of General Psychiatry*, **50**, 789-796.

Klerman, G. L., Lavori, P. N., Rice, J., *et al* (1985) Birth cohort trends in rates of major depressive disorder among relatives of patients with affective disorder. *Archives of General Psychiatry*, **42**, 689-693.

Kraepelin, E. (1922) *Manic Depressive Insanity and Paranoia* (trans. R. M. Barclay). Edinburgh: E. & S. Livingstone.

Lalouel, J. M., Rao, D. L., Morton, N. E., *et al* (1983) A unified model for complex segregation analysis. *American Journal of Human Genetics*, **35**, 816-826.

Leboyer, M., Babron, M. C. & Clerget Darpoux, F. (1990) Sampling strategy in linkage studies of affective disorders. *Psychological Medicine*, **20**, 573-579.

Leonhard, K. (1959) *Aufteilung der Engoden Psychosen.* Berlin: Akademic Verlag.

McGuffin, P. (1988) Major genes of major affective disorder. *British Journal of Psychiatry,* **153,** 591-596.

—— & Katz, R. (1986) Nature, nurture and affective disorder. In *The Biology of Depression* (ed. J. W. F. Deakin), pp. 26-51. London: Gaskell.

——, —— & Bebbington, P. (1987) Hazard, heredity and affective disorder. *Journal of Psychiatric Research,* **21,** 365-375.

——, —— & —— (1988*a*) The Camberwell Collaborative Depression: Study 3. Depression and adversity in the relatives of depressed probands. *British Journal of Psychiatry,* **152,** 775-782.

——, ——, Aldrich, J., *et al* (1988*b*) The Camberwell Collaborative Depression: Study 2. Investigation of family members. *British Journal of Psychiatry,* **152,** 766-775.

—— & Sargeant, M. (1991) Genetic markers and affective disorder. In *The New Genetics of Mental Illness* (ed. P. McGuffin & R. M. Murray), pp. 27-43. Oxford: Butterworth Heinemann.

——, Katz, R. & Rutherford, J. (1991) Nature, nurture and depression: a twin study. *Psychological Medicine,* **21,** 329-335.

—— & —— (1993) Genes, adversity and depression. In *Nature, Nurture and Psychology* (eds R. Plomin & G. E. McClearn), pp. 217-230. Washington, DC: American Psychological Association.

——, ——, Rutherford, J., *et al* (1993) Twin studies as vital indicators of phenotypes in molecular genetic research. In *Twins as Tools of Behavioral Genetics* (eds T. Bouchard & P. Propping), pp. 224-256. Chichester: Wiley.

Mendlewicz, J. & Rainer, J. D. (1977) Adoption study supporting genetic transmission in manic-depressive illness. *Nature,* **268,** 326-329.

——, Simon, P., Sevy, S., *et al* (1987) Polymorphic DNA marker and X chromosome and manic depression. *Lancet, ii,* 1230-1232.

Morton, N. E. & MacLean, C. J. (1974) Analysis of familial resemblance.III. Complex segregation analysis of quantitative traits. *American Journal of Human Genetics,* **26,** 489.

Orley, J. & Wing, J. K. (1979) Psychiatric disorders in two African tillages. *Archives of General Psychiatry,* **36,** 513-520.

O'Rourke, D. H., McGuffin, P. & Reich, T. (1983) Genetic analysis of manic-depressive illness. *American Journal of Physical Anthropology,* **62,** 51-59.

Paykel, E. S. (1978) Contribution of life events to causation of psychiatric illness. *Psychological Medicine,* **8,** 245-253.

Perris, C. (1966) A study of bipolar (manic depressive) and unipolar recurrent depressive psychoses. *Acta Psychiatrica et Neurologica Scandinavica* (suppl. 42).

——, Perris, H., Ericsson, U., *et al* (1982) The genetics of depression. A family study of unipolar and reactive depressed patients. *Archives für Psychiatrica Nervenkranken,* **232,** 137-155.

Plomin, R. (1990) The role of inheritance in behavior. *Science,* **248,** 183-188.

Pollitt, J. (1972) The relationship between genetic and precipitating factors in depressive illness. *British Journal of Psychiatry,* **121,** 67-70.

Price, J. (1968) The genetics of depressive behaviour. In *Recent Developments in Affective Disorders* (eds A. J. Coppen & A. Walk). *British Journal of Psychiatry,* Special Publication No. 2. Ashford: Headley Bros.

—— (1989) Affective disorder not linked to HLA. *Genetic Epidemiology,* **6,** 299-304.

Reich, T., Clayton, P. J. & Winokur, G. (1969) Family history studies V. The genetics of mania. *American Journal of Psychiatry,* **125,** 1358-1369.

——, James, J. W. & Morris, C. A. (1972) The use of multiple thresholds in determining the mode of transmission of semi-continuous traits. *Annals of Human Genetics,* **36,** 163-184.

——, Cloninger, C. R., Suarez, B., et al (1982) Genetics of affective disorders. In *Handbook of Psychiatry, vol. III, Psychoses of Uncertain Aetiology* (eds J. K. Wing & L. Wing). Cambridge: Cambridge University Press.

Rice, J., Reich, T., Andreasen, N. C., *et al* (1984) Sex related differences in depression - familial evidence. *Journal of Affective Disorders,* **7,** 199-210.

——, ——, ——, *et al* (1987) The familial transmission of bipolar illness. *Archives of General Psychiatry,* **44,** 441 - 447.

Shapiro, R. W. (1971) A twin study of non-endogenous depression. *Acta Jutlandica,* **42** (publication of the University of Aarhus).

Slater, E. & Shields, J. (1969) Genetical aspects of anxiety. In *Studies of Anxiety* (ed. M. H. Lader). *British Journal of Psychiatry,* Special Publication No. 3. Ashford: Headley Bros.

—— & Cowie, V. (1971) *The Genetics of Mental Disorder.* London: Oxford University Press.

Stenstedt, A. (1952) A study in manic depressive psychosis: clinical, social and genetic investigations. *Acta Psychiatrica Scandinavica Supplementum,* **79.**

—— (1966) Genetics of neurotic depression. *Acta Psychiatrica Scandinavica,* **42,** 392-409.

Sturt, E., Kumakara, N. & Der, G. (1984) How depressing life is - lifelong morbidity risk for depressive disorder in the general population. *Journal of Affective Disorder,* **7,** 109-122.

Suarez, B. K. & Croughan, J. (1982) Is the major histocompatibility complex linked to genes that increase susceptibility to affective disorder? A critical appraisal. *Psychiatry Research,* **7,** 19-45.

Torgersen, S. (1986) Genetic factors in moderately severe and mild affective disorders. *Archives of General Psychiatry,* **43,** 222-226.

Tsuang, M., Winokur, G. & Crowe, R. (1980) Morbidity risks of schizophrenia and affective disorders among first degree relatives of patients with schizophrenia, mania, depression and surgical conditions. *British Journal of Psychiatry,* **137,** 497-504.

—— & Faraone, S. B. (1990) *The Genetics of Mood Disorders.* Baltimore: Johns Hopkins University Press.

Von Knorring, A. L., Cloninger, C. R., Bodman, N., *et al* (1983) An adoption study of depressive disorders and substance abuse. *Archives of General Psychiatry,* **40,** 843-950

Wender, P. H., Kety, S. S., Rosenthal, D., *et al* (1986) Psychological disorders in the biological and adoptive relatives of individuals with affective disorders. *Archives of General Psychiatry,* **43,** 923-929.

Weissman, M. M., Gershon, E., Kidd, K. K., *et al* (1984) Psychiatric disorders in the relatives of probands with affective disorders. *Archives of General Psychiatry,* **41,** 13-21.

Weitkamp, L. R., Stancer, H. C., Persad, E., *et al* (1981) Depressive disorders and HLA: a gene on chromosome 6 that can affect behaviour. *New England Journal of Medicine,* **305,** 1301-1341.

Wing, J. K. & Sturt, E. (1978) *The PSE-ID-CATEGO System: A Supplementary Manual.* London: Institute of Psychiatry.

World Health Organization (1992) *The ICD-10 Classification of Mental and Behavioural Disorders: Clinical Descriptions and Diagnostic Guidelines.* Geneva: WHO.

Zerbin-Rudin, E. (1979) Genetics of affective disorders. In *Origin, Prevention and Treatment of Affective Disorders* (eds M. Schou & E. Strömgren), pp. 185-197. London: Academic Press.

# 7  Neurotic disorders

*Neurosis as a whole • Specific syndromes • Population-based twin studies • Mode of transmission and gene–environment interactions • Anxiety and depression • Obsessive–compulsive disorder • Twin studies of obsessional symptoms and traits • Specific phobias • Eating disorders • Conclusions*

In this chapter we will review the genetics of anxiety disorders, including panic, phobic and obsessive–compulsive disorders as well as eating disorders. We are aware, therefore, that we are using the term 'neurosis' in a broad sense and moreover that the term itself has received much criticism and is no longer used in the American Psychiatric Association's (1994) DSM–IV and only sparingly in the World Health Organization's (1992) ICD–10. Nevertheless, for descriptive purposes 'neurotic disorder' provides a useful starting point. Despite the high prevalence of such disorders, their genetics have been relatively poorly studied. This may in part result from a belief that biological factors are of comparatively minor aetiological importance in states which are, on the face of it, 'stress related'. However, it may also be that the inherent difficulties in defining and classifying neurotic disorders have deterred would-be genetic researchers. Nevertheless, animal breeding experiments have shown that a tendency to 'anxious' or avoidant behaviours is heritable in rodents and such research may, in the longer term, become basic to our understanding of human disorder.

Current classification schemes in human disorders favour splitting rather than lumping, and there is an attempt both in DSM–IV and ICD–10 to define separate syndromal clusters, mainly in terms of signs and symptoms. There have also been attempts to split the neuroses using multivariate statistical methods (e.g. factor or cluster analysis), sociodemographic details, pharmacological response, as well as symptom stability and natural history. Discussion of such methods is beyond the scope of this chapter but we will, for the time being, remain on the side of the lumpers and survey family and twin studies that have investigated neurosis as a whole.

## Neurosis as a whole

Nearly all studies using a family history method report a prevalence rate for neurosis of between 15% and 18% in the first-degree relatives of neurotic probands (Carey & Gottesman, 1981; Marks, 1986). In those studies in

**Table 7.1** Twin concordance for neurotic disorders

| Study | Diagnosis | No. of twin pairs | | Concordance rate: % | | | |
|-------|-----------|----|----|----|----|----|----|
| | | | | Same diagnosis as proband | | Any diagnosis | |
| | | MZ | DZ | MZ | DZ | MZ | DZ |
| Slater & Shields (1969) | Anxiety state | 17 | 28 | 41 | 4 | 47 | 18 |
| | Other neurosis | 12 | 21 | 0 | 0 | 25 | 24 |
| Torgersen (1983*a*) | Anxiety disorders | 32 | 53 | 34 | 17 | 53 | 38 |

which relatives were directly interviewed, rates are on average two to three times greater than this. Both methods of study, therefore, find a substantial increase in the risk to the relatives of probands over the rate of between 2% and 8% which has been estimated in the families of controls and in the general population (Marks, 1986).

In addition to an overall increased risk, some general patterns emerge. First, the risk of illness in relatives increases with the number already affected; that is, someone with two or more first-degree relatives affected is at higher risk than someone with one affected (Carey & Gottesman, 1981). Second, it appears that the more severe or long standing the disorder, the greater the risk to relatives. Thus the risk to first-degree relatives of probands with chronic anxiety in one early study (Cohen *et al*, 1951) was 21.7% compared with 5% in those of acutely ill probands. Third, irrespective of absolute rates in the relatives, the risk to female relatives is about twice as great as that for males. We will return to these findings again later, when discussing the mode of transmission of neurotic disorders.

As emphasised in Chapter 2 and throughout this book, family studies, while of great importance, do not differentiate between genetic effects and those arising from shared family environment. Data from twin and adoption studies are therefore required, although unfortunately only twin-study data are at present available for broadly defined neurotic disorder. Slater & Shields (1969) systematically ascertained 146 twin pairs from the Maudsley Twin Register where the proband had received specialist treatment for a neurotic or personality disorder. Subsequently further register-based studies were carried out by Torgersen (1983*a*) in Norway and Allgulander *et al* (1991) in Sweden. The Swedish study suggested a small genetic contribution to neurosis but did not include concordance rates. The main results from the other two studies are summarised in Table 7.1.

It is clear that there is a marked difference in concordance rates between monozygotic (MZ) and dizygotic (DZ) twins for the broad diagnosis of 'anxiety state' or anxiety disorder, suggestive of a genetic effect. There is also some evidence in the Slater & Shields study for aetiological specificity. The MZ/DZ concordance ratio, an approximate indicator of the degree of genetic determination, is greater when based on co-twins having the same diagnosis as the proband than where any diagnosis in the co-twins is allowed. Where the probands suffered from 'other neurosis' Slater & Shields found zero concordance for co-twins having the same specific category of neurosis, and approximately equal MZ and DZ concordances for any form of neurosis. In Torgersen's study there was again support for a genetic contribution to anxiety disorders, with MZ twice as high as DZ concordance, but with a lower MZ/DZ ratio when concordance was defined as any neurotic disorder in the co-twin. Interestingly, in this study, the MZ/DZ concordance ratio for neurosis as a whole was significantly greater than unity in males but not in females. This has been taken as evidence of a smaller genetic contribution to neurosis in females, but the issues here are complicated (Allgulander *et al*, 1991) and the question of sex differences is discussed in greater detail with particular reference to depressive neuroses in Chapter 6.

We can conclude that there is firm evidence that neurotic disorders show familial aggregation and that twin studies suggest that this is at least partly a consequence of genetic factors.

# Specific syndromes

### Anxiety neurosis, agoraphobia and panic

The splitting of anxiety disorders into two – generalised anxiety disorder (GAD) and panic disorder (PD) – originates from the claim that anxiety states which are manifested predominantly by panic attacks are selectively responsive to imipramine (Klein, 1964) and there have been subsequent speculations that the two disorders have differing aetiology. It has also been suggested that benzodiazepines are effective in the treatment of GAD but relatively ineffective in PD (Sheehan, 1982). The validity of the distinction between GAD and PD has received some support from epidemiology, in that GAD has an earlier and more insidious onset, a more chronic course, and patients with this disorder report fewer somatic symptoms than those with PD (Noyes *et al*, 1987).

However, we should note that despite the fairly widespread acceptance of the GAD/PD dichotomy, particularly in North America, the original pharmacological basis of this distinction has been challenged by an increasing acceptance of the usefulness of antidepressant drugs in the treatment of GAD and reports of the effectiveness of benzodiazepines in both disorders (e.g. Tyrer *et al*, 1988). The status of agoraphobia within the spectrum of anxiety disorders has also been the subject of scrutiny. Marks (1971) suggested that it be distinguished from other anxiety states largely on clinical grounds but others have argued that this is unjustified (Hallam, 1978). In DSM–IV, agoraphobia is considered to be a special form of PD in which avoidant behaviour is prominent.

Genetic studies have been employed in an attempt to shed light on some of these diagnostic issues. Crowe *et al* (1983) collected data on the relatives of 41 probands with PD and the same number of unaffected controls. The morbid risk of definite PD in the relatives of PD probands was 17.3%, with an additional 7.4% classified as probable cases. This was markedly higher than the risks in relatives of control probands, where 1.8% were found to have definite PD, with another 0.5% classified as probably affected. The risk of GAD showed no difference between the two sets of relatives, suggesting some specificity in the familial transmission of PD.

The relationship between agoraphobia and PD was examined further by the same group (Noyes *et al*, 1986). The relatives of 40 probands with agoraphobia and the same number with PD were interviewed directly or by telephone and the diagnoses (using DSM–III) were compared with those in the relatives of healthy controls. The results are summarised in Table 7.2, in which both agoraphobia and PD emerge as highly familial disorders which appear not to be associated with a high risk of GAD. The interpretation of the high risk of PD in the relatives of agoraphobic probands but no increase in agoraphobia among PD relatives is more complex. The authors suggest that agoraphobia may be a severe variant of panic disorder. However, applying a liability/threshold model (see Chapter 2) we might expect that the overall rate of both PD and agoraphobia would be increased

**Table 7.2** Morbid risks in first-degree relatives

| Proband diagnosis | Number of relatives | Morbid risks: % | | | | |
|---|---|---|---|---|---|---|
| | | PD | Agora-phobia | GAD | Alco-holism | Primary affective disorder |
| PD | 241 | 14.9 | 1.7 | 5.4 | 6.6 | 4.1 |
| Agoraphobia | 256 | 7.0 | 9.4 | 3.9 | 12.9 | 4.7 |
| Control | 113 | 3.5 | 3.5 | 3.5 | 4.4 | 7.1 |

PD = panic disorder; GAD = generalised anxiety disorder.

in the relatives of probands with the more severe form of the disorder (i.e. agoraphobia) but this does not appear to be the case.

The same group then recruited a series of probands with GAD by newspaper advertisement (Noyes *et al*, 1987) and compared the results with their earlier findings for PD and agoraphobia. The rate of GAD in the relatives of GAD probands was, at 19.5%, more than five times the risk in control families. There was no increase in the risk of agoraphobia, PD, or other psychiatric disorders but there was an increased risk of alcoholism.

Taken together, these studies suggest that GAD and PD are both familial but have separate aetiologies, while agoraphobia and PD share common familial and possibly genetic aetiological factors. However, the results must be taken as suggestive rather than conclusive since the methodological shortcomings include lack of systematic ascertainment, small sample size, and assessment of relatives that was not 'blind' to the proband diagnosis.

# Population-based twin studies

One way of overcoming the problem of small numbers in twin studies is to investigate symptoms of psychiatric disorder in larger samples of ostensibly normal twins. One such study obtained twins through the volunteer Australian twin registry, who then underwent a structured psychiatric interview carried out by researchers who were blind both to zygosity and the results of the interview with the co-twin (Andrews *et al*, 1990). Surprisingly, no significant differences were found between MZ and DZ concordances for PD or agoraphobia with panic, GAD or indeed any other form of neurotic disorder. The results would therefore seem to be at odds with the findings of Torgersen (1983*b*) and Slater & Shields (1969). However, this could be explained by a difference in severity of the disorders being studied. For example, Torgersen found that the MZ/DZ concordance ratio was 2.3 for disorders requiring in-patient treatment but little over 1 for neurotic disorders treated as out-patient cases. It might therefore be argued that more severe disorders are genetically influenced but less severe forms of anxiety and neurotic disorders have little or no genetic component. Hence, a study looking at volunteer twins who may never have come in contact with psychiatric services will tend to identify mainly mild forms of the disorder and therefore fail to find a genetic effect.

However, there are two counterarguments. First, referral to psychiatric services may be complicated by factors other than simply the severity of the disorder (Farmer & Griffiths, 1992). Second, there is other evidence from population-based studies of twins that even broadly defined disorders can be shown to be heritable. For example, Kendler *et al* (1987), in a different study of Australian twins, found evidence for a genetic contribution to broadly defined anxiety and depression. In a subsequent study of female twins in the US, Kendler *et al* (1992) were able to confirm these findings using more thorough diagnostic methods, again including structured interviews. The results were intriguing in suggesting a large overlap between the genes contributing to anxiety and depressive symptoms, and we will return to discuss this in more detail later.

In summary, the family and twin evidence taken together points to a genetic contribution to anxiety disorders. The evidence is more consistent for PD and agoraphobia, and is less clear for GAD. On balance it seems likely that there is a genetic contribution to GAD, but it may be fairly non-specific and modest in size. New ground is being explored in twin studies of post-traumatic stress disorder (PTSD) in Vietnam veterans (True *et al*, 1993) which suggests that there is some genetic contribution to breakdown after exposure to combat stress.

# Mode of transmission and gene–environment interactions

Although, from all that we have discussed so far, it is obvious that anxiety disorders as a whole are not transmitted in a Mendelian fashion, there have been attempts to identify subforms that may have major locus inheritance. Most attention has focused on PD where, as we have noted, the risk of recurrence in relatives of probands tends to be higher than for all other anxiety disorders. A single major locus (SML) model (see Chapter 2) consisting of a dominant gene with incomplete penetrance was suggested as a satisfactory explanation of one set of family data (Pauls *et al*, 1980). Subsequently a more detailed analysis taking into account sex effects (Crowe *et al*, 1983) found that a model in which there were no sporadic forms of the disorder and where 25% of male and 46% of female heterozygotes were affected provided a good statistical fit. However, a multifactorial model could explain the transmission of PD equally well. Therefore, although the idea of SML transmission has its attractions, particularly to researchers who hope to resolve the aetiology of anxiety disorders using linkage strategies, the evidence for major locus transmission is slim. Indeed, as noted earlier, there are several pointers in the general direction of polygenic, multifactorial inheritance. These include the fact that the risk increases when more than one relative is affected (Carey & Gottesman, 1981) and the general tendency for earlier onset or more severe cases of anxiety disorder to be associated with higher familial loading. It could be argued that PD shows greater familiality than GAD simply because it is a more severe form of illness.

Such factors have led some workers to make the prior assumption of multifactorial inheritance in their genetic analysis of anxiety disorders. The focus of interest is then on overlapping genetic contributions to different symptom profiles and attempts to resolve genetic, shared and non-shared environmental contributions. For example, Martin *et al* (1988) carried out a multivariate analysis of symptom correlations in twins. In females, additive genetic factors were important in explaining general neuroticism, but panic symptoms showed evidence of specific genetic dominance effects, or epistasis (i.e. gene–gene interactions). In males, general neuroticism also showed evidence of dominance effects, but the genetic factors contributing to both the somatic and the psychological symptoms of panic were non-specific. Therefore, the results suggest that if there are genetic factors specific to panic rather than other forms of anxiety, then these are important only in females. Another interesting finding was that a large proportion of the variance in anxiety symptoms in both men and women were attributable to environmental factors, but these appeared to be exclusively of the non-shared (i.e. non-familial) type.

Although, as clinicians are well aware, anxiety symptoms fluctuate greatly over time, virtually all studies have taken a 'lifetime ever' perspective. One recent exception was again based on a study of Australian twins (MacKinnon *et al*, 1990). Correlations in neurotic symptoms were examined at five different times, each separated by four-month intervals. The mean level of symptoms showed evidence of substantial genetic control but the fluctuation of symptom intensity was primarily influenced by individual environmental factors, such as adverse life events. Other environmental measures, such as level of social support and earlier relationship with parents, did not emerge as powerful aetiological factors.

# Anxiety and depression

The co-occurrence of depression and anxiety is extremely common in clinical practice. This overlap is also evident in some family studies. For example, Weissman *et al* (1984) found that the risk of depression and anxiety was increased in the families of probands who had both anxiety disorder and major depression compared with the families of probands with only depression. Using a family history method, Angst *et al* (1990) found increased rates of anxiety and depression in the parents of subjects who suffered from anxiety alone, depression alone, or anxiety and depression mixed. By contrast, other workers (Cloninger *et al*, 1981; Crowe *et al*, 1983; Noyes *et al*, 1987) found no increase in the rate of primary affective disorders in relatives of probands with anxiety disorder.

Studies based on twin samples tend to suggest that anxiety without depressive symptoms has a different genetic aetiology from mixed anxiety and depression or depression alone. We have earlier referred to the Maudsley study of Slater & Shields (1969), who found greater MZ and DZ concordance for anxiety disorders but less evidence of a genetic effect when the diagnostic criteria were broadened to consider other neuroses, which in this study consisted mainly of depressive disorders. Similar conclusions can be drawn from the twin study of Torgersen (1990), in which three proband groups were studied: probands with pure anxiety, probands with pure major depression, and probands with major depression and anxiety. For the diagnosis of anxiety, MZ concordance was greater than the DZ concordance only in the pure anxiety proband group. In contrast, in the case of probands with major depression plus anxiety, MZ concordance rates were greater than DZ concordance rates for diagnoses of major depression and major depression plus anxiety. These results suggest that pure anxiety is genetically distinct from both major depression and major depression plus anxiety.

A greater degree of genetic overlap of anxiety and depression was suggested by the twin study based on questionnaire self-report (Kendler *et al*, 1987). A subsequent, more detailed study of female twins using personal interviews found very similar results (Kendler *et al*, 1992). A bivariate path analysis was performed to estimate how much of the correlation between major depression and generalised anxiety disorder could be ascribed to additive genetic effects, shared family environment, or non-shared environmental effects. Familial environment appeared to play no role in the aetiology of either condition, but genetic factors were important for both major depression and generalised anxiety, and appeared to be identical for the two disorders. The results, therefore, suggest that the non-overlapping, non-familial environmental factors may account for the existence of two apparently different syndromes.

Although of great interest, some caution is merited in attempting to extrapolate these findings directly to clinical populations. The lifetime prevalences of major depression or GAD lasting at least one month were 31% and 24% respectively in this sample. These very high (non-age-corrected) figures are greater than the age-corrected rates generally found in family studies of the first-degree relatives of probands with anxiety. Indeed they are comparable to the rates in MZ co-twins of probands with anxiety disorder in the study of Torgersen (1983). Clearly, therefore, Kendler *et al* (1992) have interpreted the criteria liberally. This again illustrates one of the problems in studying the genetics of anxiety disorders.

# Obsessive–compulsive disorder

Early studies of obsessive–compulsive disorder (OCD), predating the use of operational criteria, have been summarised by Carey & Gottesman (1981). Although the results show wide between-study variation, with estimates of any treated psychiatric disorder in relatives ranging from 9% to 33%, for the narrower categories of hospital-treated obsessional illness agreement was closer, with risks to first-degree relatives of between 0.4% and 3.1%. None of the early studies included control groups, but it was widely accepted that the population risk of OCD was low, at round 1 in

2000, so that even the modest recurrence risks in first-degree relatives suggested a familial disorder. However, a modern epidemiological study demonstrated problems of case definition (Karno *et al*, 1988), in that the population lifetime prevalence of OCD based on structured interviews carried out by non-clinicians was 2–3% but this turned out to have disappointingly poor agreement with the result of a reinterview of a subset of the population by clinicians. The important message for family studies of OCD therefore is that a control population is essential.

Two controlled family studies of OCD have been carried out and have produced rather different results. Lenane *et al* (1990) studied the first-degree relatives of children presenting with the disorder. Seventeen per cent of their parents were found to have OCD compared with 1.5% of the parents of conduct-disordered children used as a control group. Rates of OC personality and 'subdivided' OCD were 11% and 13%, respectively, which is probably greater than expected though, unfortunately, the corresponding rates in controls for these diagnoses were not presented. There also appeared to be an increased risk of OCD in the siblings of OCD probands, who had a non-age-corrected rate of 9%. On age correction, taking into account the fact that most siblings have not lived through the period of this, the figure rose by 35%.

By contrast, McKeon & Murray (1987), who studied the relatives of 50 adult OCD patients attending a behaviour therapy clinic, found no evidence for familial aggregation of OCD as such. The lifetime prevalence of the disorder was, at 0.7%, the same in probands' relatives as in controls. There was also no difference in the mean scores of the two groups on the Leyton Obsessional Inventory. There was however an increased rate of psychiatric disorders generally among the relatives of OCD probands, with a 35% lifetime prevalence of any psychiatric disorder, mainly neurosis, compared with 17% in controls. The reasons for the different results between the two studies, with one showing an apparently specific familiality of OCD and the other showing a more general familial aggregation of neurosis, are not clear. However, it is possible that, since the study of Lenane *et al* took as the proband group patients with severe OCD starting in childhood, this is again an example of a clinically more severe variety of disorder showing a stronger and more specific familial tendency.

Two other modern studies relied upon family history and did not employ control groups but are nevertheless worthy of mention. Insel *et al* (1983) obtained family histories from 27 patients meeting DSM–III criteria for OCD; 11% of parents of index cases had either affective disorder or alcoholism requiring treatment but there were no cases of OCD and only one patient had a child with the disorder.

In another study (Rasmussen & Tsuang, 1986) the proband group consisted of 44 patients with OCD, of whom 24 had been hospitalised. Five per cent of their parents met the criteria for OCD together with a further 11% who were judged to have a significant level of obsessional traits.

Affective disorders were frequent in the parents, with 20% of mothers having a history of major depression.

In conclusion, therefore, all studies of the relatives of patients with OCD suggest increased rates of psychopathology, but there is no consistent answer as to whether this is because of a specific tendency to OCD, or a more general familial predisposition to neurotic and other psychopathology.

## Twin studies of obsessional symptoms and traits

Given the contradictory nature of the family data, evidence from twin and adoption studies would be particularly valuable. Unfortunately, no adoption data whatsoever exist on OCD, and the twin-study evidence is fairly scant. Several concordant MZ twin pairs have been reported (e.g. McGuffin & Mawson, 1980), but the inferences that can be drawn from these are limited. A small clinical sample, consisting of 15 MZ and 15 DZ pairs ascertained from the Maudsley Twin Register, has been reported by Carey & Gottesman (Table 7.3). The study included probands with OCD occurring with other disorders, but nevertheless suggests a genetic effect both for psychopathology generally and OCD specifically. The only other clinical sample was too small to allow any definite conclusion, but found no co-twins affected either in three MZ or nine DZ pairs where the proband had OCD (Torgersen, 1983*a*).

Faced with the problem of small numbers, it again may be useful to turn to data on obsessive–compulsive symptoms and traits in non-clinical population samples of twins. We have already mentioned the Australian twin study of Andrews *et al* (1990) which failed to find evidence of a genetic contribution to OCD or indeed any other form of neurosis. However,

**Table 7.3**  Concordance rates (%) in obsessive twins

|  | Any psychiatric treatment[1] | Treatment for any obsessional symptoms | Obsessive symptoms or features irrespective of treatment |
|---|---|---|---|
| MZ concordance (*n*=15) | 53 | 33 | 87 |
| DZ concordance (*n*=15) | 33 | 7 | 47 |

1. From GP or specialist.
From Carey & Gottesman (1981).

taking a dimensional rather than categorical approach, Clifford *et al* (1984) examined obsessional symptoms and traits as well as neuroticism scores in a twin sample obtained from the Institute of Psychiatry volunteer twin register. They found evidence of modest but significant heritability for scores on the Leyton Obsessional Inventory as well for neuroticism, with which there was an overlap. They concluded that OCD may result from the combined effect of both a specific inherited tendency to obsessive–compulsive symptoms and a more general tendency to neuroticism, which might neatly explain both the similarities and some of the differences in other data we have just reviewed.

# Specific phobias

Two small early studies combined give a lifetime prevalence of phobia of 12% in the first-degree relatives of probands with phobic disorder compared with 4% of controls (Solyom *et al*, 1974; Buglass *et al*, 1977). More recently a study of specific phobias excluding agoraphobia found a lifetime prevalence of 31% in the first-degree relatives of probands with simple phobia compared with 11% in controls (Fryer *et al*, 1990). There was no apparent increase in the rate of agoraphobia or other psychiatric disorders in the relatives of the probands with a simple phobia, which lends some support to the idea that agoraphobia is correctly classified with panic disorder and has a somewhat different genetic aetiology to simple or specific phobias.

Carey & Gottesman (1981) have reported a small twin series from the Maudsley register. When 'affected' status was defined as 'phobic symptoms with or without treatment', 7 out of 8 MZ pairs were concordant compared with 5 out of 13 DZ pairs. This is suggestive of a genetic contribution but the sample size makes the study too small to be definitive. Again, larger twin studies of non-clinical populations can provide further information, and Torgersen (1979) identified 99 same-sex pairs of twins from the Norwegian National Register and studied their reports of 'normal' phobias by questionnaire. Using factor analysis, phobic symptoms were classified into five types: social fears, fear of animals, fears of mutilation (blood, injury, etc.), 'nature' (heights, sharp objects, enclosed spaces), and 'separation fears', which included agoraphobia-like items. In all cases the MZ correlations were greater than DZ correlations, and in all save separation fears the MZ/DZ differences were statistically significant and therefore suggestive of a genetic contribution.

Normal fears have also been studied in volunteer twins, by Rose *et al* (1981). Substantial heritabilities were found for fears of animals and other simple phobias.

We can conclude that although the area has so far been under-studied, there probably is a genetic contribution to simple fears and phobias.

# Eating disorders

Familial influences have long been thought to be important in anorexia nervosa, but until comparatively recently these have focused on alleged psychodynamic problems or dysfunctional patterns of communication. Similarly, the tendency for obesity to run in families has often been thought to be due to environmental factors including shared diet, and learnt patterns of eating and of taking (or failing to take) exercise. However, over about the past decade there has been an increasing interest in eating disorders from a more specifically genetic standpoint, with accumulating evidence that genes do indeed play a part.

## Anorexia nervosa and bulimia

There is now a reasonable consensus that anorexia nervosa is familial, with rates in first-degree relatives at around 5–10% compared with a population rate of 0.1% (Treasure & Holland, 1991). In addition, the majority of studies have shown that there is an increased risk of major affective disorder in relatives of probands with anorexia nervosa (Hudson *et al*, 1983; Gershon *et al*, 1984; Rivinus *et al*, 1984; Logue *et al*, 1989; Kassett *et al*, 1989). Although it has been suggested that the association with affective disorders is only apparent because of the inclusion of probands who have had both affective disorder and eating disorder (Strober & Katz, 1987) most controlled studies of anorexia nervosa (Gershon *et al*, 1984; Logue *et al*, 1989) and bulimia nervosa (Hudson *et al*, 1987; Kassett *et al*, 1989; Logue *et al*, 1989) have reported increased rates of affective disorder in relatives irrespective of whether the proband has both eating disorder and affective disorder or eating disorder alone. Interestingly the rate of bipolar disorder as well as major depression is increased in the relatives of patients with eating disorders (Hudson *et al*, 1987; Kassett *et al*, 1989). In addition, several studies have suggested an increase in the risk of alcoholism and other forms of drug abuse in the relatives of patients with eating disorders (Treasure & Holland, 1991) but this is not a universal finding (Logue *et al*, 1989).

## Twin studies

There have been a number of reports of twins where one or both have suffered from anorexia nervosa, and reviewers who have attempted to compile these (e.g. Garfinkel & Garner, 1986) almost inevitably find higher MZ than DZ concordance. As mentioned in Chapter 2 and elsewhere, non-systematic reports of twins almost always turn out to be biased in favour of MZ twins who are concordant. Thus a genetic aetiology may be inferred where none actually exists. In an attempt to overcome this problem Holland *et al* (1984) studied 34 pairs of twins who, although not ascertained by a register, were a reasonably complete sample of twin pairs in contact with two large eating disorder clinics in London teaching hospitals. Out of 16 female MZ pairs, 9 were concordant compared with 1 out of 14 same-sex female DZ pairs. No attempt was made to differentiate between restricting and bulimic forms of anorexia nervosa and structured interviews were not employed. In an attempt to overcome these shortcomings, the series was expanded to include 68 sets of female twins of whom at least one had an eating disorder. These pairs were independently assessed using structured interviews, and zygosity was established by blood group testing. Although there was still a problem of non-systematic ascertainment, this sample is the biggest clinical series studied to date. The concordance rates for any form of eating disorder were 55% in MZ twins and 24% in DZ twins. When the diagnostic criteria in both probands and co-twins were narrowed to restricting anorexia nervosa (a disorder characterised by extreme dieting and avoidance of food), the size of the genetic effect increased, with a MZ concordance of 59% versus 8% in DZ twins. By contrast, a diagnosis of bulimia nervosa yielded concordances of 36% in MZ twins and 38% in DZ twins, suggesting little or no genetic contribution. In applying a simple path analytic model (see Chapter 2), a heritability ($h^2$) of 76% was estimated for anorexia nervosa, with common environment ($c^2$) contributing 19% of the variance. By contrast bulimia nervosa had a negligible heritability, with common environment explaining over 80% of the variance.

As with other disorders discussed in this chapter, it is possible to speculate that eating behaviours found in the general population might have some relevance to the development of the disorder. Therefore Rutherford *et al* (1993) studied a larger sample of female twins ascertained via the Institute of Psychiatry volunteer register. The twins were assessed using questionnaire measures including the Eating Attitudes Test (EAT) and the Eating Disorder Inventory (EDI). Scores on the EAT showed moderate heritability, with additive genetic effects ($h^2$) accounting for a little under half of the variance and the remainder accounted for by non-familial environmental effects. Common family environment ($c^2$) appeared to play little or no part. The same pattern was found for various eating disorders subscales except, interestingly, for bulimia, where the heritability appeared to be negligible and once again, as in the clinical disorder, there appeared to be a significant common family environmental contribution.

In summary, there is fairly consistent evidence that anorexia nervosa is familial and there may be an overlap with other disorders, particularly mood disorders. However, anorexia nervosa as such in clinical samples appears to be heritable and anorexia-nervosa-like symptoms in normal women are also genetically influenced. On the other hand, bulimia nervosa, which also shows familial tendency appears to be mainly environmentally influenced, and this is true both of clinical samples and bulimic symptoms in normal twins.

## Obesity

Obesity is less often identified as a psychiatric disorder than anorexia nervosa or bulimia. Nevertheless it is, as we have noted, often attributed to psychological or sociocultural factors. However, there is a large amount of evidence suggesting that people resemble their relatives with respect to body weight over the entire range. There is also some evidence that this is partly genetic. For example, Rutherford *et al* (1993), in their study of eating attitudes in normal female twins, estimated the heritability of body mass index (i.e. body weight in kilograms divided by height in metres squared) to be about 0.4. Not surprisingly, therefore, evidence from twin and adoption studies suggests a genetic contribution to obesity (Stunkard *et al*, 1989*a,b*), and this is supported by data on body weight in twins reared apart (Price & Gottesman, 1991). Although most researchers assume that inheritance is polygenic, on statistical grounds Price & Stunkard (1989) suggest that there may also be a gene of major effect.

## Genetic marker studies of neuroses and eating disorders

Given the lack of evidence of major gene effects in neuroses, it is not surprising that linkage studies have been uncommon. As discussed in Chapter 3, the aim of such studies is to examine the co-segregation of the disorder and genetic markers in families who are multiply affected in the hope of detecting departure from independent assortment and hence localising major gene effects. As discussed previously, panic disorder is the one neurotic condition where there has been considerable interest in the segregation of major loci in some pedigrees. Consequently, a study of classical genetic markers was carried out (Crowe *et al*, 1987); this provided suggestive evidence of linkage between panic disorder and the haptoglobin locus on chromosome 16q22. However, a subsequent attempt to locate this finding on a new set of pedigrees excluded linkage under most models of transmission (Crowe *et al*, 1990). In addition, linkage with various candidate genes has been excluded (e.g. Mutchler *et al*, 1990).

As also discussed in Chapter 3, association studies offer the prospect of detecting genes of smaller effect, and this approach may therefore be more relevant to neurotic disorders, where it seems likely that the genetic components are polygenic. So far, almost all association studies have been of eating disorders and there have been suggestions of classical marker associations, for example between HLA and anorexia nervosa (Biederman *et al*, 1984). However, this again has not been replicated (Kiss *et al*, 1988). Nevertheless, in the long run, association strategies using DNA polymorphisms are likely to be successful in detecting quantitative trait loci (QTL) for neurotic disorders and other traits with polygenic inheritance.

# Conclusions

Although the evidence is fragmentary and in places downright contradictory, there appears to be a general consensus that several forms of neurosis are familial and probably have a moderate genetic component. Neurotic conditions present classification problems because, by their nature, they can be seen as exaggerations of normal behaviours. Therefore it may sometimes be best to measure neuroses on continuous scales rather than as present/absent categories as in traditional psychiatric practice. Indeed, difficulties in deciding where to position the cut-off between normality and neurosis are probably partly responsible for many of the contradictory results in family and twin studies. Therefore much work still needs to be done and it is probably sensible to invest most energy in exploiting 'classical' genetic methods, that is, family, twin and adoption studies, rather than to turn straight away to techniques of molecular genetics. Nevertheless, given that genetic components are probably present, the long-term prospects for an understanding of the biological basis of neurotic disorders at a molecular level are promising.

# References

Allgulander, C., Nowak, J. & Rice, J. P. (1991) Psychopathology and treatment of 30,344 twins in Sweden. II. Heritability estimates of psychiatric diagnosis and treatment in 12,884 twin pairs. *Acta Psychiatrica Scandinavica*, **83**, 12-15.

American Psychiatric Association (1994) *Diagnostic and Statistical Manual of Mental Disorders* (4th edn) (DSM–IV). Washington, DC: APA.

Andrews, G., Stewart, G., Allen, R., *et al* (1990) The genetics of six neurotic disorders: a twin study. *Journal of Affective Disorders*, **19**, 23-29.

Angst, J., Vollrath, M., Merikangas, K., *et al* (1990) Comorbidity of anxiety and depression in the Zurich Cohort study of young adults. In *Comorbidity of Mood and Anxiety Disorders* (eds J. D. Maser & C. R. Cloninger), pp. 123-137. Washington, DC: American Psychiatric Press.

Biederman, J., Rivinus, T. M., Herzog, D. B., *et al* (1984) High frequency of HL-bW16 in patients with anorexia nervosa. *American Journal of Psychiatry*, **141**, 1109-1110.

Buglass, D., Clarke, J., Henderson, A. S., *et al* (1977) A study of agarophobic housewives. *Psychological Medicine*, **7**, 73-86.

Carey, G. & Gottesman, I. I. (1981) Twin and family studies of anxiety, phobic and obsessive disorders. In *Anxiety: New Research and Changing Concepts* (eds D. F. Klein & J. Rabkin), pp. 117-135. New York: Raven Press.

Clifford, C. A., Murray, R. M. & Faulkner, D. W. (1984) Genetic and environmental influences on obsessional traits and symptoms. *Psychological Medicine*, **14**, 791-800.

Cloninger, C. R., Lewis, C., Rice, J., *et al* (1981) Strategies for resolution of biological and cultural inheritance. In *Genetic Strategies in Psychobiology and Psychiatry* (eds E. S. Gershon, S. Matthyse, X.-D. Breakfield, *et al*). California: Boxwood Press.

Cohen, M. E., Badal, D. W., Kilpatrick, A., *et al* (1951) The high familial prevalence of neurocirculatory asthenia (anxiety neurosis, effort syndrome). *American Journal of Human Genetics*, **3**, 126-158.

Crowe, R. R., Noyes, R. J., Pauls, D. L., *et al* (1983) A family study of panic disorder. *Archives of General Psychiatry*, **40**, 1065-1069.

——, ——, Wilson, A. F., *et al* (1987) A linkage study of panic disorder. *Archives of General Psychiatry*, **44**, 933-937.

——, ——, Samuelson, S., *et al* (1990) Close linkage between panic disorder and alpha-haptoglobin excluded in 10 families. *Archives of General Psychiatry*, **47**, 377-380.

Farmer, A. E. & Griffiths, H. (1992) Labelling and illness in primary care: factors influencing general practitioners' decisions to refer patients to a psychiatrist. *Psychological Medicine*, **22**, 717-723.

Fyer, A. J., Mannuzza, S., Gallops, M. S., *et al* (1990) Familial transmission of simple phobias and fears. *Archives of General Psychiatry*, **47**, 252-256.

Garfinkel, P. E. & Garner, D. M. (1982) *Anorexia Nervosa: A Multidimensional Perspective*. New York: Bruner/Mazel.

Garner, D. M. & Garfinkel, P. E. (1982) The Eating Attitudes Test: an index of the symptoms of anorexia nervosa. *Psychological Medicine*, **9**, 273-280.

Gershon, E. S., Schreiber, J. L., Hamovit, J.R., *et al* (1984) Clinical findings in patients with anorexia nervosa and affective illness in their relatives. *American Journal of Psychiatry*, **141**, 1419-1422.

Hallam, R. S. (1978) Agoraphobia: a critical review of the concept. *British Journal of Psychiatry*, **133**, 314-319.

Holland, A. J., Hall, A., Murray, R., *et al* (1984) Anorexia nervosa: evidence for a genetic basis. *Journal of Psychosomatic Research*, **32**, 561-571.

Hudson, J. I., Pope, H. J., Jonas, J. M., *et al* (1983) Family history study of anorexia nervosa and bulimia. *British Journal of Psychiatry*, **142**, 133-138.

——, ——, ——, *et al* (1987) A controlled family history study of bulimia. *Psychological Medicine*, **17**, 883-890.

Insel, T. R., Hoover, C. & Murphy, D. L. (1983) Parents of patients with obsessive-compulsive disorder. *Psychological Medicine*, **13**, 807-811.

Kahn, R. J., McNair, D. M., Lipman, R. S., *et al* (1986) Imipramine and chlordiazepoxide in depressive and anxiety disorders, II: Efficacy in anxious outpatients. *Archives of General Psychiatry*, **43**, 79-85.

Karno, M., Golding, J. M., Sorenson, S. B., *et al* (1988) The epidemiology of obsessive-compulsive disorder in five US communities. *Archives of General Psychiatry*, **45**, 1094-1099.

Kassett, J. A., Gershon, E. S., Maxwell, M. E., *et al* (1989) Psychiatric disorders in the first-degree relatives of probands with bulimia nervosa. *American Journal of Psychiatry*, **146**, 1468-1471.

Kendler, K. S., Heath, A. C., Martin, N. G., *et al* (1987) Symptoms of anxiety and symptoms of depression. Same genes, different environments? *Archives of General Psychiatry*, **44**, 451-457.

——, Neale, M. C., Kessler, R. C., *et al* (1992) Major depression and generalized anxiety disorders. Same genes, (partly) different environments? *Archives of General Psychiatry*, **49**, 716-722.

Kiss, A., Hajek, R. & Agathe, H. A. (1988) Lack of association between HLA antigens and anorexia nervosa. *American Journal of Psychiatry*, **145**, 876-877.

Klein, D. F. (1964) Delineation of two drug-responsive anxiety syndromes. *Psychopharmacology*, **53**, 397-408.

Lenane, M. C., Swedo, S. E., Leonard, H., *et al* (1990) Psychiatric disorders in first degree relatives of children and adolescents with obsessive compulsive disorder. *Journal of the American Academy of Child and Adolescent Psychiatry*, **29**, 407-412.

Logue, C. M., Crowe, R. R. & Bean, J. A. (1989) A family study of anorexia nervosa and bulimia. *Comprehensive Psychiatry*, **30**, 179-188.

MacKinnon, A. J., Henderson, A. S. & Andrews, G. (1990) Genetic and environmental determinants of the lability of trait neuroticism and the symptoms of anxiety and depression. *Psychological Medicine*, **20**, 581-590.

Marks, I. M. (1971) The classification of phobic disorders. *British Journal of Psychiatry*, 116, 337-386.

—— (1986) Genetics of fear and anxiety disorders. *British Journal of Psychiatry*, **149**, 406-418.

Martin, N. G., Jardine, R., Andrews, G., *et al* (1988) Anxiety disorders and neuroticism: are there genetic factors specific to panic? *Acta Psychiatrica Scandinavica*, **77**, 698-706.

McGuffin, P. & Mawson, D. (1980) Obsessive–compulsive neurosis: two identical twin pairs. *British Journal of Psychiatry*, **137**, 285-287.

McKeon, P. & Murray, R. (1987) Familial aspects of obsessive-compulsive neurosis. *British Journal of Psychiatry*, **151**, 528-534.

Moran, C. & Andrews, G. (1985) The familial occurrence of agoraphobia. *British Journal of Psychiatry*, **146**, 262-267.

Mutchler, K., Crowe, R. R., Noyes, R., *et al* (1990) Exclusion of the tyrosine hydroxylase gene in 14 panic disorder pedigrees. *American Journal of Psychiatry*, **147**, 1367-1369

Noyes, R. J., Crowe, R. R., Harris, E. L., *et al* (1986) Relationship between panic disorder and agoraphobia. A family study. *Archives of General Psychiatry*, **43**, 227-232.

——, Clarkson, C., Crowe, R. R., *et al* (1987) A family study of generalized anxiety disorder. *American Journal of Psychiatry*, **144**, 1019-1024.

Pauls, D. L., Bucher, K. D., Crowe, R. R., *et al* (1980) A genetic study of panic disorder pedigrees. *American Journal of Human Genetics*, **32**, 639-644.

Price, R. A. & Stunkard, A. J. (1989) Comingling analysis of obesity in twins. *Human Heredity*, **39**, 121-135.

—— & Gottesman, I. I. (1991) Body fat in identical twins reared apart: roles for genes and environment. *Behavior Genetics*, **21**, 1-7.

Rasmussen, S. & Tsuang, M. (1986) Clinical characteristics and family history in DSMIII obsessive compulsive disorder. *American Journal of Psychiatry*, **143**, 317-322.

Rivinus, T. M., Biederman, J., Herzog, D. B., *et al* (1984) Anorexia nervosa and affective disorders: a controlled family history study. *American Journal of Psychiatry*, **141**, 1414-1418.

Rose, R. J., Miller, J. Z., Pogue-Geile, M. F., *et al* (1981) Twin-family studies of common fears and phobias. In *Twin Research 3: Intelligence, Personality and Development*, pp. 169-174. New York: Alan R. Liss.

Rutherford, J., McGuffin, P., Katz, R. J., *et al* (1993) Genetic influences on eating attitudes in a normal female twin population. *Psychological Medicine*, **23**, 425-436.

Sheehan, D. V. (1982) Current concepts in psychiatry. Panic attacks and phobias. *New England Journal of Medicine*, **307**, 156-158.

Slater, E. & Shields, J. (1969) Genetical aspects of anxiety. In *Studies of Anxiety* (ed. M. H. Lader). *British Journal of Psychiatry* Special Publication No.3. Headley: Ashford.

Solyom, L., Beck, P., Solyom, C., *et al* (1974) Some etiological factors in phobic neurosis. *Canadian Psychiatric Association Journal*, **19**, 69-78.

Strober, M. & Katz, R. (1987) Do eating disorders and affective disorder share a common aetiology? *International Journal of Eating Disorders*, **6**, 171-180.

Stunkard, A. J., Sorensen, T. I., Hanis, C., *et al* (1986*a*) An adoption study of human obesity. *New England Journal of Medicine*, **314**, 193-198.

——, Foch, T. T. & Hrubec, Z. (1986*b*) A twin study of human obesity. *Journal of the American Medical Association*, **256**, 41-54.

Torgersen, S. (1979) The nature and origin of common phobic fears. *British Journal of Psychiatry*, **134**, 343-352.

—— (1983*a*) Genetic factors in anxiety disorders. *Archives of General Psychiatry*, **40**, 1085-1089.

—— (1983*b*) Genetics and neurosis: the effects of sampling variation upon the twin concordance ratio. *British Journal of Psychiatry*, **142**, 126-132.

—— (1990) A twin-study perspective of the comorbidity of anxiety and depression. In *Comorbidity of Mood and Anxiety Disorders* (eds J. D. Maser & C. R. Cloninger), pp. 367-378. Washington DC: American Psychiatric Press.

Treasure, J. L. & Holland, A. J. (1991) Genes and the aetiology of eating disorders. In *The New Genetics of Mental Illness* (eds P. McGuffin & R. Murray), pp. 198-211. Oxford: Butterworth-Heinemann.

True, W. R., Rice, J., Eisen, S. A., *et al* (1993) A twin study of genetic and environmental contributions to liability for posttraumatic stress symptoms. *Archives of General Psychiatry*, **50**, 257-264.

Tyrer, P., Seivewright, N., Murphy, S., *et al* (1988) The Nottingham study of neurotic disorder: comparison of drug and psychological treatments. *Lancet*, *ii*, 235-240.

Weissman, M. M., Leckman, J. F., Merikangas, K. R., *et al* (1984) Depression and anxiety disorders in parents and children. Results from the Yale family study. *Archives of General Psychiatry,* **41**, 845-852.

World Health Organization (1992) *The ICD–10 Classification of Mental and Behavioural Disorders: Clinical Descriptions and Diagnostic Guidelines.* Geneva: WHO.

# 8 Personality disorders and criminal behaviours

*Genetics of normal personality • Personality disorder • Biological, chromosomal and molecular markers • Conclusions*

The concept of personality and how it should best be described and measured is controversial and complex. It is therefore not surprising that the validity and usefulness of the term 'personality disorder' has been widely questioned. Despite this, clinicians and researchers continue to use the term and both ICD–10 (World Health Organization, 1992) and DSM–IV (American Psychiatric Association, 1994) include several different categories of personality disorder.

The distinction between normal and abnormal personality is often difficult and therefore it may be more sensible to consider abnormal personalities in terms of quantitative variations from the normal akin to 'caseness' rather than as distinct categorical entities. In view of this, it is important to understand the contribution of genetic factors to continuously distributed personality traits before moving on to consider the genetics of categorically defined personality disorders.

## Genetics of normal personality

The role of genetic factors in the variation in normal personality has mainly been investigated by family, twin and adoption studies with the use of personality questionnaire assessments. However, indirect contributions have also been made by animal studies and studies of human psychophysiological measures.

### Animal studies

The selective breeding of animals for particular attributes, including temperament, is a recognised and very long established practice in the domestication of animals for food or as pets. In modern times, systematic studies of observable behaviour patterns of selectively bred animals have also been carried out. For example, 'Maudsley reactive rats' have been selectively bred for high emotional response. When placed in a brightly lit enclosure, the 'open field test', they defaecate more frequently and 'freeze' more often than Maudsley non-reactive rats (Wimer & Wimer, 1985).

Certain strains of dog such as the 'nervous pointer' have also been selectively bred. They are noticeably fearful and timid in the presence of man but act normally towards other dogs (Reese, 1979).

Although results from these sorts of studies cannot be directly extrapolated to complex human personality traits, it is of interest to note that genetic factors influence behavioural traits in animals which can be considered as crude analogues of human temperamental characteristics (see temperament in Chapter 10, p. 174).

## Psychophysiological studies

It has been suggested that psychophysiological characteristics may also provide an indirect measure of personality traits. Monozygotic (MZ) twins can be reliably distinguished from dizygotic (DZ) twins by blind assessment of their resting electroencephalography (EEG) patterns (Lennox *et al*, 1945) and MZ similarities persist even when they have been reared apart (Juel-Nielsen & Harvand, 1958). However, auditory and visual evoked responses appear to be under less genetic control (Lewis *et al*, 1972) and correlations in alpha blocking are no higher in MZ than in DZ twins (Young & Fenton, 1971). The findings of twin studies of peripheral measures suggest that habituation of the galvanic skin response (GSR) and spontaneous fluctuations in GSR and pulse rate are influenced genetically (Lader & Wing, 1966; Hume, 1973; Lykken *et al*, 1988). Therefore it seems that certain psychophysiological traits are under genetic influence, but there is as yet insufficient evidence to suggest that these can be taken as reliable predispositional, biological measures of personality attributes or abnormal personality. The genetics of individual differences in neurotransmitters relevant to functioning of the central nervous system (CNS) is little understood, but may begin to become clearer as progress is made in studies at the molecular level.

## Personality questionnaire studies

The findings of nearly all twin studies suggest that personality as measured by questionnaires is in part genetically determined (Loehlin *et al*, 1988; Eaves *et al*, 1989; Plomin & Rende, 1991). However, the degree of influence of genetic factors on the different kinds of personality traits is less consistent. In studies where the MMPI (Minnesota Multiphasic Personality Inventory) has been used, there has been some agreement about the heritability of scores on scales named 'social introversion', 'depression', 'psychopathic deviance' and 'schizophrenia' (Gottesman, 1963, 1965; Reznikoff & Honeyman, 1967). However, there has been less consistency regarding the genetic influence on other personality traits. Reanalysis of twin studies where the California Psychological Inventory has been used (Carey *et al*, 1978) has shown similar findings to studies based on the Eysenck

Personality Questionnaire (Eaves & Eysenck, 1975), in that scores relating to extraversion–introversion appear to be the most heritable.

More recently, attempts have been made to explore twin data further by model fitting (see Chapter 2). Overall, for personality traits measured by questionnaires, there appears to be a heritability of around 35–50% (Martin & Jardine, 1986; Eaves *et al*, 1989). An interesting finding is that nearly all twin data can be explained by models which do not include shared family environment. That is, although environment is the largest contributor to the variance, this is entirely of the non-shared (non-familial) type. These results, apart from being highly consistent, also challenge some traditional views about the role of family factors in personality develop-ment. The only scales in which family environment appear to be of some importance are for those related to conservatism, but even then it only explains 20% of the variance (Martin & Jardine, 1986).

In general, studies of MZ twins reared apart have shown slightly lower heritabilities than studies of reared-together twins, but have again con-firmed the negligible influences of shared familial environment (Pedersen *et al*, 1988; Tellegen *et al*, 1988; Plomin & Rende, 1991). Adoption studies show a similar, modest genetic contribution to a variety of personality traits (Loehlin *et al*, 1988).

In conclusion, virtually all studies to date suggest that questionnaire-measured personality traits are partly genetic, and that non-shared environment is of much greater importance than shared environment in determining individual differences in personality.

### Sexual orientation

Despite interest in the possibility of a biological basis to sexual orientation, there has been little systematic study of the role of genetic factors. In an early and well known twin study of male homosexuality, Kallmann (1952) reported an MZ concordance rate of 100%, with a DZ concordance of 15%. However, the methodological flaws in this study have become apparent with more recent twin findings which show lower MZ concordance rates. In the most recent genetic study (Bailey & Pillard, 1991), probands consisted of volunteer male homosexuals who were twins or who had an adoptive brother. Rates of homosexuality among MZ co-twins, DZ co-twins and adoptive brothers were 52%, 22% and 11%, respectively, and heritability for homosexuality could be estimated at between 31% and 74%. Contrary to expectations, a history of childhood non-conformity to gender role did not seem to be associated with genetic loading for subsequent homosexuality. Lesbianism and genetics is largely unexplored, but a heritable component has been claimed (Bailey *et al*, 1993).

The suggestion that homosexuality is substantially heritable is surprising given that, in an evolutionary sense, such a trait would be expected to reduce fitness – there is likely to be reduced probability of having children and thus passing on one's genes to subsequent generations. There have been speculations by sociobiologists that homosexuality is a form of altruistic behaviour, in which in earlier times an individual sacrificed their own opportunity to procreate to enhance the breeding opportunities of their kin (Wilson, 1975). However, there is little empirical evidence to support this interesting view. Although the recent twin data suggest that environmental factors are influential, once again these are largely non-familial, with minimal shared environmental effects.

# Personality disorder

As genetic factors appear to be of relevance to normal personality traits, it seems reasonable to consider the role of genes in determining personality which deviates from the normal. As mentioned earlier, there are different methods of categorising personality disorders in clinical use but little firm knowledge about their validity. Personality disorders are not only a clinically heterogeneous group but are unlikely to be homogeneous with respect to aetiology. For descriptive purposes, we have broadly divided the personality disorders into three categories: antisocial personality/ criminality, anxious and avoidant personalities, and schizoid/schizotypal personalities.

## Antisocial personality

Most studies have focused on the genetic influences on criminal behaviour, and although equating this with antisocial personality is probably an oversimplification, a record of non-trivial crime is at least a reliable trait. In an early and influential study by Lange (1931) entitled "Crime as destiny", 10 of 13 MZ pairs were concordant for criminality compared with only 2 of 17 DZ twins. The methodological flaws in this study were overcome to some extent by two later surveys which were based on twin registers and therefore avoided ascertainment biases. In a national Danish criminal register study (Christiansen, 1974; Cloninger & Gottesman, 1987 - update of results), concordance rates of 51% for MZ male twins and 30% for DZ male twins were found. However, results of another Scandinavian study (Dalgaard & Kringlen, 1976), where 41% of MZ twins were concordant compared with 26% of DZ twins, were interpreted by the authors as suggesting that genetic influences were of less importance than previously thought.

More recently, results of seven twin studies of adult male and female criminality have been pooled to give a weighted mean pairwise concordance for adult criminality of 51% in MZ twins and 22% in DZ twins (McGuffin & Gottesman, 1985). These findings suggest that genetic factors significantly influence adult criminality. However, this contrasts with the pooled results for juvenile delinquency (see Chapter 10), where concordance rates of 87% for MZ twins and 72% for DZ twins suggest that delinquency is transmitted familially but that genetic factors are generally of little aetiological importance.

Adoption studies have been noticeably consistent in their findings, despite methodological difficulties. Both studies of offspring of criminals (Crowe, 1972, 1974) and results from adoptee studies suggest that genetic factors influence antisocial behaviour and personality (Cadoret, 1978; Cadoret & Cain, 1980; Cloninger *et al*, 1982; Sigvardsson *et al*, 1982; Cadoret *et al*, 1985). However, environmental factors also appear to be contributory. For example, in one series, the risk of criminality was higher for men who had been in multiple temporary placements and where the adoptive home was of low social status. Similarly, prolonged institutional care and urban rearing increased the risk of criminality for women.

Findings based on adoptive studies also suggest that criminality is a heterogeneous group of behaviours and that genetic factors influence the type of crime committed. It seems that recidivist property offences are particularly heritable, whereas violent crime may be associated with (secondary to or interactive with a genetic predisposition to) alcoholism (Bohman *et al*, 1982; Mednick *et al*, 1984).

A cross-fostering design enables examination of both genetic factors and family environment at the same time. In such a study based on the Danish national criminal register (Mednick *et al*, 1984), 13.5% of adoptees had been convicted where neither biological nor adoptive parents were known to the police. This was not significantly different from a rate of 14.7% among adoptees where the adoptive father only had a police record. However, 20% of the adoptees had a criminal record where only the biological father was known to the police and this rose to 24.5% where both biological and adoptive fathers were known to the police. These results not only suggest that genetic factors influence criminality but also that family environmental factors interact where there is already a genetic disposition.

In most of these studies criminal behaviour/ antisocial personality have been considered as separate and distinct categories from 'normals'. However, rather than using dichotomies, it may be easier to consider these behaviours in terms of a continuously distributed liability. Using this type of model it is possible to explain the lower rates of criminality among women than men by assuming two thresholds. The threshold for women is assumed to be higher than for men and therefore female criminals will have a greater genetic loading than their male counterparts. This type of model appears to be compatible with the Danish twin data (Cloninger *et al*, 1978).

Multiple-threshold models have also been used to explain familial associations between antisocial personality disorder and other types of abnormal personality. There has been particular interest in the apparent familial association between somatisation disorder or Briquet syndrome and antisocial personality disorder. It has been suggested that as relatives of women with Briquet syndrome show a high rate of antisocial disorder (Guze *et al*, 1967; Cloninger & Guze, 1973; Cloninger *et al*, 1975), the two disorders are different expressions of the same underlying liability. A genetic association between antisocial personality and Briquet syndrome is also supported by the results of an adoption study (Cadoret, 1978).

In conclusion, despite methodological problems in defining antisocial personality, it seems that genetic factors do play a role.

## Anxious and neurotic personalities

A major problem encountered in studying the genetics of anxious personality is in distinguishing between anxiety disorders and more stable and enduring anxious personality traits. It seems that genetic factors are in part influential in the transmission of anxiety disorders and that other forms of anxiety such as panic disorder and simple phobia also aggregate in families (see Chapter 7).

Several studies have focused on the genetics of 'normal phobias'. In a twin study based on the Norwegian national register, responses to a phobia questionnaire were analysed (Torgersen, 1979). MZ twins were more similar than DZ twins in their fears of animals, social fears, mutilation fears (e.g. medical procedures, blood), 'nature fears' (e.g. heights, enclosed spaces) and separation fears. MZ/DZ differences were significant for all these types of fears except for separation fears. In a study of college-age twins (Rose *et al*, 1981), once again genetic factors contributed to the transmission of many common fears. As for normal personality, common environment appears to contribute very little to the variance for common fears.

These recent findings which suggest that genetic factors are of considerable importance in determining fears are predated by observations made by Charles Darwin. He had pointed out the evolutionary advantages conferred by inheritance of fears of threats such as snakes and spiders. This contrasts with more modern-day dangers such as guns, knives or fast cars, which are rarely associated with phobic responses (Marks, 1986).

## Obsessional personality

Again, the distinction between obsessional personality disorder and obsessive–compulsive disorder is a difficult one. Although a number of family studies of obsessional disorder have shown increased rates of obsessional traits among family members, estimated rates have varied widely, from 5% (Carey *et al*, 1978) to 37% (Lewis, 1935). There have been several case reports of MZ twins concordant for obsessional disorder and traits (McGuffin & Mawson, 1980; Marks, 1986), but only one systematic twin study has been carried out (Carey & Gottesman, 1981). In this study of obsessive–compulsive probands using consecutive admissions on the Maudsley twin register, 13 of 15 MZ twins were concordant for obsessional features compared with 7 of 15 DZ twins (see also Table 7.3, p. 137).

The results of twin studies of obsessional personality traits have been conflicting. In one well designed study of volunteer twins, where the Leyton Obsessional Inventory was used, the estimated heritabilities were 0.4 for obsessional traits and 0.47 for obsessional symptoms (Clifford *et al*, 1984). There was also a highly significant correlation between obsessional symptom scores and neuroticism. It has therefore been suggested that genetic factors contribute to both obsessional personality traits and a more general neurotic tendency, with a combination of both presenting as obsessional symptoms. However, in contrast, in another twin study (most of whom were obtained from the general population), obsessive traits were not heritable (Torgersen, 1980), and obsessional symptoms measured on the MHQ (Middlesex Health Questionnaire) among another group of twins (not cases) were also not genetically influenced (Young *et al*, 1971).

It seems likely that these conflicting results may well be due to methodological differences between the studies. However, it is of note that the study of Clifford *et al* (1984), which showed that genetic factors did contribute moderately to obsessional traits, is probably the best designed and the only one to carry out formal testing of genetic models.

## Hysterical personality

The concept of hysteria has so many different meanings that it is hardly surprising that there has been so much inconsistency in both the definition of hysterical personality disorder and in the results of genetic studies. In Gottesman's (1963) twin study of normal adolescents, genetic factors were of negligible importance in determining hysterical personality traits as measured by the MMPI. However, in another twin study, Torgersen (1980) found that a hysterical personality factor appeared to be heritable, especially among women. Similarly, a twin study based on the MHQ found that hysterical personality traits were genetically influenced (Young *et al*, 1971). However, there is also doubt concerning whether the personality trait being measured in this study was actually extraversion rather than hysteria.

There has only been one twin study of classic conversion or dissociative hysterical symptoms (Slater, 1961). In this study, genetic factors did not appear to be influential. More recently, interest has been focused on somatisation disorder or Briquet syndrome, a rather different concept of hysteria, first put forward by a 19th-century French physician, which has been more accepted in some quarters in the United States. This is a disorder predominantly found in women, and it consists of presenting multiple physical symptoms in multiple systems with numerous investigations, treatments and operations, all negative for organic pathology. Although this condition is classified as an axis I disorder in DSM–III (American Psychiatric Association, 1980), it appears to be familially related to antisocial personality (see earlier), and because of its early onset and enduring nature it seems more akin to an abnormal personality type than a discrete illness. There may also be some 'culture-bound' components in somatisation disorder since the full-blown syndrome is apparently common only in some parts of the United States and the diagnosis is seldom made in the United Kingdom or other parts of Europe. Shields (1982) has reviewed the earlier literature.

## Schizoid–schizotypal personality

It has long been thought that relatives of schizophrenics show high rates of abnormal personalities, with some features similar to those of schizophrenia. The original concept of 'schizoid disease' put forward in Heston's (1970) monogenic theory of schizophrenia was very broad in that it included creative and intellectual abilities as well as more commonly recognised schizoid and paranoid traits.

The Danish adoption studies have been especially influential in delineating the so-called 'schizophrenia spectrum disorders', which were commoner among the biological relatives of schizophrenic adoptees than among adoptive relatives or controls (Kety *et al*, 1971). However, even this concept seemed unacceptably broad, and more restricted operational criteria for schizotypal personality were then derived from further analysis of the Danish adoption data (Spitzer *et al*, 1979). Later modification of this definition was then incorporated into DSM–III.

Most family studies have been on samples ascertained through schizophrenic probands, and these have nearly all shown an excess of schizotypal personality disorder and schizophrenia among first-degree relatives (Kendler *et al*, 1984; Baron *et al*, 1983, 1985*a*). Schizotypal personality disorder also appears to aggregate familially (Baron *et al*, 1985*b*; Siever *et al*, 1990). However, most family studies have failed to demonstrate an increased risk of schizophrenia among relatives of probands who have schizotypal personality disorder (Soloff & Millward, 1983; Baron *et al*, 1985*b*; Schulz *et al*, 1986). This may simply result from lack of statistical power. In addition, results from a more recent Italian family study (Battaglia *et al*, 1991) suggest that relatives of patients with pure schizotypy, not mixed schizotypal/borderline probands (who have been included in other study samples), may be at significantly greater risk for schizophrenia than controls.

A liability threshold model could provide an explanation for most of the findings so far, by assuming that schizophrenia and schizotypy occupy different positions on the same liability continuum, with schizotypy being a milder, commoner condition with a lower threshold for being affected and schizophrenia being a narrower, more severe disorder with a higher threshold needed for being affected. This type of model would mean that a very large sample size would be required to demonstrate an excess of schizophrenia among relatives of schizotypal probands.

Findings based on a reanalysis of a twin study of schizophrenia (Gottesman & Shields, 1972) also suggest that schizophrenia and schizotypal personality disorder maybe genetically related (Farmer *et al*, 1987). A suggestively higher MZ/DZ concordance ratio was found when the definition of illness included both schizophrenia and schizotypal personality disorder. Although there are limits on the usefulness of the MZ/DZ ratio as an indicator of the degree of genetic determination, these results suggest that the inclusion of schizotypal personality disorder with schizophrenia may result in a more genetically valid phenotype.

As mentioned earlier, the original criteria for schizotypal personality disorder were derived from the Danish adoption data and therefore the reanalysis of these data applying a DSM–III definition could be seen as circular. Nevertheless, such an adoption data reanalysis has provided some interesting results. When DSM–III criteria for schizophrenia and schizotypal personality disorder were applied (Kendler *et al*, 1981) the rates of disorder were 22% in the biological relatives of the schizophrenic adoptees compared with 2% among the adoptive relatives and controls (Kendler *et al*, 1981) (see also more recent results summarised in Table 5.2, p. 91). These results suggest that the DSM–III definition of schizotypal personality is more meaningful than the earlier and broader concept of spectrum disorder. A more extensive review of the relationship between schizotypal personality disorder and schizophrenia has been provided by Prescott & Gottesman (1993), who conclude that it should probably be included in the liability spectrum with schizophrenia.

Another way of defining schizotypy is by regarding it as a continuous measure rather than as a discrete disorder. Scales attempting to measure schizotypy have been devised (Claridge, 1988; Venables *et al*, 1990). Although one twin study has demonstrated that scores are influenced genetically (Claridge & Hewitt, 1987), schizotypy measurements tend to be positively correlated with neuroticism scores, which suggests that the schizotypy scales are neither highly specific nor pure. Schizotypy scores derived from the MMPI also appear to be familial and have a pattern of distribution compatible with major factor inheritance (Moldin *et al*, 1990). The refinement of continuous measures of schizotypy is of great importance in terms of the potential for their use in both determining a mode of transmission and in linkage studies.

## Borderline personality disorder

The different concept of borderline states has been extensively used in the psychoanalytic literature and particularly described by Gunderson & Singer (1975). There has been some confusion about the term, in that schizophrenia spectrum disorders have also been referred to as borderline schizophrenia. However, it seems that borderline states as defined by Gunderson & Singer are characterised more by depressive than by schizophrenia-like features (Stone, 1981). Furthermore, although described as a 'state', borderline patients seem to show a cluster of more or less enduring traits. Following on from this, a modified form of borderline state was then defined by Spitzer *et al* (1979) and called 'unstable personality' and this has since been incorporated into the DSM and termed 'borderline personality disorder'.

Family studies mostly suggest that borderline personality has no familial relationship with schizophrenia or schizotypal personality disorder, but rather that borderline probands and their relatives show higher rates of affective disorder (Loranger *et al*, 1982; Baron *et al*, 1985*b*). It also seems that there are higher rates of borderline personality among relatives of borderline probands, but this is not specific in that there is also an increased rate of histrionic and antisocial personality among family members (Pope *et al*, 1983). There has only been one small twin study of borderline personality, and these results suggested that although borderline personality disorder may be a familial condition it does not seem to be genetically influenced (Torgersen, 1984).

# Biological, chromosomal and molecular markers

Little is known about the biological basis of personality disorder and as yet there are no good biological markers. Although lowered platelet monoamine oxidase (MAO) activity is no longer thought to be a useful marker for schizophrenia (Reveley *et al*, 1986), there has been some interest in its value as a marker for personality types. In particular, an association has been reported between scores on scales of sensation seeking and platelet MAO levels (Buchsbaum *et al*, 1976). However, the importance and certainty of this finding remains unclear (Zuckerman, 1991). A report of a family in which mild X-linked mental retardation is associated with aggressive behaviour and a probable mutation in the MAO-A gene (Brunner *et al*, 1993*a,b*) has renewed interest in this area.

Much greater attention has focused on the possible relationship between personality disorder and chromosomal anomalies. A study of the inmates of a hospital for mentally abnormal offenders by Jacobs *et al* (1968) which revealed that 3% of them had an extra Y chromosome (XYY karyotype) raised the possibility of an aetiological link with this form of aneuploidy. However, it seems that the majority of individuals affected with XYY have no obvious abnormality other than being taller and less bright than average. Only a minority are institutionalised. In a population survey of over 4000 men taller than 1.84 m, 12 (0.3%) individuals were found to have the 47XYY karyotype, and of these 5 (42%) had criminal records (Witkin *et al*,

1976). This compared with a rate of only 9% among the normal XY men. However, most of the crimes were relatively minor and non-violent. This suggests that although XYY males may show increased rates of social deviance, this does not usually include serious criminality.

The evidence already reviewed suggests that the mode of transmission for personality is complex and cannot be explained by single genes having a major influence on particular personality types. It is much more likely that personality traits and abnormalities are influenced polygenically, with environmental factors also contributing. A multifactorial type of trans-mission means that classical linkage studies are unlikely to be fruitful. However, recent experiments in plant and laboratory animal breeding have demonstrated that genes of minor effect can also be studied and located using DNA markers. For example, from a complete genetic linkage map of the tomato, it was possible to identify so-called quantitative trait loci (QTL), which influence certain forms of continuous variation such as fruit mass, fruit pH and liquid-soluble concentrations (Paterson *et al*, 1988). Broadly similar strategies have been used to identify loci affecting blood pressure in the rat (Hilbert *et al*, 1991). Although these results show that polygenes for some simple continuous traits can be localised, a search for QTL for human personality traits would be considerably more complex and time consuming. However, mapping of the human genome is progressing so rapidly that the eventual localisation of most functional genes including QTL seems inevitable (see Chapter 3).

# Conclusions

Despite the problems in defining meaningful phenotypes, findings from family, twin and adoption studies suggest that genetic factors are of importance in determining both normal personality traits and some personality disorders. Personality disorders are a heterogeneous group of disorders and do not appear to be transmitted in a Mendelian fashion. Environmental factors are also influential, with non-familial environmental factors appearing to be of greater importance than shared family factors in determining normal personality. However, this does not necessarily also apply to personality disorder, as shared environmental factors have been shown for example to contribute to the familial transmission of criminality.

As transmission of personality and personality disorder appears to be polygenic, it seems unlikely that classical linkage studies will prove to be successful. Recent work has demonstrated that polygenes involved in determining simple continuous traits in plants can be identified. These results, in conjunction with the rapid progress in mapping of the human genome, suggest that the localisation of some genes with detectable effects on personality is a real possibility in the foreseeable future.

# References
American Psychiatric Association (1980) *Diagnostic and Statistical Manual of Mental Disorders* (3rd edn) (DSM–III). Washington, DC: APA.

—— (1994) *Diagnostic and Statistical Manual of Mental Disorders* (4th edn) (DSM–IV). Washington, DC: APA.

Bailey, J. M. & Pillard, R. C. (1991) A genetic study of male sexual orientation. *Archives of General Psychiatry*, **48**, 1089-1096.

——, ——, Neale M.C., *et al* (1993) Heritable factors influence sexual orientation in women. *Archives of General Psychiatry*, **50**, 217-223.

Baron, M., Gruen, R., Asnis, L., *et al* (1983) Familial relatedness of schizophrenic and schizotypal states. *American Journal of Psychiatry*, **140**, 1437-1442.

——, ——, Rainer, J. D., *et al* (1985*a*) A family study of schizophrenic and normal control probands: implications for the spectrum concept of schizophrenia. *American Journal of Psychiatry*, **142**, 447-455.

——, ——, Asnis, L., *et al* (1985*b*) Familial transmission of schizotypal and borderline personality disorders. *American Journal of Psychiatry*, **142**, 927-934.

Battaglia, M., Gasperini, M., Sciuto, G., *et al* (1991) Psychiatric disorders in the families of schizotypal subjects. *Schizophrenia Bulletin*, **17**, 659-665.

Bohman, M., Cloninger, R., Sigvardsson, S., *et al* (1982) Predisposition to petty criminality in Swedish adoptees. Genetic and environmental heterogeneity. *Archives of General Psychiatry*, **39**, 1233-1241.

Brunner, H.G., Nelen, M.R., van Zandvoort, P., *et al* (1993*a*) X-linked borderline mental retardation with prominent behavioural disturbance: phenotype, genetic localization and evidence for disturbed monoamine metabolism. *American Journal of Human Genetics*, **52**, 1032-1039.

——, ——, Breakefield, X.O., *et al* (1993*b*) Abnormal behaviour linked to a point mutation in the structural gene for monoamine oxidase A. *Psychiatric Genetics*, **3**, 122.

Buchsbaum, M. S., Cowsey,R. D. & Murphy, D. L (1976) The biochemical high risk paradigm. Behavioural and family correlates of low platelet monoamine oxidase activity. *Science*, **194**, 339-341.

Cadoret, R. J. (1978) Psychopathology in adopted-away offspring of biologic parents with antisocial behaviour. *Archives of General Psychiatry*, **35**, 176-184.

—— & Cain, C. (1980) Sex differences in predictors of antisocial behaviour adoptees. *Archives of General Psychiatry*, **37**, 1171-1175.

——, O'Gorman, T. W., Troughton, E., *et al* (1985) Alcholism and antisocial personality – interrelationships, genetics and environmental factors. *Archives of General Psychiatry*, **42**, 161-167.

Carey, G., Goldsmith, H. H., Tellegen, A., *et al* (1978) Genetics and personality inventories. The limits of replication with twin data. *Behavior Genetics*, **8**, 299-313.

—— & Gottesman, I. I. (1981) Twin and family studies of anxiety, phobic and obsessive disorders. In *Anxiety: New Research and Changing Concepts* (eds D. F. Klein & J. Rabkin), pp. 117–135. New York: Raven Press.

Christiansen, K. O. (1974) The genesis of aggressive criminality. Implications of a study of crime in a Danish twin study. In *Determinants and Origins of Aggressive Behaviour* (eds J. De Wit & W. W. Hartup). The Hague: Mouton.

Claridge, G. (1988) Schizotypy and schizophrenia. In *Schizophrenia: The Major Issues* (eds P. Bebbington & P. McGuffin), pp. 187-200. Oxford: Heinemann Medical.

—— & Hewitt, J. K. (1987) A biometrical study of schizotypy in a normal population. *Personality and Individual Differences*, **8**, 303-312.

Clifford, C.A., Murray, R. M. & Fulker, D. W. (1984) Genetic and environmental influences on obsessional traits and symptoms. *Psychological Medicine*, **14**, 791-800.

Cloninger, C. R. & Guze, S. B. (1973) Psychiatric illness in the families of female criminals. A study of 288 first-degrees relatives. *British Journal of Psychiatry*, **127**, 697-703.

——, Reich, T. & Guze, S. B. (1975) The multifactorial model of disease transmission III. Familial relationship between sociopathy and hysteria (Briquet's syndrome). *British Journal of Psychiatry*, **127**, 23-32.

——, Christiansen, K. O., Reich, T., *et al* (1978) Implications of sex differences in the prevalences of antisocial personality, alcoholism and criminality for familial transmission. *Archives of General Psychiatry*, **35**, 941-945.

——, Sigvardsson, S., Bohman, M., *et al* (1982) Predisposition to petty criminality in Swedish adoptees II. Cross-fostering analysis of gene–environment interaction. *Archives of General Psychiatry*, **39**, 1242-1247.

—— & Gottesman, I. I. (1987) Genetic and environmental factors in antisocial behavior disorders. In *Causes of Crime: New Biological Approaches* (eds S. A. Mednick, T. E. Moffitt & S. A. Stack). Cambridge: Cambridge University Press.

Crowe, R. R. (1972) The adopted offspring of women criminal offenders – a study of their arrest records. *Archives of General Psychiatry*, **27**, 600-603.

—— (1974) An adoption study of antisocial personality. *Archives of General Psychiatry*, **31**, 785-791.

Dalgaard, O. S. & Kringlen, E. (1976) A Norwegian study of criminality. *British Journal of Criminology*, **16**, 213-232.

Eaves, L. J. & Eysenck, H. J. (1975) The nature of extraversion: a genetical analysis. *Journal of Personality and Social Psychology*, **32**, 102-112.

——, —— & Martin, N. (1989) *Genes, Culture and Personality*. New York: Academic.

Farmer, A. E., McGuffin, P. & Gottesman, I. I. (1987) Twin concordance for DSM–III schizophrenia. Scrutinising the validity of the definition. *Archives of General Psychiatry*, **44**, 634-641.

Gottesman, I. I. (1963) Heritability of personality: a demonstration. *Psychological Monograph*, **77**, 1-21.

—— (1965) Personality and natural selection. In *Methods and Goals in Human Behaviour Genetics* (ed. S. G. Vanderberg). New York: Academic.

—— & Shields, J. (1972) *Schizophrenia: The Epigenetic Puzzle*. New York: CUP.

Gunderson, J. G. & Singer, M. T. (1975) Defining borderline patients: an overview. *American Journal of Psychiatry*, **132**, 1-10.

Guze, S. B., Wolfgram, E .D., McKinnery, J. K., *et al* (1967) Psychiatric illness in the families of convicted criminals. A study of 519 first-degree relatives. *Diseases of the Nervous System*, **28**, 651-659.

Heston, L. L. (1966) Psychiatric disorders in foster home-reared children of schizophrenic mothers. *British Journal of Psychiatry*, **112**, 819-825.

—— (1970) The genetics of schizophrenia and schizoid disease. *Science*, **167**, 249-256.

Hilbert, P., Lindpaintner, K., Beckmann, J. S., *et al* (1991) Chromosomal mapping of two genetic loci associated with blood-pressure regulation in hereditary hypertensive rats. *Nature*, **353**, 521-529.

Hume, W. I. (1973) Physiological measures in twins. In *Personality Differences and Biological Variations: A Study of Twins* (eds G. Claridge, S. Canter & W. I. Hume). Oxford: Pergamon Press.

Jacobs, P. A., Price, W. H., Cower-Brown, W. M., *et al* (1968) Chromosome studies on men in maximum security hospitals. *Annals of Human Genetics*, **31**, 339-358.

Juel-Nielsen, N. & Harvand, B. (1958) The electroencephalogram in uniovular twins brought up apart. *Acta Genetica*, **8**, 57-64.

Kallmann, F. J. (1952) Twin and sibship study of overt male homosexuality. *American Journal of Human Genetics*, **4**, 136-146.

Kendler, K. S., Gruenberg, A. M. & Strauss, J. S. (1981) An independent analysis of the Copenhagen sample of the Danish adoption study of schizophrenia. II. The relationship between schizotypal personality disorders and schizophrenia. *Archives of General Psychiatry*, **38**, 982-984.

——, Masterson, C. C., Unigaro, R., *et al* (1984) A family history study of schizophrenic related personality disorders. *American Journal of Psychiatry*, **141**, 424-427.

Kety, S. S., Rosenthal, D., Wender, P. H., *et al* (1971) Mental illness in the biological and adoptive families of adopted schizophrenics. *American Journal of Psychiatry*, **128**, 302-306.

Lader, M. & Wing, L. (1966) *Physiological Measures, Sedative Drugs and Morbid Anxiety*. Oxford: Oxford University Press.

Lange, J. (1931) *Crime as Destiny*. London: Allen & Unwin.

Lennox, W. G., Gibbs, E. L. & Gibbs, F. A.(1945) The brain wave pattern: an hereditary trait. Evidence from 74 'normal' pairs of twins. *Journal of Heredity*, **36**, 233-243.

Lewis, A. (1935) Problems of obsessional illness. *Proceedings of the Royal Society of Medicine*, **29**, 325-336.

Lewis, E. G., Dustman, R. E. & Beck, C. (1972) Evoked response similarity in monozygotic, dizygotic and unrelated individuals: a comparative study. *Electroencephalography and Clinical Neurophysiology*, **32**, 309-316.

Loehlin, J. C. & Nichols, R. C. (1976) *Heredity, Environment and Personality. A study of 850 Sets of Twins*. Texas: University of Texas Press.

——, Willerman, L. & Horn, J. M. (1988) Human behaviour genetics. *Annual Review of Psychology*, **39**, 795-799.

Loranger, A. W., Oldham, J. M. & Tulis, E. H. (1982) Familial transmission of DSM–III borderline personality disorders. *Archives of General Psychiatry*, **39**, 795-799.

Lykken, D. T., Iacono, W. G., Haroian, K., *et al* (1988) Habituation of the skin conductance response to strong stimuli: a twin study. *Psychophysiology*, **25**, 4-15.

Marks, I. (1986) Genetics of fear and anxiety disorders: a review. *British Journal of Psychiatry*, **149**, 406-418.

Martin, N. & Jardine, R. (1986) Eysenck's contributions to behaviour genetics. In *Hans Eysenck: Consensus and Controversy* (eds S. Modgil & C. Modgil), pp. 13-47. Philadelphia: Falmer.

McGuffin, P. & Mawson, D. (1980) Obsessive–compulsive neurosis: two identical twin pairs. *British Journal of Psychiatry*, **137**, 285-287.

—— & Gottesman, I. I. (1985) Genetic influences on normal and abnormal development. In *Child Psychiatry: Modern Approaches* (2nd edn) (eds M. Rutter & L. Hersov). London: Blackwell.

Mednick, S. A., Gabrielli, W. F. Jr & Hutchings, B. (1984) Genetic influences in criminal convictions. Evidence from an adoption cohort. *Science*, **22**, 891-894.

Moldin, S. O., Rice, J. P., Gottesman, I. I., *et al* (1990) Transmission of a psychometric indicator for liability to schizophrenia in normal families. *Genetic Epidemiology*, **7**, 163-176.

Paterson, A. H., Lander, E. S., Hewitt, J. D., *et al* (1988) Resolution of quantitative traits into mendelian factors by using a complete linkage map of restriction fragment length polymorphisms. *Nature*, **335**, 721-726.

Pedersen, N. L., Plomin, R., McLearn, G. E., *et al* (1988) Neuroticism, extraversion and related traits in adult twins reared apart and reared together. *Journal of Personality and Social Psychology*, **55**, 950-957.

Plomin, R. & Rende, R. (1991) Human behaviour genetics. *Annual Review of Psychology*, **42**, 161-190.

Pope, H. G., Jonas, J. M., Hudson, J. I., *et al* (1983) The validity of DSM–III borderline personality disorder: a phenomenologic, family history, treatment response, and long term follow-up study. *Archives of General Psychiatry*, **40**, 23-30.

Prescott, C.A. & Gottesman, I. I. (1993) Genetically mediated vulnerability to schizophrenia. *Psychiatric Clinics of North America*, **16**, 245-267.

Reese, W. G. (1979) A dog model for human psychopathology. *American Journal of Psychiatry*, **136**, 1168-1172.

Reveley, M. A., Reveley, A. M., Clifford, C., *et al* (1986) Genetics of platelet MAO activity in discordant schizophrenic and normal twins. In *Contemporary Issues in Schizophrenia* (eds A. Kerr & P. Smith), pp. 310-317. London: Gaskell.

Reznikoff, M. & Honeyman, M. S. (1967) MMPI profiles of monozygotic and dizygotic twin pairs (Abstract). *Journal of Consulting Psychology*, **31**, 100.

Rose, R.J., Miller, J. Z., Pogue-Geille, M. F., *et al* (1981) Twin-family studies of common fears and phobias. In *Twin Research 3: Intelligence, Personality and Development*, pp.169-174. New York: Alan R. Liss.

Schulz, P. M., Schulz, S. C., Goldberg, S. C., *et al* (1986) Diagnoses of the relatives of schizotypal outpatients. *Journal of Nervous and Mental Diseases*, **174**, 457-463.

Shields, J. (1982) Genetic studies of hysterical disorders. In *Hysteria* (ed. A Roy), pp. 41-56. Chichester: Wiley.

Siever, L. J., Silverman, K. M., Horvath, T. B., *et al* (1990) Increased morbid risk for schizophrenia related disorders in relatives of schizotypal personality disordered patients. *Archives of General Psychiatry*, **47**, 634-640.

Sigvardsson, S., Cloninger, C. R., Bohman, M., *et al* (1982) Predisposition to petty criminality in Swedish adoptees. III. Sex differences and validation of the male typology. *Archives of General Psychiatry*, **39**, 1248-1253.

Slater, E. (1961) The Thirty-fifth Maudsley lecture: 'Hysteria 311'. *Journal of Mental Science*, **107**, 359-381.

Soloff, P. H. & Millward, J. W. (1983) Psychiatric disorders in the families of borderline patients. *Archives of General Psychiatry*, **40**, 37-44.

Spitzer, R. L., Endicott, J. & Gibbon, M. (1979) Crossing the border into borderline personality and borderline schizophrenia. *Archives of General Psychiatry*, **356**, 17-24.

Stone, M. H. (1981) Psychiatrically ill relatives of borderline patients: a family study. *Psychiatric Quarterly*, **58**, 71-83.

Tellegen, A., Lykken, D. T., Bouchard, T. J., *et al* (1988) Personality similarity in twins reared apart and together. *Journal of Personality and Social Psychology*, **54**, 1031-1039.

Torgersen, S.(1979) The nature and origin of common phobic fears. *British Journal of Psychiatry*, **134**, 343-351.

—— (1980) The oral obsessive and hysterical personality syndrome. A study of heredity and environmental factors by means of the twin method. *Archives of General Psychiatry*, **37**, 1272-1277.

—— (1984) Genetic and nosological aspects of schizotypal and borderline personality disorders. A twin study. *Archives of General Psychiatry*, **41**, 546-554.

Venables, P. H., Wilkins, S., Mitchell, D. A., *et al* (1990) A scale for the measurement of schizotypy. *Personality and Individual Differences*, **11**, 481-495.

Wilson, E. O. (1975) *Sociobiology, the New Synthesis*. Cambridge: Harvard University Press.

Wimer, R. E. & Wimer, C. C. (1985) Animal behavior genetics: a search for the biological foundations of behavior. *Annual Review of Psychology*, **36**, 171-218.

Witkin, H. A., Mednick, S. A., Schulsinger, F., *et al* (1976) Criminality in XYY and XXY men. *Science*, **193**, 547-555.

Young, J. P. R. & Fenton, G. W. (1971) An investigation of the genetic aspects of the alpha attenuation response. *Psychological Medicine*, **1**, 365-371.

——, —— & Lader, M. H. (1971) The inheritance of neurotic traits: a twin study of the Middlesex Hospital Questionnaire. *British Journal of Psychiatry*, **119**, 393-398.

World Health Organization (1992) *The ICD–10 Classification of Mental and Behavioural Disorders: Clinical Descriptions and Diagnostic Guidelines*. Geneva: WHO.

Zuckerman, M. (1991) *Psychobiology of Personality*. Cambridge: CUP.

# 9 Alcoholism

---

*Family studies • Twin studies • Adoption studies • Genes, environment
and subtypes of alcoholism • Biological basis of alcoholism •
Conclusions*

---

There has been a long-standing acceptance by most clinicians that
alcoholism sometimes shows a tendency to run in families. However,
psychiatrists specialising in its treatment have only comparatively recently
taken seriously the proposition that genetic factors might be important.
This may in part be because of the irregular pattern of familial transmission,
but probably more influential was the recognition of obvious environmental factors, particularly availability of alcohol and the assumption that
family members pass on drinking habits 'by example' rather than via their
genes (Kessel & Walton, 1965). A greater willingness to acknowledge that
genetic factors may contribute to the familiality of alcoholism has
resulted from a series of genetic epidemiological studies carried out over
the past two decades. An additional factor in influencing more recent
opinion has been the advance in knowledge of the molecular pharma-
cology of alcohol and an increasing interest in the potential power of
molecular genetic studies.

## Family studies

There have been many studies of alcoholism consistently showing an
increase risk of the disorder in the relatives of alcoholics. For example,
Cotton (1979) combined the data from over 30 studies to give a weighted
average frequency of alcoholism of 27% in the fathers of alcoholics, and
over twenty studies to give a weighted average frequency of alcoholism
of 5% in alcoholics' mothers. However, studies with rigorous methods
have been the exception rather than the rule (Merikangas, 1989). Only
a handful have used standardised diagnostic criteria on personally
interviewed relatives and have included control groups. Such studies show
that, just as in the population as a whole, more male relatives are affected
than females. For example, Reich & Cloninger (1990), using the Feighner
criteria, report lifetime prevalences of alcoholism of between 15% in
the sisters and 57% in the brothers of male probands (see Table 9.1).
Interestingly, the risk of alcoholism in the first-degree relatives of female
alcoholics was very similar, suggesting that the sex of the proband has

161

**Table 9.1**  Frequency of alcoholism in spouses and first-degree relatives of 300 alcoholic probands

|  | Male probands | | | Female probands | | |
|---|---|---|---|---|---|---|
|  | *n* | % affected | Mean age | *n* | % affected | Mean age |
| Fathers | 80 | 37.5 | 54.1 | 13 | 38.5 | 61.2 |
| Mothers | 125 | 20.8 | 51.2 | 27 | 3.7 | 59.3 |
| Brothers | 192 | 56.8 | 29.3 | 36 | 52.8 | 36.7 |
| Sisters | 196 | 14.8 | 31.3 | 49 | 20.4 | 35.3 |
| Sons | 28 | 32.1 | 23.8 | 20 | 50.0 | 26.3 |
| Daughters | 47 | 19.1 | 23.1 | 18 | 16.7 | 24.9 |
| Spouses | 100 | 13.0 | 35.9 | 25 | 56.0 | 41.0 |

Data from Reich & Cloninger (1990).

little influence on the familial distribution of the disorder. It is also noteworthy that the lifetime prevalence of alcoholism in the husbands of alcoholic women was, at 56%, similar to that in their male biological relatives. Likewise the 13% prevalence in alcoholic men's wives was comparable to the frequency in their sisters. This suggests that either there is assortative mating for alcoholism, or that people become similar to their spouses in their drinking habits, or a combination of the two.

Although some authors have suggested rates of alcoholism as much as seven times higher in relatives of alcoholics than in controls (Stone & Gottesman, 1993), the family data reported by Reich & Cloninger have to be compared with survey data from their own department which show general population lifetime prevalences of alcohol abuse of over 20% in men and 5% in women up to the age of 44. Nevertheless, this still supports the hypothesis that alcoholism is familial. However, there are two other observations on the familial aggregation of male alcoholism that make it unlikely that a purely genetic explanation will suffice. The first is that grandfather/grandson pairs may be as concordant as father/son pairs (Kaij & Dock, 1975). Secondly, in a study of half-siblings, concordances similar to those in full siblings were found (Schuckit *et al*, 1972). That is, there was as much resemblance in pairs of relatives sharing only a quarter of their genes as in those who on average share one half. Despite this, the existence of definite familial effects make genetic factors worthy of further exploration, so long as it is done with an open mind and with an awareness of the possible existence of heterogeneity (Sher, 1991).

# Twin studies

Twin studies of alcoholism and alcohol abuse or dependence are listed in Table 9.2, and some of the main findings with respect to concordance rates are summarised. The earliest study, by Kaij (1960), was based partly on interviews and supplemented by official records from a 'Temperance Board Register'. Most cases would probably now be classified as alcohol abusers rather than suffering from dependence. The study by Hrubec & Omenn (1981) was based on Veterans Hospital records and questionnaire data. None of the subjects was actually interviewed by the researchers and again, as in the study of Kaij, all were men. Both of these studies appeared to indicate a genetic contribution to alcohol abuse, but the first study to use standardised interviews, operational diagnostic criteria and to include women as well as men, showed no difference between monozygotic (MZ) and dizygotic (DZ) concordances (Gurling *et al*, 1981). Although the samples were small when divided by sex there was not even a suggestion of a genetic effect in either men or women. These results contrast with two more recent studies (Pickens *et al*, 1991; Caldwell & Gottesman, 1991) both of which, for the broad criteria of alcohol abuse and/or dependence, found higher concordance in male MZ than DZ twins. In the Caldwell & Gottesman study, ascertainment was carried out systematically via a consecutive hospital series. Recruitment in the Pickens study and the subsequent report by McGue *et al* (1992) was not systematic but precautions were taken to overcome ascertainment biases, and DSM–III criteria were used. The results suggest a moderate heritability ($h^2$) in males, but a more modest effect in females, where heritability was variously estimated at 0%

**Table 9.2** Twin studies of alcohol abuse or dependence

| Study | Sex | MZ | | DZ | |
|---|---|---|---|---|---|
| | | *n* | Concord-ance: % | *n* | Concord-ance: % |
| Kaij (1960) | M | 32 | 53 | 142 | 28 |
| Hrubec & Omen (1981) | M | 271 | 26 | 442 | 12 |
| Gurling *et al* (1981) | M&F | 29 | 29 | 40 | 33 |
| Pickens *et al* (1991) | M | 50 | 76 | 64 | 61 |
| | F | 31 | 36 | 24 | 25 |
| Caldwell & Gottesman (1991) | M | 28 | 68 | 26 | 46 |
| | F | 17 | 47 | 3 | 42 |
| McGue *et al* (1992) | M | 85 | 77 | 96 | 54 |
| | F | 44 | 39 | 43 | 42 |
| Kendler *et al* (1992) | M | 81 | 32 | 79 | 24 |

(McGue *et al*, 1992), 8% (Caldwell & Gottesman, 1991) and 26% (Pickens *et al*, 1991). When the criteria were narrowed to require alcohol dependence (with or without abuse), the difference between MZ and DZ concordance rates increased. For example, Pickens *et al* found that the male concordance was 59% in MZ and 36% in DZ twins, while the female concordance was 25% for MZ and 5% for DZ subjects. These concordances correspond to heritabilities of just under 60% for alcohol dependence in men and 42% in women (Pickens *et al*, 1991). By contrast for alcohol abuse (dependence not a requirement) there was evidence of substantial shared environmental effects ($c^2$), accounting for 48% of the variance in liability in men and 47% in women.

It was also of interest that when Pickens *et al* examined the particular items that contributed to the diagnosis of alcoholism, they found the greatest MZ/DZ differences (and by implication the largest genetic effects) in multiple binges, continued use of alcohol despite a worsening condition, alcohol-related job or school trouble, and morning drinking. The same pattern was not observed in women, where the only item which showed a significant difference between MZ and DZ concordance was heavy use of alcohol for a period of two weeks.

Kendler *et al* (1992) were unusual in studying only female twins in the general population, where they found higher MZ than DZ concordance for DSM–III–R alcoholism and estimated that the heritability was 56%. Also, in contrast to other recent studies, they have found no effect of shared environment.

Therefore, in summary, despite diagnostic differences, marked variation in reported concordance rates and one small study showing no evidence for genetic effect, it seems probable that there is at least a modest genetic contribution to broadly defined alcohol abuse or dependence. When consideration is restricted to alcohol dependence, the recent studies suggest moderate heritability ($h^2$) in both men and women. However, in concluding this we should not overlook the fact that nearly all of the twin data suggest that the environmental contribution to alcoholism is large (McGue, 1993). Recent studies where the components of environmental variance have been estimated, most, but not all, find evidence of marked shared (i.e. familial) environment effects ($c^2$) which seem to be particularly important for alcohol abuse.

## Twin studies of 'normal' alcohol use

An alternative approach to focusing on alcohol misuse is to study drinking patterns in normal twins. Such a study was carried out by Clifford *et al* (1984), who found that additive genetic effects (i.e. $h^2$) accounted for about 40% of the variance in total weekly alcohol consumption, with shared environment ($c^2$) accounting for 32%. Very similar overall results were found in men in the study of normal twins by Jardine *et al* (1984), although here only genetic factors appeared to be an important source of resemblance in female twins. However, results from a study of Finnish twins separated before the age of 11 years (Kaprio *et al*, 1984) suggest that both genes and family environment are influential in levels of alcohol consumption. Thirty MZ and 95 DZ twin pairs were matched with twins reared together. Correlations for alcohol consumption were greater in twins reared together than those brought up apart, but in men concordance rates for heavy alcohol use were greater in all MZ than DZ pairs. More recently, Heath *et al* (1993) have suggested the need to consider alcohol use as consisting of separate underlying dimensions related to abstention, consumption frequency and level of consumption. They have presented twin-study evidence suggesting that each of them is heritable to varying degrees.

# Adoption studies

Given the importance of shared environmental effects on drinking behaviour, adoption studies would seem to be a particularly attractive way of investigating the causes of alcoholism, since they provide the means of controlling family environment. The results for adoption studies are summarised in Table 9.3 and show the frequency of the disorder in adopted-away offspring of affected individuals as compared with that in control adoptees.

**Table 9.3**  Adoption studies of alcoholism

| Study | Sex | Adoptees | | | |
|---|---|---|---|---|---|
| | | Experimental | | Controls | |
| | | *n* | % affected | *n* | % affected |
| Roe & Burks (1945) | M + F | 27 | 70 | 27 | 64 |
| Goodwin *et al* (1976) | M | 55 | 18 | 70 | 5 |
| Goodwin *et al* (1977) | F | 49 | 4 | 48 | 4 |
| Cadoret (1978) | M | 6 | 33 | 78 | 1 |
| Cadoret *et al* (1985) | M | 127 | 62 | 28 | 24 |
| | F | 87 | 33 | 24 | 5 |
| Bohman *et al* (1978) | M | 131 | 36 | 23 | 13 |
| | F | 51[1] | 10 } | 577 | 3 |
| | F | 285[2] | 4 } | | |

1. Mother or both parents affected.
2. Only father affected.

The first study (Roe & Burks, 1945) found no evidence of a genetic contribution to alcoholism, but has been criticised in terms of both the small sample and the uncertain definition of the disorder. The next study, published three decades later by Goodwin *et al* (1976), was based on a national adoption register in Denmark, and its finding of an almost fourfold increase in the frequency of alcoholism in male adoptees whose biological father was alcoholic proved to be very influential in persuading sceptics about the role of genes. Nevertheless, it has been pointed out (Murray *et al*, 1983) that the apparent genetic effect in this study was crucially dependent on where the cut-off between 'problem drinking' and alcoholism was taken, since in both the experimental group and controls the frequency of problem drinking and alcoholism combined was the same. Furthermore, the same group of workers failed to find evidence of a genetic contribution to alcoholism in their study of female adoptees. Subsequent work in both the United States (Cadoret, 1978; Cadoret *et al*, 1985) and in Sweden (Bohman, 1978; Bohman *et al*, 1981) confirmed that male adoptees with an alcoholic biological parent were at increased risk of alcoholism and in addition suggested that the same was true of females. However, in the Swedish study alcoholism was increased only in the daughters of female alcoholics (Bohman, 1981).

Thus, as in the twin-study evidence, there is greater consistency in the data for men than for women, but overall and taken together with the findings from family and twin studies, the results suggest low to moderate genetic contributions to the liability to alcoholism in both sexes.

## Genes, environment and subtypes of alcoholism

One of the problems facing researchers in alcoholism is that it is frequently found in combination with other psychiatric disorders. Detailed discussion of this 'co-morbidity' problem is beyond the scope of this chapter, but its bearing on genetic studies has been reviewed cogently by Merikangas (1990). One of the most common overlaps in clinical practice is between depressive disorders and alcoholism. The overlap in families between alcoholism and depression, together with the excess of alcoholism in men and the higher rate of depression in women, has led Winokur *et al* (1975) to postulate the existence of 'depression spectrum disorder', in which alcoholism (or antisocial personality) may present as a sort of male equivalent of depression. However, data from the adoption study of Goodwin *et al* mentioned earlier argue for an environmental rather than genetic connection between depression and alcoholism. An increased risk of depression in the daughters of alcoholic fathers only occurred in those who were raised by their natural parents and not in those who were adopted away. Further genetic analyses by Reich *et al* (1975), applying the sorts of two-threshold models discussed in Chapter 2, suggest that depression and alcoholism are not merely different phenotypic manifestations of the same genotype. This conclusion has subsequently been supported by a large-scale family study carried out by other workers (Merikangas *et al*, 1985).

Threshold analysis can also be applied to test whether different amounts of familial liability can account for the different rates of alcoholism for men and women. Under the simplest model, alcoholic women should occupy a more extreme position on the liability continuum, since they are less common than alcoholic men. Moreover, this predicts that studies of families of affected women should produce more cases than families of affected men, and as we have discussed earlier this does not happen (Reich & Cloninger, 1990). The rates of alcoholism in family members are similar whether one starts with a male or a female proband, and the data fit better with an isoproportional or 'environmental' model (Cloninger *et al*, 1981) (see also Chapter 2), where the difference between men and women can be best explained by non-familial environmental exposure to risk factors for alcoholism.

## Subtypes of alcoholism

The question of subtypes for alcoholism is an unresolved issue, but an influential and much discussed classification is that put forward by Cloninger *et al* (1981), based on an extension and reanalysis of the adoption data of Bohman. These data allowed a detailed cross-fostering analysis to be performed. That is, the investigators were able to compare biological offspring of alcoholics raised by normal parents and biological offspring of non-alcoholic parents raised by alcoholics. As a result of this and a sophisticated multivariate statistical treatment of the Swedish data, Cloninger *et al* proposed that the existence of type 1 or 'milieu-limited' abuse, which occurs in both men and women, is characterised by mild, adult-onset abuse and is influenced by both genetic and environmental factors. By contrast, type 2, or 'male limited', abuse is characterised by teenage onset in men. Here the history of alcohol abuse is usually severe and is associated with criminality in the biological fathers. Type 2 alcoholism is strongly influenced by genes and there is negligible influence from the postnatal environment.

Cloninger (1987) has postulated that these subtypes are associated with personality traits which in turn reflect inherited neuroadaptive mechanisms. He suggests that type 1 alcoholism is typically associated with low novelty seeking, high harm avoidance and high reward dependence. Type 2 alcoholics are in most ways opposite, showing high novelty seeking and both low harm avoidance and reward dependence. Although work elsewhere does not entirely support the hypothesis of these two positive forms of alcoholism (Schuckit & Irwin, 1989) there is much other data to suggest that a strong family history of alcoholism and a personal history of maladaptive behaviour in males is frequently associated with a type 2 profile (McGue *et al*, 1992).

# Biological basis of alcoholism

Despite methodological flaws and inconsistencies as well as freely acknowledged influences of social/cultural factors, the classical genetic studies suggest that alcoholism has a partly genetic and therefore biological basis. Broadly speaking, the ways in which this has been explored fall into three groups. These are studies of metabolic and central nervous system (CNS) response to alcohol, animal studies, and studies using molecular genetic methods. We will consider each in turn.

## Metabolic and CNS response to alcohol

In normal humans, genetic factors seem to exert an important influence on alcohol metabolism. Early studies of ethanol elimination rates showed moderate to high heritability, and more recently Martin *et al* (1985), in a study of normal volunteer Australian twins, estimated that the heritability for peak blood alcohol concentration after ingestion of a test dose was 62%, while the heritability of rate of elimination was 50%. This appeared to be fairly stable, in that the results on a subset of pairs who were retested suggested that only a minor proportion of the variation could be attributed to differences in drinking experience or habits. Inter-racial as well as inter-individual differences have also been described, and the molecular basis of some of these differences have been suggested by recent studies (see below).

An alternative form of investigation is to search for specific CNS responses to alcohol which may characterise alcoholics or potential alcoholics. For example, twin-study evidence suggests that the brain's response as reflected in electroencephalogram (EEG) patterns is genetically influenced (Propping, 1977, 1992). Alcoholics are said to show more alpha wave expression on the EEG, but this may be related to the effects rather than the causes of heavy drinking. However, it is of interest from the genetic viewpoint that MZ twins concordant for poor alpha wave expression are 'cured' of the EEG variant by the intake of alcohol (Propping, 1977). EEG event-related potentials (ERP) also show abnormalities in alcoholics. ERP consist of the EEG response to visual or other stimuli that have been averaged by computer. One such potential called the P300 is flattened in alcoholics, but has also been reported to show flattening in their adolescent sons (Begleiter *et al*, 1984) and has therefore been suggested as a marker of vulnerability to alcoholism.

Simpler measures of CNS response have also been investigated. For example one report suggested that ethanol-induced body sway is significantly less in a sample of healthy young men with an alcoholic first-degree relative than in a group of controls without such a family history (Schuckit *et al*, 1985).

## Animal studies

Selective breeding experiments on rats and mice have successfully produced strains which consistently prefer dilute alcohol to water as well as strains which differ in other ways, such as behavioural response to alcohol intake or withdrawal (reviewed by Crabb & Belknap, 1992). As well as suggesting a genetic contribution to alcohol preference and metabolism, breeding experiments suggest that individual differences among animals are best considered as quantitative traits (i.e. measured on a continuous scale rather than as a present/absent dichotomy) and that such traits are probably influenced by several genes, each of comparatively small effect. This can be inferred from breeding experiments where investigators can go on producing divergence between selected lines over many generations by continuing to select for high or low scores on a particular measure (Plomin, 1990). If strain differences were due to only one or even several genetic loci, then divergence should occur rapidly and not increase on selection continued over many subsequent generations. In current strategies DNA markers are employed to detect linkage in back-crosses (see Chapter 3) to detect quantitative trait loci (QTL) which may influence preference or alcohol metabolism (Crabb & Belknap, 1992). Another strategy, which is somewhat analogous to performing an association study in human beings, is to investigate the relationship between genetic markers and various traits in so-called recombinant inbred (RI) strains which result from repeated crossing of the offspring of two or more strains which differ with respect to a phenotype of interest (Plomin, 1990; Plomin & McClearn, 1993).

## Molecular genetic studies in humans

In humans, too, the advent of recombinant DNA technology has brought a shift of emphasis and a greater concentration on attempting to understand the genetics of alcoholism at a molecular level. Much attention has been directed to the alcohol metabolising enzymes alcohol dehydrogenase (ADH) and acetaldehyde dehydrogenase (ALDH) (reviewed by Hodgkinson *et al*, 1991). It is now known that there are three genes coding for class 1 ADH, all of which are located on the long arm of chromosome 4. Mitochondrial acetaldehyde dehydrogenase (ALDH 2), which is thought to account for most acetaldehyde oxidation, is coded for by a gene on chromosome 12. About half of all Orientals have a point mutation in the ALDH 2 gene. This results in an inactive variant of the enzyme which contributes to the characteristic 'Antabuse-like' reaction on ingestion of alcohol which occurs in many of this ethnic group. Interestingly, the inactive variant is found in only 5% of Japanese alcoholics, the rest of whom have the active type which is found in the greater majority of Caucasians (Hodgkinson *et al*, 1991).

Studies using 'random' genetic markers for linkage analysis in families multiply affected by alcoholism have also yielded positive results. For example, there has been suggestion of linkage with a classical genetic marker, the MNS blood group (Hill *et al*, 1988). Unfortunately this has not been replicated, and in the face of the evidence from family, twin and adoption studies, as well as hints from animal work, the likelihood of their being any major locus for alcoholism as opposed to several genes of small effect is low. Therefore the chances of linkage analysis succeeding must be fairly low. However, association studies, which, as we have discussed in Chapter 3, are capable of detecting genes of comparatively small effect, may hold more promise. Essentially the general assumption is that several (perhaps many) genes plus environment contribute to the liability to alcoholism, which is continuously distributed in the population, and only those individuals who at sometime exceed the threshold become affected (see Chapter 2). Thus association studies in humans are attempting to detect the QTL that contribute to liability to alcoholism.

Most recent interest has focused on a Taq-$I$ polymorphism at the gene encoding the dopamine receptor $D_2$ (DRD2). Five different groups have reported a positive association between the less common (A1) allele and either alcoholism or alcoholism plus drug misuse (reviews by Stone & Gottesman, 1993; Uhl *et al*, 1992). However at least two other research teams were not able to replicate this finding. Given the mixed ethnic backgrounds of the inhabitants of the USA, where nearly all of the studies were conducted, it is possible that at least some of the positive results can be explained by population stratification (Chapter 3). That is, we need to be sure that this apparent association has not arisen as a result of a mixture of subpopulations coincidentally differing both in their frequency of alcoholism and of DRD2 alleles. Despite these caveats, the general strategy of looking for associations in 'candidate' genes is worth pursuing, providing we remember the possible pitfalls (see Chapter 3) and bear in mind the probability that molecular basis of susceptibility to alcoholism is likely to be heterogeneous (Devor, 1993).

# Conclusions

The findings in alcoholism and alcohol use are complex but there are strong hints of genetic components in both. The usefulness of 'classic' genetic methods, including twin and adoption studies, has not been exhausted in alcoholism, and such studies have hardly been applied at all in other forms of drug dependence, where much basic work is needed. Linkage studies where there is an attempt to search for genes of major effect in alcoholism are probably less promising than studies of 'candidate' genes which may influence patterns of normal drinking as well as the development of alcoholism. These are probably best studied at present using association strategies. However, animal studies aiming to detect QTL are potentially promising and there is increasing evidence in breeding experiments of a genetic influence for preference or response to alcohol and other drugs of dependence. The usefulness of a search for QTL in animals and the relevance to human polygenic disorder is already apparent from studies of hypertension and diabetes in rodents. Genetic research into alcoholism is therefore likely to be one of the first areas where animal studies inform molecular genetic studies in humans.

# References

Begleiter, H., Porjesz, B., Bihari, B., *et al* (1984) Event-related brain potentials in boys at risk for alcoholism. *Science*, **225**, 1493-1496.

Bohman, M. (1978) Some genetic aspects of alcoholism and criminality: a population of adoptees. *Archives of General Psychiatry*, **35**, 269-276.

——, Sigvardsson, S. & Cloninger, C. R. (1981) Maternal inheritance of alcohol abuse: cross-fostering analysis of adopted women. *Archives of General Psychiatry*, **38**, 965-969.

Cadoret, R. (1978) Evidence for genetic inheritance of primary affective disorder in adoptees. *American Journal of Psychiatry*, **135**, 463-466.

——, O'Gorman, T. W., Troughton, E., *et al* (1985) Alcoholism and antisocial personality: interrelationships, genetic and environmental factors. *Archives of General Psychiatry*, **42**, 161-167.

Caldwell, C. B. & Gottesman, I. I. (1991) Sex differences in the risk for alcoholism: a twin study. *Behavioral Genetics*, **6**, 563.

Clifford, C. A., Fulker, D. W. & Murray, R. M. (1984) Genetic and environmental influences on drinking patterns in normal twins. In *Alcohol Related Problems* (eds N. Krasner, J. S. Madden & R. J. Walker), pp. 115-126. New York: Wiley.

Cloninger, C. R. (1987) Neurogenetic adaptive mechanisms in alcoholism. *Science*, **236**, 410-416.

——, Bohman, M. & Sivardsson, S. (1981) Inheritance of alcohol abuse: cross-fostering analysis of adopted men. *Archives of General Psychiatry*, **38**, 861-868.

Cotton, N. S. (1979) The familial incidence of alcoholism. *Journal of Studies of Alcohol*, **40**, 89-116.

Crabb, J. C. & Belknap, J. K. (1992) Genetic approaches to drug dependence. *Trends in Pharmacological Sciences*, **13**, 212-219.

Devor, E. J. (1993) Why there is no gene for alcoholism? *Behavior Genetics*, **23**, 145-151.

Goodwin, D. W., Schulinger, F., Müller, N., *et al* (1976) Drinking problems in adopted and non-adopted sons of alcoholics. *Archives of General Psychiatry*, **31**, 164-169.

——, ——, Knop, J., *et al* (1977) Psychopathology in adopted and non-adopted daughters of alcoholics. *Archives of General Psychiatry*, **34**, 1005-1009.

Gurling, H. M. D., Murray, R. M. & Clifford, C. A. (1981) Investigations into the genetics of alcohol dependence and into its effect on brain function. In *Twin Research 3, Part C. Epidemiological and Clinical Studies* (eds L. Gedda, P. Parisi & W. E. Nance), pp. 77–87. New York: Alan R. Liss.

Heath, A. (1993) What can we learn about the determinants of psychotherapy and substance abuse from studies of normal twins? In *Twins as a Tool of Behavioural Genetics* (eds T. J. Bonehard & P. Propping), pp. 273-285. Chichester: Wiley.

Hill, S. Y., Aston, C. & Rabin, B. (1988) Suggestive evidence of genetic linkage between alcoholism and the MNS blood group. *Alcoholism Clinical and Experimental Research*, **12**, 811-814.

Hodgkinson, S., Mullan, M. & Murray, R. M. (1991) The genetics of vulnerability to alcoholism. In *The New Genetics of Mental Illness* (eds P. McGuffin & R. Murray), pp. 182-197. London: Mental Health Foundation.

Hrubec, Z. & Omenn, G. S. (1981) Evidence of genetic predisposition to alcoholic cirrhosis and psychosis. *Alcoholism Clinical and Experimental Research*, **5**, 207-215.

Jardine, R., Martin, N. G. & Henderson, A. S. (1984) Genetic covariation between neuroticism and the symptoms of anxiety and depression. *Genetic Epidemiology*, **1**, 89-107.

Kaij, L. (1960) *Alcoholism in Twins*. Stockholm: Almqvist and Wiksell.

—— & Dock, J. (1975) Grandsons of alcoholics. *Archives of General Psychiatry*, **32**, 1379-1381.

Kaprio, J., Koskenvuo, M. & Langinvainio, H. (1984) Finnish twins reared apart. IV: Smoking and drinking habits. A preliminary analysis of the effect of heredity and environment. *Acta Genetica Medica Gemellologiae*, **33**, 425-33.

Kendler, K. S., Heath, A. C., Neale, M. C., *et al* (1992) A population-based twin study of alcoholism in women. *Archives of General Psychiatry*, **49**, 257.

Kessel, N. & Walton, H. (1965) *Alcoholism*, p. 71. London: Penguin.

Martin, N. G., Oakeshott, J. G., Gibson, J. B., *et al* (1985) A twin study of psychomotor and physiological responses to an acute dose of alcohol. *Behavior Genetics*, **15**, 305-347.

McGue, M. (1993) From proteins to cognitions: the behavioral genetics of alcoholism. In *Nature, Nurture and Psychology* (eds R. Plomin & G. E. MacLearn), pp. 245-268. Washington, DC: American Psychological Association.

——, Pickens, R. W. & Svikis, D.-S. (1992) Sex and age effects on the inheritance of alcohol problems: a twin study. *Journal of Abnormal Psychology*, **101**, 3-17.

Merikangas, K. R. (1989) Genetics of alcoholism: a review of human studies. In *Genetics of Neuropsychiatric Diseases* (ed. L. Wetterberg), pp. 269–271. London: Macmillan.

—— (1990) The genetic epidemiology of alcoholism. *Psychological Medicine*, **20**, 11-22.

——, Leckman, J. F., Prusoff, B. A., *et al* (1985) Familial transmission of alcoholism and depression. *Archives of General Psychiatry*, **42**, 367-372.

Murray, R. M., Clifford, C. A. & Gurling, H. M. D. (1983) Twin and adoption studies: how good is the evidence for a genetic role. In *Recent Developments in Alcoholism* vol. 1 (ed. M. Galanter), pp. 25–48. New York: Plenum Press.

Pickens, R. W., Svikis, D. S., McGue, M., *et al* (1991) Heterogeneity in the inheritance of alcoholism. *Archives of General Psychiatry*, **48**, 19-28.

Plomin, R. (1990) The role of inheritance in behavior. *Science*, **248**, 183-188.

—— & McClearn, G. E. (1993) Quantitative trait loci (QTL) analysis and alcohol-related behaviors. *Behavior Genetics*, **23**, 197-211.

Propping, P. (1977) Genetic control of ethanol action on the central nervous system. An EEG study in twins. *Human Genetics*, **35**, 309-334.

—— (1992) Alcoholism. In *The Genetic Basis of Common Diseases* (eds R. A. King, J. I. Rotter & A. G. Motulsky), pp. 837-848. Oxford: Oxford University Press.

Reich, T., Winokur, G. & Mullaney, J. (1975) The transmission of alcoholism. In *Genetics Research in Psychiatry* (eds R. R. Fieve, D. Rosenthal & H. Brill), pp. 259-269. Baltimore: Johns Hopkins University Press.

—— & Cloninger, R. (1990) Time-dependent model of the familial transmission of alcoholism. In *Banbury Report 33: Genetics and Biology of Alcoholism*, pp. 55-73. Cold Spring Harbor Press.

Roe, A. & Burks, B. (1945) *Adult Adjustment of Foster-Children of Alcoholic and Psychotic Parentage and the Influence of the Foster Home*. Memoirs of the Section on Alcoholic Studies No. 3. New Haven: Yale University Press.

Schuckit, M. A. (1985) Ethanol-induced body sway in men at high alcoholism risk. *Archives of General Psychiatry*, **42**, 375-379.

——, Goodwin, D. & Winokur, G. (1972) A study of alcoholism in half siblings. *American Journal of Psychiatry*, **128**, 122-125.

—— & Irwin, M. (1989) An analysis of the clinical relevance of type 1 and type 2 alcoholics. *British Journal of Addiction*, **84**, 869-876.

Sher, K. J. (1991) *Children of Alcoholics: A Critical Appraisal of Theory and Research*. Chicago: University of Chicago Press.

Stone, W. S. & Gottesman, I. I. (1993) A perspective on the search for the causes of alcoholism: slow down the rush to genetic judgements. *Neurology, Psychiatry and Brian Research*, **1**, 123-132.

Uhl, G. R., Persico, A. M. & Smith, S. S. (1992) Current excitement with D2 dopamine receptor gene alleles in substance abuse. *Archives of General Psychiatry*, **49**, 157-160.

Winokur, G., Cadoret, R., Baker, M., *et al* (1975) Depression spectrum versus pure depressive disease: some further data. *British Journal of Psychiatry*, **127**, 75-77.

# 10    Childhood disorders

---

*Temperament • Infantile autism • Depression • Anxiety disorders •
Conduct disorders • Hyperactivity • Enuresis • Developmental reading
disorders • Tics and Tourette's syndrome • Conclusions*

---

Genetic research into childhood psychiatric disorders has until relatively
recently been a rare pursuit. This may in part have been due to the
commonly misplaced belief that genetic aetiology is incompatible with
effective therapeutic intervention. However, this misconception is apparent
when long established successes are considered; for example, treatment
of phenylketonuria by diet as well as the dramatic successes of molecular genetics studies of single-gene disorders and the potential of 'gene
therapy'.

The traditional dichotomisation of nature versus nurture (*either* genes
*or* environment) has also been restrictive. This may be especially true for
child psychiatry, where many disorders are viewed as quantitative variations
from the normal rather than as 'illnesses' and where treatment approaches
have traditionally been non-biological.

Over the last decade, however, there has been increased recognition of
the value of genetic research in studying the aetiological roles and interplay
of both genes and environmental factors in child psychiatry. We will discuss
the most important findings in this chapter and will begin with the general
topic of temperament before going on to review the findings for a selected
range of disorders for which data are available.

## Temperament

There has been considerable debate about the very concept of temperament in childhood (Rutter, 1987), although there seems to be little doubt
that certain, reasonably enduring differences between individuals can be
observed from an early age. Furthermore, childhood temperament appears
to have implications for the development of later changes in behaviour,
including abnormal behaviour.

Much of the research has consisted of twin studies and, at first sight,
results are conflicting. In two large studies, genetic factors did not appear
to contribute significantly to the variance (Goldsmith & Campos, 1986;
Wilson & Matheny, 1986), yet in studies which have relied on parental
rather than laboratory ratings, most traits have been found to be heritable
in infancy (Torgersen & Kringlen, 1978; Cyphers *et al*, 1990).

Temperament in older children, however, does appear to be moderately heritable (Goldsmith & Gottesman, 1981; Torgersen, 1987). Most twin studies have explored temperamental dimensions based on the acronym EASI (emotionality, activity, sociability, and impulsivity) and of these, activity appears to be the most consistently heritable trait. Interestingly, common environmental factors contribute minimally, and this is similar to twin-study findings for adult personality.

In contrast to many twin studies, adoption studies (Loehlin *et al*, 1981; Plomin *et al*, 1988) have consistently shown only very small genetic influences for temperament. Again, this might partly be explained because of their focus on younger children.

In summary, certain general conclusions can be drawn. Firstly, when parental ratings of childhood temperament are used, genetic influences are found to be of greater importance than when blind laboratory assessments are made. Although parental ratings are subject to biases, laboratory assessments may also be affected by the necessarily artificial situation. Secondly, genetic factors become more influential as the child approaches adulthood, particularly for traits such as sociability, emotionality and activity. These findings highlight the importance of developmental changes and the advantages of longitudinal genetic studies. Thirdly, shared environment is of minor importance in determining temperament.

# Infantile autism

As early as 1943, when autism was first described, Kanner suggested that the underlying defect may well be innate. The findings of later studies then suggested that autism was not strongly influenced genetically (Hanson & Gottesman, 1976). However, interest has once again been revived by the results of more recent and better-designed family and twin studies.

## Family studies

Based on a review of studies, the rate of autism among siblings of affected individuals has been estimated at about 3% (Smalley *et al*, 1988) and this has been confirmed in the most recent family study, where standardised methods of assessment were used, and where the rate of autism among siblings was also found to be 3% (MacDonald *et al*, 1989). On initial inspection of these rates, autism does not therefore appear to be a markedly familial disorder. However, it is important to remember that autism is a rare disorder and compared with a general population frequency of 2–4 per 10 000, the rate among siblings of autistic individuals is 75–150 times greater.

The existence of a kind of 'autistic spectrum disorder' is suggested by the results of family studies, which nearly all show familial loading for a broader range of cognitive disabilities, particularly speech and language abnormalities, and social deficits. In some studies this familial loading of cognitive abnormalities has been mostly confined to affected children with additional mental retardation (Baird & August, 1985). However, in more recent work, the familiality of cognitive abnormalities has also been demonstrated for probands with normal intelligence (MacDonald *et al*, 1989; Piven *et al*, 1990). In the family study of MacDonald *et al*, the siblings of autistic probands showed higher rates of cognitive deficits compared with siblings of controls (15% v. 4.5%) and a similar excess of social difficulties (12% v. 0%).

Overall, it appears that both narrowly defined autism and a broader range of cognitive /social deficits aggregate in families of children suffering from autism.

### Twin studies

The first systematic twin study, carried out at the Institute of Psychiatry, London, was published in 1977 (Folstein & Rutter) and the findings provided the first empirical evidence that autism is a heritable disorder. Pairwise concordance rates were 36% for monozygotic (MZ) twins and 0% for dizygotic (DZ) twins. When the phenotype was broadened to include cognitive disabilities the concordance rates rose to 82% for MZ twins and 10% for DZ twins.

Similar results were found in a Scandinavian study (Steffenberg *et al*, 1989), where pairwise concordance rates were significantly higher for MZ twins than for DZ twins (91% v. 0%), although the findings for cognitive disabilities were not replicated. More recently, in an extended Institute of Psychiatry twin study with larger numbers, concordance rates for autism were once again found to be higher for MZ twins (69%) than for DZ twins (0%) (Bailey, 1993). Like the original Folstein & Rutter study, concordance rates were higher for a broader phenotype including cognitive/social difficulties (88% for MZ twins versus 9% for DZ twins).

Overall, twin data not only suggest that autism is a heritable disorder but also that cognitive and social disabilities can properly be regarded as part of the autistic phenotype.

### Models of transmission

Autistic individuals rarely have children, and there is also evidence that after the birth of an autistic child some parents decide to have no further children (Jones & Szatmari, 1988). These factors make investigation of the mode of transmission of autism difficult.

In general, family and twin data are not consistent with single-gene transmission. Although in one study segregation patterns appeared to suggest autosomal recessive transmission (Ritvo *et al*, 1985), this has not been replicated (Smalley *et al*, 1988). However, most data appear compatible with a multifactorial or mixed mode of transmission. A multifactorial liability model with different thresholds for narrowly defined autism and the less severe cognitive/social disabilities could explain some of the family and twin data. Similarly, a liability model with different thresholds for males and females is an attractive explanation of the excess of autistic males, although model fitting has been disappointingly inconclusive (Tsai & Beisler, 1983). There have been many reports of the association of autism with single-gene disorders such as fragile X, tuberose sclerosis and phenylketonuria, and chromosomal abnormalities (Reiss *et al*, 1986). Despite early enthusiasm about these associations, they probably only account for a small percentage of autistic individuals.

Thus, single-gene transmission for most cases of autism is unlikely, although these associations suggest that it is a genetically heterogeneous disorder.

## Biological markers and risk factors

The pathophysiology of autism is unknown, and so far proposed markers such as increased levels of platelet 5-HT, monoamine oxidase activity and low dopamine β-hydroxylase activity have not been particularly useful. However, imaging studies have demonstrated cerebellar abnormalities in some autistic individuals. These findings are of particular interest because of similar cerebellar changes found among individuals with fragile X. Imaging may help define a subgroup of affected individuals, although unfortunately the abnormalities found so far are too inconsistent to serve as reliable markers for autism.

## Gene–environment interaction

The roles of perinatal adversity and congenital malformations in the aetiology of autism are subjects of continuing debate. In both the British (Folstein & Rutter, 1977) and Scandinavian (Steffenberg *et al*, 1989) twin studies, concordance for autism could not be explained by obstetric complications. However, there was evidence of increased perinatal adversity among the autistic co-twins of discordant MZ twin pairs (but not among discordant co-twins of those with cognitive/social abnormalities).

On these grounds it was suggested that perinatal hazards may make the difference between full-blown autism and cognitive/social abnormalities in the genetically predisposed (Folstein & Rutter, 1977). However, others proposed that perinatal hazards and genes are discrete aetiological causes (Steffenberg *et al*, 1989). However, the association of perinatal complications with autism in singletons is weak and recent twin evidence suggests that obstetric hazards are a consequence rather than a cause of autism (Bailey, 1993). Thus at present it seems highly unlikely that perinatal adversity alone could determine some forms of autism.

## Molecular genetics

As mentioned earlier, autism is associated with several different single-gene disorders and chromosomal abnormalities. Of these, fragile X is the commonest disorder and this association is therefore of the greatest interest to geneticists. However, recent estimates suggest that the rate of fragile X among autistics is no more than 5% (Rutter *et al*, 1990) and it now seems unlikely that the fragile X site, at Xq27.3, is in any way genetically linked to a major locus for autism.

So far there have been few association and linkage studies of autism and no positive findings (Spence *et al*, 1985). Although much of the human genome remains unstudied, there is no certain evidence that a gene of major contribution exists. However, recent advances in identifying quantitative trait loci (see Chapter 3) mean that genes of relatively small effect may also be detected and localised.

# Depression

There is consistent evidence of an important genetic contribution to depression in adult life (see Chapter 6) and increasing evidence of continuities between depression in childhood and later recurrences as an adult (Harrington *et al*, 1990). It might be expected therefore that genetic factors influence childhood depression.

Family studies can be broadly divided into two groups: those where the offspring of adult probands have been studied, and those which have focused on the adult relatives of depressed children. Several family studies have shown evidence of an association between parental depression and psychopathology, especially depression, in their offspring (Weissman *et al*, 1984). In general it appears that children of depressed probands are at greater risk of developing major depression, not only when more first- and second-degree relatives are affected, but especially when parental depression is of early onset (Weissman *et al*, 1987; Orvaschel *et al*, 1988).

A problem associated with many family studies where the probands are adults is the reliance on parental ratings for the children. There is evidence that parental ratings may reflect more about the mood state of the parent than that of the child (Angold *et al*, 1987). However, there have been similar findings of increased rates of depression when children have been directly interviewed (Weissman *et al*, 1987, 1992; Orvaschel *et al*, 1988; Orvaschel, 1990) and among relatives where the probands have been children with unipolar depression (Livingston *et al*, 1985; Puig Antich *et al*, 1989; Kutcher & Marton, 1991) and children with bipolar illness (Strober *et al*, 1988; Dwyer & Delong, 1989; Kutcher *et al*, 1991). These findings suggest that childhood depression and depression in adulthood tend to aggregate in the same families.

One point of note concerns comorbidity. For a number of childhood psychiatric disorders, patterns of familial transmission appear to vary according to whether the disorder is 'pure' or coexists with another disorder. For example, pure depression in childhood appears to be rare and most commonly coexists with anxiety or conduct disorder, and there is some evidence that suggests that depression coexistent with conduct disorder maybe less familial than pure depression (Puig Antich *et al*, 1989).

Of course familiality does not necessarily demonstrate a genetic influence, but to date there has been only one published twin study and this was of subclinical depressed mood in childhood (Wierzbicki, 1987). The results showed that MZ twins resembled one another more closely than DZ twins on several measures, but the sample was not systematically ascertained. More recently, preliminary results from a systematic, population-based twin sample suggest that there is substantial heritability of depression symptom scores in adolescence and that shared environmental factors are more important in younger children (Thapar & McGuffin, 1994).

Overall, there is evidence that depression in childhood aggregates familially and that early-onset depression is more familial, if not necessarily more genetic. Twin studies currently underway should provide further information about the genetic nature of childhood depression, but adoption studies are also clearly desirable.

# Anxiety disorders

There have been few family studies of childhood anxiety. Studies of offspring of parents with anxiety disorders have mostly suggested that anxiety disorders cluster familially (Berg, 1976; Weissman *et al*, 1984). In the most recent study where probands were children with anxiety disorders, relatives showed significantly higher rates of anxiety disorders than relatives of controls (Last *et al*, 1991). Thus such evidence as is available suggests that anxiety disorders in childhood are transmitted familially.

However, the familiality of specific types of anxiety disorders is less clear. There is some suggestion of specificity for the familial transmission of obsessive–compulsive disorders (OCD) and panic disorder (i.e. a trend for relatives of probands with OCD to also show OCD; relatives of probands with panic disorder to also show panic disorder (Last *et al*, 1991)). Evidence for the specific familial transmission of other DSM–III–R anxiety subtypes such as overanxious disorder and separation anxiety (American Psychiatric Association, 1987) is as yet unconvincing. At present it can only be concluded that broadly defined anxiety appears to cluster in families. There is insufficient evidence to draw conclusions about the familiality of most specific types of anxiety disorders. Again, in order to determine whether genes contribute to this familiality, twin and adoption studies are needed.

# Conduct disorder

Results of twin and adoption studies of adult criminality and antisocial personality suggest that genetic factors are of considerable aetiological significance (see Chapter 8). Unfortunately, there have been fewer genetic studies of juvenile delinquency and even less interest in the genetics of conduct disorder, despite the relatively high prevalence rates of these conditions.

## Family and twin studies

Criminality in a parent appears to be a major risk factor for juvenile delinquency (Rutter & Giller, 1983), a finding which is compatible with learning or genetic theories. The pooled concordance rates obtained from five twin studies of juvenile delinquency were 87% for MZ twins and 72% for DZ pairs (McGuffin & Gottesman, 1985). These findings suggest a strong familial environmental influence on juvenile delinquency, but in marked contrast to studies of adult criminality, genetic factors appear to be of much less importance.

## Adoption studies

Again, most adoption studies have focused on adult criminality, although a few have combined data on childhood and adult antisocial behaviour.

In one study of 10- and 11-year-old adoptees, there was no increased rate of antisocial behaviour among the offspring of criminal biological fathers (Bohman, 1972). By contrast, in the only adoption study of conduct disorders specifically, a relatively high rate of personality disorder was found among the biological mothers of affected adoptees (Jary & Stewart, 1985).

In summary, twin and adoption data mostly suggest that familial environmental factors are of greater importance than genes in the transmission of juvenile delinquency. In keeping with this are findings of associations between family discord, large family size, poor parenting practices, and conduct disorder/delinquency. There have been too few genetic studies of conduct disorder to draw adequate conclusions about its transmission. However, conduct disorder often coexists with other disorders. More is known about the genetics of conduct disorder as a comorbid condition, which will be discussed further in the section on hyperactivity (see below).

It seems surprising that adult criminality and antisocial disorder, which appear to be genetically influenced, are almost invariably preceded by juvenile conduct problems, which appear to be mainly environmental (Robins, 1978). However, this may in part be related to the fact that rates of juvenile delinquency are much higher than those of adult criminality, but most juvenile offenders do not progress into adult criminality.

# Hyperactivity

A major problem in studying the genetics of childhood hyperactivity is in defining a meaningful phenotype. DSM–III–R attention deficit hyperactivity disorder (ADHD) and DSM–III attention deficit disorder with hyperactivity (ADDH) (American Psychiatric Association, 1980) are broader concepts of hyperactivity than those usually applied outside of North America. These transatlantic diagnostic differences mean that a number of cases of DSM–III attention deficit disorder would probably be classified as conduct disorder by British clinicians. An additional difficulty, for both researchers and those interpreting the results of genetic studies, is that of comorbidity. Hyperactivity commonly coexists with other psychiatric disorders, in particular conduct disorder.

Genetic research findings can broadly be divided into two groups, firstly those concerned with the genetic transmission of hyperactivity, and secondly results which focus on the genetic relationship between hyperactivity and other psychiatric disorders.

## Family studies

In two of the early family studies, parents and second-degree relatives of hyperactive children showed higher rates of a history of hyperactivity than controls (Morrison & Stewart, 1971; Cantwell, 1972). Higher rates have also been found among full siblings of severely affected children when compared to half-siblings (Nichols & Chen, 1981).

Similar results were found in the most recent family study where standardised methods of assessment and diagnosis were used (Biederman *et al*, 1986), and significantly higher rates of DSM–III attention deficit disorder were found among both parents and siblings of affected individuals (31.5% v. 5.7% of controls).

These studies all suggest that hyperactivity aggregates in families. However, as mentioned earlier, many affected children do not show 'pure' hyperactivity. The effect of comorbid conditions on the familiality of hyperactivity is an important consideration, which has only been studied quite recently.

## Comorbidity

Attention deficit disorder appears to aggregate familially even when coexistent with conduct disorder or oppositional defiant disorder. In fact, familial risk for ADD seems to be highest when probands show both ADD and conduct disorder (Faraone *et al*, 1991). In earlier studies, where comorbidity was not considered, there was some suggestion of links between antisocial personality in parents and hyperactivity in their offspring on the basis of both family (Stewart *et al*, 1980; Morrison, 1980) and adoption data (Morrison & Stewart, 1973; Cantwell, 1975). More recent work, however, suggests that the significantly higher rates of antisocial disorders (antisocial personality, oppositional defiant disorder and childhood conduct disorder) among relatives are accounted for by relatives of children with both attention deficit disorder *and* conduct disorder or oppositional disorder, and not relatives of those with 'pure' ADD (Biederman *et al*, 1987). These results lend support to the idea that pure hyperactivity is an entity distinct from hyperactivity with a comorbid condition. In fact, a separate diagnostic category of hyperkinetic conduct disorder is included in ICD–10 (World Health Organization, 1992).

## Twin studies

Unfortunately, there have been few systematic twin studies of hyperactivity. One of the earliest studies, which did not use a systematically ascertained sample or standardised measurements, showed that MZ twins were significantly more alike than DZ twins for both activity levels and hyperactivity (Willerman, 1973).

In a more recent questionnaire-based but systematic twin study, genetic factors accounted for about half of the variance. Probandwise concordance rates for situational and pervasive hyperactivity were 51% for MZ twins and 33% for DZ twins (Goodman & Stevenson, 1989). These studies suggest that genetic factors play an important role in the familial transmission of hyperactivity.

Despite popular theories about the role of perinatal factors, perhaps rooted in the early concept of minimal brain dysfunction, the association between perinatal adversity and hyperactivity is difficult to interpret. A recent study showed significant but only small effects of obstetric and perinatal complications (Chandola *et al*, 1992). In short, although genetic factors cannot explain all the observed variance, a specific environmental risk factor of major contribution has not yet been identified.

## Adoption studies

Increased rates of hyperactivity (or a history of hyperactivity) have been found among both adopted-away siblings of children with hyperactivity (Safer, 1973) and among the natural parents of hyperactive boys when compared with controls (Morrison & Stewart, 1973; Cantwell, 1975). Although there are limitations to these studies, these results when taken with the twin data strongly suggest that hyperactivity is a heritable condition.

# Enuresis

Enuresis is a familial disorder. In an early study (Hallgren, 1958), 70% of families with an enuretic child had another affected member, and in a study of kibbutz children, a quarter of the enuretic children had a sibling who was similarly affected (Kaffman, 1962).

However, there have been surprisingly few twin studies. In one study of enuretics (Bakwin, 1971), concordance rates were 68% for MZ twins and 36% for DZ twins. Hallgren (1960) had similarly found higher concordance rates for MZ twins compared with DZ twins in an earlier study.

Although few systematic genetic studies of enuresis have been done, current evidence suggests that this line of investigation should be pursued.

# Developmental reading disorders

## Family studies

A large number of studies have shown that reading disabilities aggregate in families. In one of the earliest studies, the risk to first-degree relatives of probands was found to be 41%, which compares with a risk of between 5% and 10% in the general population (Hallgren, 1950). In another family study, 45% of the relatives of affected children also had reading difficulties (Finucci *et al*, 1976).

Similar results have been demonstrated when a representative sample has been used. In the Colorado Family Reading Study (Vogler *et al*, 1985), for boys with reading difficulties the frequency of affected fathers was 40% and of affected mothers 35%. For girls, the frequency of affected parents was considerably lower (17–18%). Overall, there is strong evidence of familial clustering of reading difficulties, and estimates of familial risk have mostly varied between 36% and 45% (Pennington, 1990).

## Twin studies

Findings from an early but non-systematic twin study (Bakwin, 1973) suggested that reading disability is genetically influenced (MZ concordance rate of 84% versus DZ concordance rate of 29%). A later study, which used a larger twin sample, reported a heritability of 30% for reading difficulties (DeFries *et al*, 1987). In particular, significant heritability was found for single-word reading, spelling and digit span, but not for reading comprehension or perceptual motor speed.

In contrast to these findings, a study of 13-year-old twins rather surprisingly showed low concordance rates for reading difficulties for both MZ and DZ twins (Stevenson *et al*, 1987).Genetic factors appeared to be of greater importance for spelling, with an estimated heritability of 73%.

An analysis of reading skills among twins from the Colarado reading project (Olson *et al*, 1989) provides some interesting results. Significant heritability was found for a phonological measure (non-word reading performance) but not for orthographic skill (recognition of which of two spellings was correct). There is increasing evidence that underlying phonological processing deficits are of especial importance (Snowling, 1991), so it is of particular interest that these skills have been found to be heritable.

## Mode of transmission and molecular genetics

A number of different modes of transmission for reading difficulties have been postulated. However, complex segregation analysis has been used in only one sample (Lewitter *et al*, 1980), of 133 nuclear families. There was no support for single major locus transmission for the whole population, but there was evidence of genetic heterogeneity.

The hypothesis of genetic heterogeneity is strengthened by unreplicated linkage findings. Great interest was generated by the initial positive finding of linkage between reading disability and a marker on the short arm of chromosome 15 (Smith *et al*, 1983). However, this result was obtained for a minority of families where there appeared to be autosomal dominant transmission and has not, as with recent schizophrenia and bipolar linkage findings (see Chapters 5 and 6), been replicated in other populations. However, a recent analysis has treated reading disability as a quantitative trait rather than a dichotomous one in an attempt to detect so-called quantitative trait loci (QTL, see Chapter 3). The results, though not conclusive, are interesting and suggest a general approach to detecting loci in this and other disorders where more than one gene is likely to be involved (Fulker *et al*, 1991).

In conclusion, current evidence suggests that genetic factors are an important influence in the transmission of reading disabilities. However, it seems highly unlikely that reading difficulties in general will be accounted for by a single gene.

# Tics and Tourette's syndrome

## Family studies

In the original description of Tourette's syndrome (TS), Gilles de la Tourette suggested that the disorder may well be familial. Since then a number of family studies have been carried out and the findings have supported this hypothesis. Moreover, it appears that relatives of probands with TS show increased rates of chronic tics as well as full-blown TS (Pauls *et al*, 1984; Pauls & Leckman, 1986; Robertson & Gourdie, 1990).

It has been suggested that simple tics, chronic tics and full-blown TS lie on the same continuum of increasing severity. However, whereas TS and chronic tics are relatively rare, simple tics can occur in up to 10% of the population, and there is no convincing evidence of familial aggregation of common simple tics.

Interestingly, several family studies have shown that OCD also aggregates with chronic tics and TS in the families of TS probands (Montgomery *et al*, 1982; Pauls *et al*, 1986; Robertson & Gourdie, 1990). These findings give rise to the question of what behaviours should be included in the TS phenotype. Although there has been interest in associations between TS and conditions such as attention deficit disorder, there is insufficient evidence to suggest that these should be included in the TS phenotype. Overall, there is now considerable evidence that TS, chronic tics and some obsessive–compulsive disorders are familially related.

## Twin studies

Most reports of twins with TS have been anecdotal. One study included 43 pairs of twins who were identified through the Tourette Syndrome Association (Price *et al*, 1985). Concordance rates for TS were significantly higher among MZ twins than among DZ twins (53% v. 8%). When the phenotype was broadened to include tics, the concordance rates rose to 77% for MZ twins and 23% for DZ twins. However, the twin sample was not systematically ascertained. Thus, although the results suggest that TS is transmitted genetically, systematic twin studies are needed, and these could be of particular use in helping to define a meaningful TS phenotype.

## Mode of transmission and molecular genetics

Testing models of transmission is difficult when there are uncertainties about the boundaries of the phenotype and the population prevalence of the disorder. Although complex segregation analyses suggest that a single major locus is compatible with family data, there is little agreement about the level of penetrance, the number of phenocopies, and indeed the definition of the phenotype itself. An autosomal dominant gene with variable penetrance has been proposed to explain family data for a phenotype consisting of both TS and tics (Comings *et al*, 1984; Price *et al*, 1988) as well as for a broader phenotype of TS, tics and obsessive–compulsive disorder (Pauls & Leckman, 1986). It has even been suggested that there may be sex-specific expression of the gene, with tics and TS commoner in males and OCD commoner in females (Pauls & Leckman, 1986). However, it must be remembered that results of complex segregation analyses can be deceptive and should be interpreted with caution, especially when dealing with a difficult to define behavioural trait.

So far there have been no positive association or linkage findings. It could be argued that such a search is premature, given the uncertainties about the phenotype and the lack of systematic twin data.

# Conclusions

There is now considerable evidence showing that many childhood disorders aggregate familially. However, this of course could be due to shared family environment and not necessarily imply genetic influences. Simple Mendelian transmission alone is unlikely to explain the pattern of inheritance for most child psychiatric disorders. Even for disorders such as autism where there is strong evidence of a genetic effect, the possibility of genetic heterogeneity seems to be more plausible.

As yet, few linkage studies have been carried out for childhood psychiatric disorders. It is likely that molecular genetic techniques, in particular the mapping of QTLs, will be of relevance to the study of childhood disorders at some stage. However, before embarking on searches for genes at a molecular level, at present for most child psychiatric disorders there is a lack of basic knowledge as to whether genes do contribute and if so to what extent they do so. There is therefore still a need for further traditional twin and adoption studies.

In the past, previous popular misconceptions about genetic studies may have led child psychiatrists to doubt the relevance of this type of work to their specialty. However, it is now increasingly evident that genetic studies can shed light on the role of both genetic and environmental influences, and that understanding of the aetiology of childhood psychiatric disorders has implications for their prevention as well as their treatment.

Similarly, geneticists may have previously ignored the importance of psychiatric disorders in this age group, but there is now increasing evidence of continuities between childhood psychiatric disorders and those in adulthood (Robins, 1978; Harrington *et al*, 1990). There are also suggestions that, in general, early-onset disorders are more severe and more genetically influenced.

For all of these reasons, it seems likely that the genetics of childhood disorders is likely to become an area of expanding interest for a more thorough application of classic family, twin and adoption studies as well as exploitation of molecular genetic methods (LaBuda *et al*, 1993; McGuffin, 1987).

# References

American Psychiatric Association (1980) *Diagnostic and Statistical Manual of Mental Disorder* (3rd edn) (DSM–III). Washington, DC: APA.

—— (1987) *Diagnostic and Statistical Manual of Mental Disorder* (3rd edn, revised) (DSM–III–R). Washington, DC: APA.

Angold, A., Weissman, M. M., John, K., *et al* (1987) Parent and child reports of depressive symptoms in children at low and high risk of depression. *Journal of Child Psychology and Psychiatry*, **28**, 901-915.

Bailey, A. (1993) The biology of autism. *Psychological Medicine*, **23**, 7-11.

Baird, T. D. & August, G. J. (1985) Familial heterogeneity in infantile autism. *Journal of Autism and Developmental Disorders*, **15**, 315-321.

Bakwin, H. (1971) Enuresis in twins. *American Journal of Diseases of Childhood*, **121**, 222-225.

—— (1973) Reading disability in twins. *Developmental Medicine and Child Neurology*, **15**, 184-187.

Berg, I. (1976) School phobia in the children of agorophobic women. *British Journal of Psychiatry*, **128**, 86-89.

Biederman, J., Munir, K., Knee, D., *et al* (1986) A family study of patients with attention deficit disorder and normal controls. *Psychiatry Research*, **20**, 263-274.

——, —— & —— (1987) Conduct and oppositional disorder in clinically referred children with attention deficit disorder: a controlled family study. *Journal of the American Academy of Child and Adolescent Psychiatry*, **26**, 724-727.

Bohman, M. (1972) A study of adopted children, their background, environment and adjustment. *Acta Paediatrica Scandinavica*, **61**, 90-97.

Cantwell, D. P. (1972) Psychiatric illness in families of hyperactive children. *Archives of General Psychiatry*, **27**, 414-417.

—— (1975) Genetic studies of hyperactive children: psychiatric illness in biological and adopting parents. In *Genetic Research in Psychiatry* (eds R. R. Fieve, D. Rosenthal & H. Brill), pp. 273-280. Baltimore: Johns Hopkins University Press.

Chandola, C. A., Robling, M. R., Peters, T. J., *et al* (1992) Pre- and perinatal factors and the risk of subsequent referral for hyperactivity. *Journal of Child Psychology and Psychiatry*, **33**, 1077-1090.

Comings, D. E., Comings, B. G., Devor, E. J., *et al* (1984) Detection of major gene for Gilles de la Tourette syndrome. *American Journal of Human Genetics*, **36**, 586-600.

Courchesne, E., Yeung-Courchesne, R., Press, G. A., *et al* (1988) Hypoplasia of cerebellar vermal lobules VI and VII in autism. *New England Journal of Medicine*, **318**, 1349-1354.

Cyphers, L. H., Phillips, K., Fulker, D., *et al* (1990) Twin temperament during the transition from infancy to early childhood. *Journal of the American Academy of Child and Adolescent Psychiatry*, **29**, 392-397.

DeFries, J. C., Fulker, D. W. & LaBuda, M. C. (1987) Evidence for a genetic aetiology in reading disability of twins. *Nature*, **329**, 537-539.

Dwyer, J. T. & Delong, G. R. (1987) A family history study of 20 probands with childhood manic depressive illness. *Journal of the American Academy of Child and Adolescent Psychiatry*, **26**, 176-180.

Faraone, S. V., Biederman, J., Keenan, K., *et al* (1991) Separation of DSM–III attention deficit disorder and conduct disorder: evidence from a family-genetic study of American child psychiatric patients. *Psychological Medicine*, **21**, 109-121.

Finucci, J. M., Guthrie, J. T., Childs, A. L., *et al* (1976) The genetics of specific reading disability. *Annals of Human Genetics*, **40**, 1-23.

Folstein, S. & Rutter, M. (1977) Infantile autism: a genetic study of 21 twin pairs. *Journal of Child Psychology and Psychiatry*, 18, 297-321.

Fulker, D. W., Cardon, L. R., DeFries, J. C., *et al* (1991) Multiple regression analysis of sib pair data on reading to detect quantitative trait loci. *Reading and Writing Journal*, **3**, 299-313.

Goldsmith, H. H. & Gottesman, I. I. (1981) Origins of variation in behavioral style: a longitudinal study of temperament in young twins. *Child Development*, **52**, 91-103.

—— & Campos, J. J. (1986) Fundamental issues in the study of early temperament: the Denver Twin Temperament Study. In *Advances in Developmental Psychology*, vol. 4 (eds M. E. Lamb, A. L. Brown & B. Rogoff), pp. 231-283. Hillsdale: Erlbaum.

Goodman, R. & Stevenson, J. (1989) A twin study of hyperactivity II. The aetiological role of genes, family relationships and perinatal adversity. *Journal of Child Psychology and Psychiatry*, **30**, 691-709.

Hallgren, B. (1950) Specific dyslexia (congenital word blindness): a clinical and genetic study. *Acta Psychiatrica et Neurologica Supplement*, **65**, 1-287.

—— (1958) Nocturnal enuresis: etiologic aspects. *Acta Pediatrica* (suppl.), **118**, 66.

—— (1960) Nocturnal enuresis in twins. *Acta Psychiatrica Scandinavica*, **35**, 73.

Hanson, D. R. & Gottesman, I. I. (1976) The genetics, if any, of infantile autism and childhood schizophrenia. *Journal of Autism and Childhood Schizophrenia*, **6**, 209-233.

Harrington, R., Fudge, H., Rutter, M., *et al* (1990) Adult outcomes of childhood and adolescent depression. *Archives of General Psychiatry*, **47**, 465-473.

Jary, M. L. & Stewart, M. A. (1985) Psychiatric disorder in the parents of adopted children with aggressive conduct disorder. *Neuropsychobiology*, **13**, 7-11.

Jones, M.B. & Szatmari, P. (1988) Stoppage rules and genetic studies of autism. *Journal of Autism and Developmental Disorders*, **18**, 31-40.

Kaffman, M. (1962) Enuresis among kibbutz children. *Journal of the Medical Association of Israel*, **63**, 251.

Kanner, L. (1943) Autistic disturbances of affective contact. *Nervous Children*, **2**, 217-250.

Kutcher, S. & Marton, P. (1991) Affective disorders in first degree relatives of adolescent onset bipolars, unipolars and normal controls. *Journal of the American Academy of Child and Adolescent Psychology*, **30**, 75-78.

LaBuda, M. C., Gottesman, I. I. & Pauls, D. L. (1993) Usefulness of twin studies for exploring the aetiology of childhood and adolescent psychiatric disorders. *American Journal of Medical Genetics: Neuropsychiatric Genetics*, **48**, 47-59.

Last, C. G., Hersen, M., Kazdin, A., *et al* (1991) Anxiety disorders in children and their families. *Archives of General Psychiatry*, **48**, 928-934.

Lewitter, F. J., DeFries, J. C. & Elston, R. C. (1980) Genetic models of reading disabilities. *Behavior Genetics*, **10**, 9-30.

Livingston, R., Nugent, H., Rader, L., *et al* (1985) Family histories of depressed and severely anxious children. *American Journal of Psychiatry*, **142**, 1497-1499.

Loehlin, J. C., Horn, J. M. & Willerman, L. (1981) Personality resemblance in adoptive families. *Behavior Genetics*, **11**, 309-330.

Macdonald, H., Rutter, M., Rios, P., *et al* (1989) *Cognitive and Social Abnormalities in the Siblings of Autistic and Down's Syndrome Probands*. Paper given at the

First World Congress on Psychiatric Genetics, Churchill College, Cambridge, 3–5 August.

McGuffin, P. (1987) The new genetics and childhood psychiatric disorder. *Journal of Child Psychology and Psychiatry*, **28**, 215-222.

—— & Gottesman, I. I. (1985) Genetic influences on normal and abnormal development. In *Child and Adolescent Psychiatry: Modern Approaches* (2nd edn) (eds M. Rutter & L. Hersov), pp. 17-33. Oxford: Blackwell Scientific.

Montgomery, M. A., Clayton, P. J. & Friedhoff, A. J. (1982) Psychiatric illness in Tourette syndrome patients and first degree relatives. In *Gilles de La Tourette Syndrome* (eds T. N. Chase & A. J. Friedhoff), pp. 335-339. New York: Raven Press.

Morrison, J. R. (1980) Adult psychiatric disorders in parents of hyperactive children. *American Journal of Psychiatry*, **137**, 825-827.

—— & Stewart, M. A. (1971) A family study of the hyperactive child syndrome. *Biological Psychiatry*, **3**, 189-195.

—— & —— (1973) The psychiatric status of the legal families of adopted hyperactive children. *Archives of General Psychiatry*, **28**, 888-891.

Nichols, P. L. & Chen, T. C. (1981) *Minimal Brain Dysfunction: A Prospective Study*. Hillsdale: Erlbaum.

Olson, R., Wise, B., Conners, F., *et al* (1989) Specific deficits in component reading and language skills: genetic and environmental influences. *Journal of Learning Disabilities*, **22**, 339-348.

Orvaschel, H. (1990) Early onset psychiatric disorder in high risk children and increased familial morbidity. *Journal of the American Academy of Child and Adolescent Psychiatry*, **29**, 184-188.

——, Walsh-Allis, G. & Ye, W. (1988) Psychopathology in children of parents with recurrent depression. *Journal of Abnormal Child Psychology*, **16**, 17-28.

Pauls, D. I., Kruger, S. D., Leckman, J. F., *et al* (1984) The risk of Tourette's syndrome and chronic multiple tics among relatives of Tourette's syndrome patients obtained by direct interview. *Journal of the American Academy of Child and Adolescent Psychiatry*, **23**, 134-137.

—— & Leckman, J. F. (1986) The inheritance of Gilles de la Tourette's syndrome and associated behaviours. Evidence for autosomal dominant transmission. *New England Journal of Medicine*, **315**, 993-997.

——, Tourbin, K. E., Leckman, J. F., *et al* (1986) Gilles de la Tourette's syndrome and obsessive compulsive disorder. *Archives of General Psychiatry*, **43**, 1180-1182.

Pennington, B. F. (1990) The genetics of dyslexia. *Journal of Child Psychology and Psychiatry*, **31**, 193-201.

Piven, J., Gayle, J., Chase, G., *et al* (1990) A family history study of neuropsychiatric disorders in the adult siblings of autistic individuals. *Journal of the American Academy of Child and Adolescent Psychiatry*, **29**, 177-184.

Plomin, R., DeFries, J. C. & Fulker, D. W. (1988) *Nature and Nurture in Infancy and Early Childhood*. New York: Cambridge University Press.

Price, R. A., Kidd, K. K., Cohen, D. J., *et al* (1985) A twin study of Tourette syndrome. *Archives of General Psychiatry*, **42**, 815-820.

——, Pauls, D. L., Kruger, S. D., *et al* (1988) Family data support a dominant major gene for Tourette syndrome. *Psychiatry Research*, **24**, 251-261.

Puig Antich, J., Goetz, D., Davies, M., *et al* (1989) A controlled family history study of prepubertal major depressive disorder. *Archives of General Psychiatry*, **45**, 406-418.

Reiss, A. L., Feinstein, C. & Rosenbaum, K. N. (1986) Autism and genetic disorders. *Schizophrenia Bulletin*, **12**, 724-728.

Ritvo, E. R., Spence, M. A., Freeman, B. J., *et al* (1985) Evidence for autosomal recessive inheritance in 46 families with multiple incidences of autism. *American Journal of Psychiatry*, **142**, 187-192.

Robertson, M. M. & Gourdie, A. (1990) Familial Tourette's syndrome in a large British pedigree. Associated psychopathology, severity and potential for linkage analysis. *British Journal of Psychiatry*, **156**, 515-521.

Robins, L. N. (1978) Sturdy childhood predictors of adult antisocial behavior: replications from longitudinal studies. *Psychological Medicine*, **8**, 611-622.

Rutter, M. (1987) Temperament, personality and personality disorders. *British Journal of Psychiatry*, **150**, 443-458.

—— & Giller, H. (1983) *Juvenile Delinquency: Trends and Perspectives*. Harmondsworth: Penguin.

——, MacDonald, H., LeCouteur, A., *et al* (1990) Genetic factors in child psychiatric disorders – II. Empirical findings. *Journal of Child Psychology and Psychiatry*, **31**, 39-83.

Safer, D. J. (1973) A familial factor in minimal brain dysfunction. *Behavior Genetics*, **3**, 175-186.

Smalley, S. L., Asarnow, R. F. & Spence, M. A. (1988). Autism and genetics: a decade of research. *Archives of General Psychiatry*, **45**, 953-961.

Smith, S. D., Kimberling, W. J., Pennington, B. F., *et al* (1983) Specific reading disability: identification of an inherited form through linkage analysis. *Science*, **219**, 1345-1347.

Snowling, M. J. (1991) Developmental reading disorders. *Journal of Child Psychology and Psychiatry*, **32**, 49-77.

Spence, M. A., Ritvo, E. R., Marazota, M. L., *et al* (1985) Gene mapping studies with the syndrome of autism. *Behavior Genetics*, **15**, 1-13.

Steffenberg, S., Gillberg, C., Hellgren, L., *et al* (1989) A twin study of autism in Denmark, Finland, Iceland, Norway and Sweden. *Journal of Child Psychology and Psychiatry*, **30**, 405-416.

Stevenson, J., Graham, P., Fredman, G., *et al* (1987) A twin study of genetic influences on reading and spelling ability and disability. *Journal of Child Psychology and Psychiatry*, **28**, 229-247.

Stewart, M. A., Deblois, C. S. & Cummings, C. (1980) Psychiatric disorder in the parents of hyperactive boys and those with conduct disorder. *Journal of Child Psychology and Psychiatry*, **21**, 283-292.

Strober, M., Morrell, W., Burroughs, J., *et al* (1988) A family study of bipolar I disorder in adolescence. *Journal of Affective Disorders*, **15**, 255-268.

Thapar, A. & McGuffin, P. (1994) A twin study of depressive symptoms in childhood. *British Journal of Psychiatry* (in press).

Torgersen, A. M. (1987) Longitudinal research on temperament in twins. *Acta Genetica Medica Gemellologea*, **36**, 145-154.

—— & Kringlen, E. (1978) Genetic aspects of temperamental differences in infants. *Journal of the American Academy of Child Psychiatry*, **17**, 433-444.

Tsai, L. Y. & Beisler, J. M. (1983) The developmental of sex differences in infantile autism. *British Journal of Psychiatry*, **142**, 373-378.

Vogler, G. P., DeFries, J. C. & Decker, S. N. (1985) Family history as an indicator of risk for reading disability. *Journal of Learning Disabilities*, **18**, 419-421.

Weissman, M. M., Leckman, J. F., Merikangas, K. R., *et al* (1984) Depression and anxiety disorders in parents and children. *Archives of General Psychiatry*, **41**, 845-852.

——, Gammon, G. D., John, K., *et al* (1987) Children of depressed parents: increased psychopathology and early onset of major depression. *Archives of General Psychiatry*, **44**, 847-853.

——, Fendrich, M., Warner, *et al* (1992) Incidence of psychiatric disorder in offspring at high and low risk for depression. *Journal of the American Academy of Child and Adolescent Psychiatry*, **31**, 640-648.

Wierzbicki, M. (1987) Similarity of monozygotic and dizygotic child twins in level and lability of subclinically depressed mood. *American Journal of Orthopsychiatry*, **57**, 33-40.

Willerman, L. (1973) Activity level of hyperactivity in twins. *Child Development*, **44**, 288-293.

Wilson, R. S. & Matheny, A. P. Jr (1986) Behavior-genetics research in infant temperament: the Louisville Twin Study. In *The Study of Temperament* (eds R. Plomin & J. Dunn), pp. 81-97. Hillsdale: Erlbaum.

World Health Organization (1992) *The ICD–10 Classification of Mental and Behavioural Disorders.* Geneva: WHO.

Zausmer, D. M. & Dewey, M. E. (1987) Tics and heredity. A study of the relatives of child ticquers. *British Journal of Psychiatry*, **150**, 628-634.

# 11  Dementia

*Alzheimer's disease* • *Multi-infarct dementia* • *Huntington's disease* •
*Pick's disease* • *The spongiform encephalopathies*

Dementia is a common clinical syndrome, with a prevalence after the age of 65 years estimated to range from 4.5% to 18.5% (Amaducci & Lippi, 1992), which can result from many different disease processes. In the present chapter, we shall review the genetics of several of the so-called 'primary dementias', in which cerebral function is impaired by intrinsic degeneration of the brain. We shall also briefly discuss multi-infarct dementia which, although strictly speaking a secondary dementia, warrants mention because of its high incidence.

Neuropathological studies indicate that approximately 50% of cases of severe dementia are due to Alzheimer's disease (AD), 20% to multi-infarct dementia (MID), 20% to mixed AD/MID, and the remainder to various other diseases (Tomlinson *et al*, 1970). AD and MID, like 'functional' psychiatric disorders and other common diseases with a genetic component such as coronary artery disease and diabetes mellitus, do not show clear patterns of Mendelian transmission. However, like these common disorders, there is probably aetiological heterogeneity, and it seems increasingly likely that a small proportion of cases of AD and MID are the result of defects in single genes. As with other complex disorders, cases with a high genetic loading tend to have an earlier age of onset than is typical. Among the less common primary dementias there are several single-gene disorders, as well as those where genes operate as part of a more complex aetiological picture. Recent advances in the molecular genetics of Alzheimer's disease, Huntington's disease and the spongiform encephalopathies offer real hope for understanding the pathogenesis of these disorders and for therapeutic advance.

## Alzheimer's disease

The prevalence of AD increases steeply with age, from less than 1% at 65 years to approximately 15% in the ninth decade (Skoog *et al*, 1993). The senile plaques and neurofibrillary tangles that are characteristically seen in the brains of people dying with AD were first described in 1907 by a Bavarian psychiatrist, Alois Alzheimer, a colleague of Kraepelin's in Munich at the time. In the last 10 years there has been a rapid advance in understanding the molecular events that underlie these neuropathological changes. Some of this work will be briefly discussed here, as it forms the background to recent studies in molecular genetics.

Protein sequencing has revealed that senile plaques consist of extracellular deposits of a protein fragment, approximately 40 amino acids long, which is now generally known as amyloid beta protein or beta-amyloid (Glenner & Wong, 1984; Masters *et al*, 1985). This arises by cleavage of a much larger protein called beta-amyloid precursor protein (APP) (Kang *et al*, 1987). In 'mature' plaques, the central core of beta-amyloid is surrounded by abnormal neurites and glial cells. Recent immunohistochemical studies have identified abundant, amorphous, non-filamentous deposits of beta-amyloid in AD brain tissue. These 'diffuse' plaques contain little or no degenerating neurites or reactive glial cells (Yamaguchi *et al*, 1988). The strongest evidence that they are the precursors of mature plaques is their abundance in the brains of younger subjects with Down's syndrome (DS) (Mann *et al*, 1989). Since virtually all those with DS who live beyond 40 years develop classical senile plaques identical to those seen in AD (Oliver & Holland, 1986), this implies that beta-amyloid deposition precedes the alteration of neurones and gliosis, and may well be the primary event in plaque formation (Selkoe, 1991).

Beta-amyloid is also abnormally deposited in the walls of meningeal blood vessels in AD, and was in fact first isolated from this source (Glenner & Wong, 1984). Small deposits have been found in and around blood vessels in a variety of tissues outside the brain, which suggests that the protein may be produced locally in many organs or be derived from a circulating precursor, as in other human amyloidoses (Joachim *et al*, 1989).

The other main neuropathological feature of AD is the presence of numerous neurofibrillary tangles. These consist of dense bundles of abnormal fibres, or paired helical filaments (PHFs), in the cytoplasm of certain neurones. They are composed, at least in part, of an altered form of the microtubule associated protein, tau. The remaining constituents of PHFs are unknown (Hardy & Allsop, 1991). In particular, the question of whether beta-amyloid is an intrinsic component of PHFs is as yet unanswered (Hardy & Allsop, 1991).

Neither senile plaques nor neurofibrillary tangles are specific to AD. They are found in a number of other chronic cerebral conditions. Moreover, both are found in non-demented elderly people, though here they tend to be restricted to the hippocampus and surrounding structures of the temporal lobes. In AD, plaques and tangles are much more numerous. The temporal lobes are most severely affected, but so are other areas of the cerebral cortex and basal ganglia and also the diencephalon and brainstem as well as sometimes the cerebellum. AD can therefore be viewed, neuropathologically at least, as an accentuation and acceleration of the normal ageing process.

Many epidemiological studies have been carried out in order to try to identify risk factors for AD (see Henderson, 1986, and Amaducci & Lippi,

1992, for reviews), and there is increasing recognition that considerable aetiological heterogeneity might exist. Apart from increasing age, only one variable has consistently been identified: the presence of a family history of the disorder (Heyman *et al*, 1984; Brody, 1982). To this should be added the well established fact, already mentioned, that the majority of individuals with DS (trisomy 21) who reach the fourth decade of life develop the characteristic neuropathology of AD (Oliver & Holland, 1986). These findings suggest that genetic factors may play a role in the aetiology of AD and that a gene, or genes, on chromosome 21 might be important in causing AD in individuals without DS. Other risk factors of less certain relevance include head injury and increasing maternal age (Amaducci & Lippi, 1992).

## Genetic epidemiology

Genetic studies of AD face a number of difficulties, most of which are shared with other forms of dementia. The first is that certain diagnosis depends upon both the presence of dementia during life and subsequent histopathological examination. The accuracy of clinical diagnosis alone is less than 100% and, since Alzheimer's-like neuropathological changes are common in the elderly, AD cannot always be diagnosed with certainty solely upon the basis of information obtained post-mortem.

Many early studies are difficult to interpret because of the lack of explicit diagnostic criteria. More recently, diagnostic criteria have been developed (McKhann *et al*, 1984). These are mainly concerned with the exclusion of MID and other secondary dementias, and allow clinical diagnoses of 'possible' or 'probable' AD to be made. The diagnosis of 'definite' AD requires additional histopathological evidence. Follow-up studies in elderly populations (>65 years old) indicate that a diagnosis of 'probable AD' is confirmed at autopsy in 80–90% of cases (Joachim *et al*, 1988). Its accuracy in presenile dementia, where exclusion of other primary dementias may be more important, has not been systematically tested.

The second major difficulty is that AD has a late age of onset. This has several important consequences for genetic studies. First, it can be assumed that some, perhaps many individuals who are genetically predisposed to AD will die of other causes before they express the disease. This will have the effect of reducing familial clustering and will result in the genetic contribution to the disorder being underestimated unless statistical correction is made. Secondly, relatives might be studied before the age at which the disease is expressed, again resulting in underestimation of familiality. These problems can be at least partly addressed by standard methods of age correcting (see Chapter 2) or by actuarial techniques such as life tables and survival analysis (Chase *et al*, 1983; Sturt, 1986).

A third problem is that affected relatives of probands with AD will usually be dead, and will have been so for some years in the case of those from preceding generations. Thus, diagnosis of secondary cases is often retrospective and unsupported by histopathological data, leading to low sensitivity and specificity however rigorously the probands are ascertained and diagnosed.

Late age at onset also reduces the power of linkage studies since living, affected individuals in whom marker typing is possible are only available from a single generation. The exception to this occurs when markers can be typed using archival pathological specimens from dead individuals.

Finally, it is worth bearing in mind that, given the sharp rise in incidence in later life, familial clustering in AD may reflect genetic influences on longevity as well as any possible effects of more specific inherited factors.

Early family studies found increased rates of illness in the relatives of probands with AD. Sjögren *et al* (1952) studied the families of 34 cases with AD of presenile onset (<65 years of age) and found eight secondary cases, three with onset before age 65, in 255 first-degree relatives. They concluded that multifactorial transmission was the most likely explanation of their findings. Larsson *et al* (1963) studied the relatives of 377 cases of senile dementia and found a fourfold increase in the morbidity risk for dementia in the first-degree relatives. They suggested that this could be explained by the transmission of a dominant mutation in a single gene, but with simple Mendelian ratios obscured by the late age of onset of the disorder. However, it has subsequently been argued that their findings are also compatible with multifactorial/polygenic transmission (Wright & Whalley, 1984) and a segregation analysis failed to demonstrate evidence for a major gene (McGuffin *et al*, 1991). Heston *et al* (1981) studied the relatives of probands ascertained on the basis of autopsy data. They found higher rates of illness in the relatives of early-onset cases rather than late-onset cases. These findings were widely interpreted as supporting the view that early-onset AD has a greater genetic component than late-onset disease.

During the mid and late 1980s, a number of family studies were published. These differed from earlier investigations in that the clinical grounds for the selection of cases were more stringent, though autopsy evidence was seldom available. In three of them (Mohs *et al*, 1987; Huff *et al*, 1988; Martin *et al*, 1988), probands were required to satisfy the now widely used modern diagnostic criteria for AD (McKhann *et al*, 1984). In the fourth, they were required to have agraphia and aphasia as well as amnesia (Breitner & Folstein, 1984). The probands in all these studies were unselected for age of onset and therefore consisted predominantly of senile cases. In all four, after age correction was applied, the cumulative risk of dementia in first-degree relatives did not differ significantly from 50% by age 85–90 years. These results have been interpreted as supporting the view that the aetiology of AD has a major genetic component which shows autosomal dominant transmission with age-dependent penetrance. The failure of some earlier studies to show such high rates of illness in relatives was said to have resulted from the inclusion among the probands of individuals who did not have AD.

The findings of Heston *et al* (1981) in the relatives of probands with disease of late onset are more difficult to reconcile with the recent family studies. It can be argued that an over-reliance on neuropathological findings may have led to over-diagnosis of AD in an elderly population where senile plaques and neurofibrillary tangles can be abundant in the absence of any history of dementia. Conversely, the family history method employed by workers such as Breitner & Folstein (1984), while no doubt under-estimating the total number of cases of dementia, might well have overestimated the number of secondary cases of AD by including cases with other dementias, in particular MID. Another possibility is that ascertainment bias operated to increase the number of cases with high familial loading. Farrer *et al* (1989) examined this issue by identifying all the probands in their series who were likely to have been referred because their illness appeared familial. When these were included, the maximum cumulative incidence was 44% ± 8%, an estimate close to those derived from the previous studies. However, when the non-randomly ascertained cases were excluded, the cumulative incidence of Alzheimer's-type dementia in first-degree relatives with probable AD was maximally 39% but probably closer to 24% when risk estimates were weighted for accuracy of diagnosis.

Farrer *et al* (1989) also divided their families into two groups according to the median age of onset in their probands of 67 years. This showed that the cumulative risk of disease was not significantly higher in the relatives of early-onset probands, but that these had a significantly earlier age of onset. This was because the risk to relatives of late-onset cases 'caught up' in the ninth and tenth decades. Interestingly, similar results were obtained when the relatives of AD probands were compared with those of controls. Over a lifespan of 90 years, the proportion of relatives who became affected did not differ between the two groups. However, the relatives of controls developed the disease significantly later than the relatives of the probands with AD. These results should be interpreted cautiously as they are critically dependent upon data from the small number of relatives who lived into the ninth and tenth decades. However, if confirmed in a larger study, these findings have implications for the understanding of genetic mechanisms. They suggest that what may be under genetic control is not so much whether the disorder develops but when, in which case genetic susceptibility to AD might reflect perturbation of processes involved in normal ageing.

## Twin studies

Unfortunately there is little persuasive evidence from twin or adoption studies that the aggregation of AD in families occurs as a result of genetic rather than shared environmental factors. There has been no adoption study, and this no doubt reflects the practical difficulties of studying a disease of such late onset. There have been a number of reports of discordant MZ twin pairs and, providing that the unaffected co-twin survived for many years without developing the disorder, these are good evidence that AD is not entirely genetic in origin (reviewed recently by Wright, 1991, and Breitner *et al*, 1992). The only series of adequate size was that of Kallmann (1956), which contained 54 monozygotic (MZ) and 54 dizygotic (DZ) pairs with at least one member suffering from 'senile psychosis', a diagnostic category that included patients with both AD and MID as well as a number of other disorders (Jarvik *et al*, 1980). Concordance in MZ twins was 43% compared with 8% in DZ. However, in a more recent study (Nee *et al*, 1987) using modern diagnostic practices but based upon a sample of only 22 pairs (17 MZ and 5 DZ), the MZ and DZ concordances were virtually identical, at 40% and 41% respectively. These findings do not refute the hypothesis of genetic transmission because of the small size of the sample and the lack of adequate follow-up or systematic ascertainment. No study of a systematically ascertained sample has yet been completed. Several are underway in the USA and Scandinavia, and preliminary findings are of substantially greater concordance in MZ than DZ pairs (Breitner *et al*, 1992). However, we are in the somewhat uneasy position of having a wealth of evidence for familial aggregation but little indication from twin studies as to whether this really reflects a substantial genetic component to aetiology.

### Familial Alzheimer's disease: a genetic subtype

Perhaps the most striking evidence implicating genetic factors in the aetiology of AD is the existence of families in which the disease is transmitted through several successive generations in an apparently autosomal dominant fashion (e.g. Nee *et al*, 1983). The term 'familial Alzheimer's disease' (FAD) is sometimes used to refer to cases that show this pattern of familial aggregation, although they do not show consistent clinical or neuropathological features that would allow them to be distinguished from those with non-familial disease. Over 100 FAD families have been reported and the great majority contain cases with onset of the disease in the presenium. A particularly striking feature of FAD is the low intrafamilial variation in age of onset (Van Duijn *et al*, 1991*a*), and this might account, at least in part, for the predominance of early-onset cases, since potential late-onset cases are more likely to die from other causes before manifesting the disease. For the same reason, as we shall discuss below, it is hard to estimate what proportion of cases of AD have an apparently autosomal dominant form of the disorder. However, clear evidence for this type of genetic transmission from segregation through three generations is present in only between 0.1% and 1% of all cases.

## What is the mode of transmission of 'common-or-garden' Alzheimer's disease?

As we shall see when we discuss molecular genetic studies, there is now evidence that strongly suggests autosomal dominant transmission in at least a small proportion of families with FAD. However, most cases of AD do not show such striking patterns of familial transmission, and there are two main competing hypotheses to explain their mode or modes of inheritance.

First, it is possible that the great majority reflect a dominantly inherited mutation, or mutations, whose penetrance increases with advancing age. As we have seen, this explanation was first proposed by Larsson *et al* in 1963. It gained further in popularity as the existence of FAD became more widely known, and has also gained support from those recent family studies showing cumulative risks of dementia in first-degree relatives of AD probands that do not differ significantly from 50% by age 85–90 years. However, it cannot readily explain the many reports of discordant MZ twins nor the evidence of Farrer and colleagues that a cumulative risk of 50% may be an overestimate.

These findings are more in accord with the second hypothesis, which is that transmission reflects the operation of a major gene, or genes, against a polygenic/multifactorial background. This hypothesis has also gained some recent support from a complex segregation analysis of the families of a large series of consecutively ascertained probands (Farrer *et al*, 1991). This study suggested that a major autosomal dominant allele acting with a multifactorial component best explains the clustering of AD in these families. Modes of transmission postulating a single major locus, a multifactorial component only, autosomal recessive inheritance or no genetic susceptibility to AD were all strongly rejected, and the results suggested that a major gene for AD is responsible for as little as 24% of the total variance. One interpretation of this finding is that liability to AD is dependent upon both the inheritance of a major gene and the possession of other genes or environmental risk factors which modify its expression. This can explain the non-familial occurrence of most cases of AD, even though the disease allele may be common.

As Farrer and colleagues point out, their best model also supports the hypothesis of aetiological heterogeneity. According to this view, in some multiply affected families the disease is caused primarily by a major gene, whereas in others, perhaps the majority, as well as most sporadic cases, it results from polygenic/multifactorial transmission. The large FAD kindreds described above and the stability of age of onset seen within them support the view that both early-onset, and some late-onset, families are the result of autosomal dominant transmission, whereas other genetic and shared environmental factors contribute to transmission in a substantial proportion of late-onset families (Farrer *et al*, 1991).

## The molecular genetics of Alzheimer's disease

When viewed as a whole, the genetics of Alzheimer's disease may appear complex. However, as we have seen, it appears likely from family studies that at least a subset of the disorder (FAD) reflects a dominantly inherited defect in an autosomal gene. FAD is clearly amenable to linkage studies using DNA markers in attempting to locate and ultimately isolate the genetic defect responsible. Even if, as seems likely, such cases turn out to be the exception rather than the rule, understanding their pathogenesis should give great insight into the disorder as a whole.

### Chromosome 21 and FAD

The occurrence of Alzheimer's-like neuropathology in DS suggested that the genetic defect responsible for FAD might reside upon chromosome 21. This was therefore the first of the 22 autosomes to be tested using a genetic linkage strategy. In 1987 St George-Hyslop *et al* reported linkage between AD and several DNA markers (loci D21S1/S11 and D21S16) that map to the long arm of chromosome 21 in four extended kindreds multiply affected by early-onset disease. The majority of evidence for linkage in fact came from one very large French-Italian family. At about the same time as this linkage was reported, the gene coding for APP was cloned and localised to the same region of the long arm of chromosome 21 (Kang *et al*, 1987; Goldgaber *et al*, 1987; Tanzi *et al*, 1987*b*). This led to the suggestion that the APP gene might be the site of the primary genetic defect in FAD. Further excitement was generated by a report claiming that this gene was duplicated in several cases of 'sporadic' disease (Delabar *et al*, 1987).

Taken together with the presence of Alzheimer's-like changes in DS, it appeared that the neuropathology of AD could be the result of overexpression of the APP gene as a consequence of possessing either a mutation or an extra copy of the gene. However, further findings soon led to this hypothesis being rejected. First, there were two reports of recombination occurring between AD and the APP gene in several multiply affected families, demonstrating that inheritance of a defect in this gene cannot be responsible for AD in these families (Van Broeckhoven *et al*, 1987; Tanzi *et al*, 1987*c*). Secondly, a number of studies failed to replicate the finding of a duplication of the APP gene in sporadic cases of AD (Warren *et al*, 1987; Tanzi *et al*, 1987*d*; Podlisny *et al*, 1987).

However, the finding of linkage to markers on chromosome 21 was confirmed in other families with early-onset disease (Goate *et al*, 1989). This study also extended the original observations by placing the disease locus close to D21S16 and thus a considerable genetic distance centromeric of D21S1/S11 and even further from APP (Owen *et al*, 1990) (see Fig. 11.1). In contrast, two other early studies failed to find linkage between these markers and AD (Schellenberg *et al*, 1988; Pericak-Vance *et al*, 1988). The majority of pedigrees studied by Pericak-Vance *et al* were small and contained cases of late-onset disease (>60 years), whereas Schellenberg *et al* studied American descendants of a number of so-called 'Volga German' families. These contained cases of early-onset disease (<65 years), and all had ancestors who could be traced to a small ethnic German population who had settled in Russia around 1765 on the banks of the Volga river, suggesting the presence of a founder effect.

One interpretation of these early findings was that aetiological, and possibly genetic, heterogeneity exists, with chromosome 21 linkage restricted to a subset of early-onset families. In order to test this hypothesis, St George-Hyslop *et al* (1990) undertook a collaborative analysis of data from a number of markers on chromosome 21 in 48 families. The lod score analyses supported the earlier findings of linkage. They also showed evidence for heterogeneity when the families were divided into two groups according to whether the mean age of onset was above or below 65 years. When the data from the late-onset families were analysed, the lod scores were quite strongly negative. Evidence for chromosome 21 linkage came only from early-onset families. Moreover, it appeared that not all early-onset families were linked.

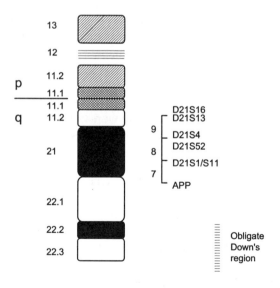

**Fig. 11.1**  An ideogram of human chromosome 21 indicating the approximate positions of the polymorphic loci showing linkage to FAD. The genetic distances between the loci are shown in centimorgans

Subsequent work by Schellenberg *et al* (1991*a*) did find weak evidence for linkage to chromosome 21 markers in some of their families with early-onset disease who were not of Volga German origin. However, their results confirmed that some forms of early-onset FAD, including that represented by the Volga German kindreds, are highly unlikely to be due to a genetic defect on chromosome 21. They also confirmed the absence of linkage to chromosome 21 in families with late-onset disease.

## Late-onset AD: more than one locus?

Pericak-Vance *et al* (1991) have also reported more recent work on their collection of predominantly late-onset pedigrees. Since the mode of inheritance in late-onset families is less clearly established, they also analysed their data using the non-parametric affected pedigree member method (APM), which does not require specification of penetrance parameters or gene frequency (Weeks & Lange, 1988). They confirmed their initial findings of an absence of significant evidence for linkage to chromosome 21 in late-onset families, although interestingly, there was some evidence for linkage using the APM, suggesting either that a subset of late-onset families is linked to a gene on chromosome 21, or that the mode of transmission was seriously mis-specified in the lod score analysis. They also found evidence for linkage to markers on chromosome 19 using both lod score analysis and the APM, but this was apparently present only in late-onset families. This region of chromosome 19 had previously been implicated in AD by the finding of association between an allele of the apolipoprotein CII (Apo CII) gene and the disease in ten multiply affected families (Schellenberg *et al*, 1987), an observation that has been extended to an expanded set of 23 families (Schellenberg *et al*, 1992*a*). In the later study, the association was significant when data from all families were analysed, but appeared stronger in early- than in late-onset cases. Lod score analyses were also performed, and while these were weakly positive in late-onset families, close linkage was apparently excluded in those of early onset, at least under the assumptions of the two sets of genetic parameters tested.

Heston *et al* (1991) found evidence for linkage between AD and D21S1/S11 in both early- and late-onset families using sib-pair analysis. Interestingly, lod score analysis assuming autosomal dominant inheritance with penetrance by age 75 of 85%, which should have been more powerful if the genetic model had been specified accurately, produced only very weakly positive scores. These findings are clearly similar to those of Pericak-Vance *et al* (1991) and suggest that a locus on chromosome 21 may be conferring susceptibility to late-onset FAD but that this is not transmitted in a simple autosomal dominant fashion.

In summary, the results of those linkage studies reviewed so far suggest that FAD is aetiologically and probably also genetically heterogeneous.

Evidence for a dominantly inherited pathogenic mutation on chromosome 21 has come from some early-onset families, though a locus on this chromosome might contribute to late-onset familial disease as well. However, not all early-onset families are linked to chromosome 21. The data from late-onset families are more difficult to interpret because the mode of transmission is less clear cut. In particular, there are problems raised by the higher probability of phenocopies occurring even within families with multiple cases due to genetic transmission. However, currently available evidence suggests that there may be loci on both chromosome 21 and chromosome 19 involved in late-onset familial disease. It seems reasonable to hypothesise on the grounds of parsimony that the former is the same as that involved in early-onset FAD, though the precise molecular pathology may be different.

## APP mutations

The demonstration of heterogeneity in FAD suggested that the APP gene had probably been dismissed too hastily, and this in fact turned out to be the case. Renewed interest in the possible role of APP in FAD was stimulated by the finding that hereditary cerebral haemorrhage with amyloidosis of the Dutch type (HCHWA-Dutch) is caused by a mutation in exon 17 of the APP gene at codon 693 (Levy *et al*, 1990; Van Broeckhoven *et al*, 1990). HCHWA-Dutch is a rare genetic disorder found in two villages in The Netherlands. Those affected die in middle age from cerebral haemorrhages caused by extensive deposition of beta-amyloid in the cerebral blood vessels. Exons 16 and 17 encode the beta-amyloid peptide.

The fact that beta-amyloid angiopathy is seen in both HCHWA-Dutch and AD led Goate *et al* (1991) to sequence exon 17 in a British family with FAD. This family was large enough to display significant evidence for chromosome 21 linkage on its own, and showed no recombination between the APP gene and the disease. Sequencing revealed a C to T transition segregating with the disease causing a valine to isoleucine substitution at amino acid 717. This mutation was also detected in an American family with early-onset FAD. Subsequently it has been found in several other families, including two from Japan (Naruse *et al*, 1991) but not in several hundred unaffected individuals.

Subsequent work has revealed two other families with mutations in codon 717 segregating with the disease, one resulting in a valine to glycine substitution (Chartier-Harlin *et al*, 1991*a*) and the other in valine to phenylalanine (Murrell *et al*, 1991). The identification of three mutations in the same codon strongly suggests that they are pathogenic. Mutations in APP 717 are rare, since they have not been found in many cases of FAD or in a large number of non-familial cases (Schellenberg *et al*, 1991*b*; Van Duijn *et al*, 1991*b*; Tanzi *et al*, 1992).

Two other apparently pathogenic mutations in APP have been reported. Mullan *et al* (1992*a*) identified a double mutation at codons 670 and 671 in exon 16 which cosegregated with the disease in two large and probably related early onset Alzheimer's families from Sweden. This mutation occurs just outside the amino terminal of beta-amyloid, whereas the codon 717 mutations occur just outside the carboxy terminal, so that the two sites flank the beta-amyloid sequence. Hendriks *et al* (1992) reported a mutation at codon 692 adjacent to that causing HCHWA-D. However, in this family some individuals with the mutation developed a disease very similar to HCHWA-D, whereas others developed presenile dementia, though neuro-pathological data were not available on the latter cases.

The discovery of apparently pathogenic mutations in APP is of profound significance, even though they are apparently rare. It suggests that beta-amyloid deposition is central to the pathogenesis of the disorder, and that other neuropathological changes, such as widespread cell loss and the formation of neurofibrillary tangles, are likely to be secondary. An important step will be to construct transgenic mice with the apparently pathogenic APP mutations in order to prove that they are indeed pathogenic. The creation of a successful animal model will itself represent an important achievement, since it will allow disease pathogenesis to be studied and interventions to be evaluated.

The most plausible explanation of how mutations in the APP gene lead to AD is that they result in a protein that is mismetabolised. Normally, APP is cleaved within the beta-amyloid region by a secretase, thus preventing deposition of this fragment (Esch *et al*, 1990). However, since beta-amyloid is found in small amounts even in normal brains, alternative processing pathways must exist that leave intact this region of the molecule. Recently, evidence has been obtained that this is indeed the case, and that potentially amyloidogenic molecules are produced in lysosomes (Estus *et al*, 1992; Golde *et al*, 1992). It seems likely that the pathogenic mutations in APP result in an altered molecule which is preferentially processed by these or other metabolic pathways which do not result in cleavage of APP within the beta-amyloid region. In this respect, it is interesting that the 717 and the 670/671 mutations flank the beta-amyloid molecule, and the 693 and 692 mutations lie close to the site of secretase cleavage (Hardy & Mullan, 1992). We may also presume that in DS the overexpression of APP that results from an extra copy of the gene leads to the excess protein being diverted down the alternative processing pathways and the accumulation of amyloidogenic molecules.

The development of highly polymorphic markers within or close to the gene (Mant *et al*, 1991) has allowed ready confirmation of the fact that not all families are linked to this locus. The inclusion of a mixture of linked and unlinked families in linkage studies probably led to mislocalisation of the disease gene to the pericentromeric region of chromosome 21, rather than the existence of a second locus in this region, as has been suggested recently (Schellenberg *et al*, 1991*b*; Tanzi, 1991). This is supported by further data from one of the families in the study by Goate *et al* (1989) which first provided evidence for a pericentromeric localisation. Recent unpublished findings suggest that the pathogenic locus in this family is not on chromosome 21 at all. It was an assumed recombination event in this family which was responsible for placing the disease gene centromeric to D21S1/S11!

## Chromosome 14 linkage

The existence of families with early-onset FAD showing apparently clear patterns of autosomal dominant segregation but which are unlinked to chromosome 21 suggested that mutations at another locus or loci can cause the disease. This was recently confirmed when Schellenberg *et al* (1992*b*) found linkage between markers on chromosome 14 and FAD in early-onset non-Volga German families. This finding was replicated by a number of other groups (St George-Hyslop *et al*, 1992; Van Broeckhoven *et al*, 1992; Mullan *et al*, 1992*b*) and work is now under way to try to identify the defective gene. Plausible candidate genes will be those involved in the regulation of APP expression and in the metabolism and degradation of beta-amyloid. It would seem that the locus on chromosome 14 probably accounts for the majority of families with FAD. However, the fact that the Volga German FAD kindreds are not linked to either APP or chromosome 14 implicates the existence of at least a third locus.

## The molecular genetics of 'common-or-garden' Alzheimer's disease

The question remains as to how we should approach the study of the great majority of cases of AD that do not show clear patterns of autosomal dominant transmission. As we have seen, there is evidence from genetic epidemiology for one or more genes of major effect. However, the evidence also favours the existence of aetiological heterogeneity such that in some multiply affected families the disease is caused predominantly by a major gene, whereas in others, as well as in most sporadic cases, aetiology is apparently more complex. Linkage studies will therefore be hampered by these uncertainties and by difficulties in identifying those families who have a simple, single-gene pathology. Moreover, we cannot say at present how many such families actually exist. If, as seems likely, aetiology in many familial cases, particularly those of late onset, is more complex, then this will have important methodological implications. In particular, the maximum likelihood method of linkage analysis should be used with great caution. One way of proceeding in the face of uncertainties concerning the mode of transmission is to adopt an exploratory approach to data analysis, testing a range of possible genetic models including those that specify low penetrance, the presence of linkage heterogeneity or a high phenocopy rate. An alternative is to study affected families using non-parametric methods of linkage analysis, such as the affected pedigree member method (Weeks & Lange, 1988) and extended sib-pair analysis (Sandkuijl, 1989), which do not require the mode of transmission to be specified. As we have seen, when these approaches have been taken, evidence for linkage to markers on both chromosomes 21 and 19 has been obtained in late-onset families (Heston *et al*, 1991; Pericak-Vance *et al*, 1991); these findings urgently require replication. Further candidate genes and loci are likely to be identified by future studies of early-onset FAD, as well as by those of the genes involved in controlling the expression and metabolism of APP.

As we have seen, a complementary approach is to study individual genes for allelic association, looking either directly for functional mutations that determine disease susceptibility or for DNA polymorphisms that are in linkage disequilibrium with them. This approach has the great advantage of being able to detect genes of relatively small effect. At present, together with non-parametric linkage methods, it should enable us to determine whether susceptibility to late-onset AD depends upon genetic variation at APP. However, recent work has revealed a strong, and at first sight surprising, association of both familial and sporadic late-onset AD with the e4 allele of apolipoprotein E (Strittmatter *et al*, 1993a; Saunders *et al*, 1993). The frequency of the e4 allele was 0.52 in affected members of late-onset multiply affected pedigrees and 0.40 in *post-mortem* confirmed cases of late-onset AD, compared with approximately 0.15 in controls. Similar findings have been obtained by other groups (e.g. Poirier *et al*, 1993; Liddell *et al*, 1994). Risk for AD apparently increases with increasing number of e4 alleles (i.e. the e4 allele acts in a co-dominant fashion) and mean age of onset decreases. In multiply affected families, over 90% of e4 homozygotes seem to develop the disorder by age 80 (Corder *et al*, 1993). In the general population, the risk to e4/e4 homozygotes is probably of the order of 40% at age 85 (Owen *et al*, 1994). However, current estimates suggest that some 40–50% of cases do not possess an e4 allele, so other aetiological factors and probably other genes must also be involved. If we assume a polygenic multifactorial mode of transmission then e4 accounts for about 17% of the variance in the liability to develop the disorder in the general population (Owen *et al*, 1994).

Apolipoprotein E (apo E) is produced in many tissues, including liver and nerve, and is known to function in the transport and distribution of lipids by interacting with lipoprotein receptors (Mahley, 1988). The three common genetic variants of apo E (designated E2, E3, and E4) result from different alleles coding for proteins with single amino-acid substitutions. The contribution made by apo E to the pathogenesis of AD is unclear. Of course, it is logically possible that the APOE gene merely acts as a neutral marker for some other gene with which it is in linkage disequilibrium and which predisposes to AD. However, a number of lines of evidence point to the direct involvement of apo E in the pathogenesis of AD. Like APP, it is known to be a neuronal stress protein, as its synthesis is greatly increased following injury to the nervous system (Ignatius *et al*, 1986; Snipes *et al*, 1986; Boyles *et al*, 1989; Hardy & Allsop, 1991). Apo E has been identified as a constituent of AD amyloid plaques and has also been found intracellularly in neurofibrillary tangles (Namba *et al*, 1991). Although apo E is also found in association with the amyloid plaques of various other amyloid-forming diseases (e.g. Creutzfeld–Jakob disease, familial amyloidotic polyneuropathy, and Down's syndrome), the e4 allele is not enriched in these diseases. Recent findings suggest that apo E4 may facilitate the deposition of beta-amyloid. Strittmatter *et al* (1993a,b) have shown that apo E binds avidly to synthetic beta-amyloid and have gone on to show that the E4 form, at physiological pH, binds more avidly to beta-amyloid peptide than the E3 form. Schmechel *et al* (1994) have shown that AD brains from patients with one or two e4 alleles have increased amyloid deposition compared with brains from those who do not possess this allele. These findings suggest that apo E4 might increase the rate at which amyloid deposits accumulate. More recently, speculation has focused on the possibility that the interaction between apo E and microtubules may be critical. There is evidence that apo E3 might increase the stability of microtubules, thus preventing or retarding the accumulation of tau in the form of neurofibrillary tangles.

# Multi-infarct dementia

Multi-infarct dementia is the second commonest form of dementia and its incidence, like that of Alzheimer's disease, is strongly age-related. This reflects the fact that the incidences of both atheromatous disease and hypertension increase with age, and it is these that predispose to multi-infarct dementia. It is important to note that there are probably as many cases of dementia resulting from mixed AD/MID pathology as result from MID alone. The finding by Hendricks *et al* (1992) mentioned above of a mutation in APP possibly predisposing to both FAD and hereditary cerebral haemorrhage suggests that mixed cases might reflect more than the chance co-occurrence of two common pathogenic mechanisms.

The genetics of MID have been little studied and as a consequence are poorly understood. Such evidence as is available from family studies suggests that there is increased morbidity in the first-degree relatives of probands (Constantinidis *et al*, 1962; Akesson, 1969), which supports a role for genetic factors. Unfortunately, there is no good evidence from twin or adoption studies to allow us to evaluate the contribution of genes as opposed to shared environmental factors. However, it seems clear that arterial disease and hypertension are under genetic control and, like other continuously distributed traits, reflect the operation of polygenic multi-factorial inheritance, although recent evidence (including some from animal studies) suggests that identifiable genes probably operate in some familial cases (Bell, 1992).

There are rare single-gene disorders that cause cerebral haemorrhage and multi-infarct dementia. We have already mentioned HCHWA-Dutch, which is caused by mutations in the APP gene showing autosomal dominant patterns of inheritance. Another autosomal dominant condition leading to hereditary cerebral haemorrhage with amyloidosis is the Icelandic type (HCHWA-Icelandic), in which the amyloid fibrils are composed not of beta-amyloid but of a variant of gamma trace basic protein, called cystatin C. This disease is caused by mutations in the cystatin C gene (Palsdottir *et al*, 1988). Several families have been reported with an autosomal domin- ant disorder consisting of recurrent subcortical ischaemic strokes and dementia with onset usually in the presenium (e.g. Sourander & Walinder, 1977; Tournier-Lasserve *et al*, 1991). Pathologically, the condition is characterised by a non-arteriosclerotic, non-amyloid angiopathy affecting mainly the small arteries penetrating the white matter and basal ganglia. Infarcts can be detected by magnetic resonance imaging and are often seen in asymptomatic offspring of affected parents. Recently, this disorder has been linked to microsatellite markers on chromosome 19q12 in two unrelated French families (Tournier-Lasserve *et al*, 1993). This should lead to identification of the disease gene in the next few years. It will then be important to determine whether different defects in the same gene confer susceptibility to the more common forms of stroke and vascular dementia.

# Huntington's disease

Huntington's disease (HD) is a comparatively uncommon progressive neuropsychiatric disorder which is characterised by choreiform movements and dementia. It is named after George Huntington, a general practitioner from New England, who described the disease in 1872. Its prevalence in northern Europe is only 5–7 per 100 000 and is lower still in southern European countries such as Italy. It is very rare in oriental countries and no cases have been described among Australian Aborigines, Maoris or Eskimos (Morris & Harper, 1991). The finding of a remarkable genetic isolate near Lake Maracaibo in Venezuela with a prevalence of 700 per 100 000 (Avila-Giron, 1973) would later provide vital clues allowing the HD mystery to be solved.

Huntington's disease shows a clear pattern of autosomal dominant inheritance with virtually 100% penetrance, although onset is usually delayed until between the ages of 25 and 50 years, with an average in the mid-40s. Thus the illness only very rarely skips a generation, and approximately 50% of the offspring of an affected parent develop the disease, with an equal incidence in males and females. Progression of the disease is accompanied by neuronal cell loss and gliosis, with the caudate nucleus and putamen particularly affected. The fundamental biochemical abnormality has not been determined, and for this reason HD was one of the first conditions for which 'positional cloning' was attempted and with initially promising results. In 1983 Gusella *et al* in Boston discovered close genetic linkage between the disease and a DNA marker (G8) which detects a locus D4S10 on the short arm of chromosome 4. This study was remarkable not only for the fact that linkage was detected after only 12 polymorphisms had been studied, but also for the fact that the linkage obtained was extremely close. There is little doubt that this success greatly fuelled optimism that molecular genetic approaches would bear fruit in the study of other neuropsychiatric disorders, just as the discovery of defective dopamine neurotransmission in Parkinson's disease led to the enthusiastic application of neurochemical techniques to these conditions.

Gusella's findings were replicated in a large number of studies from all over the world which have confirmed that D4S10 and the HD locus are about 4cM apart, with no evidence for non-allelic heterogeneity. Subsequently, the segregation of many new polymorphic sequences in this region of chromosome 4 was studied in an attempt to find markers flanking the HD locus. Genetic mapping was combined with a number of physical mapping techniques, such as pulsed field gel electrophoresis and radiation hybrid mapping, so that this region of chromosome 4 became one of the most extensively characterised areas in the genome. Initially, results of genetic mapping studies placed the disease locus close to the telomere. However, subsequent studies detected strong linkage disequilibrium between HD and the loci D4S95 and D4S98 (Snell *et al*, 1989). This confirmed the low mutation rate for the disease and also suggested that the HD gene must be extremely close to these loci and some distance proximal to the telomere. Further analysis of linkage disequilibrium in this region revealed that many different haplotypes are associated with the disease mutation, but that about a third of disease chromosomes have similar haplotypes with a conserved core region covering the 500 kb interval between D4S180 and D4S182 and containing the marker D4S95 (MacDonald *et al*, 1992). A number of genes from this region were identified. One of them, called IT15, was found to contain 21 tandemly repeated copies of the trinucleotide CAG near its 5' end and within the putative coding sequence. Polymerase chain reaction studies of this repeat showed that normal chromosomes contain between 11 and 34 copies, whereas disease chromosomes have from 42 up to at least 66 (Huntington's Disease Collaborative Research Group, 1993). The mutational mechanism therefore appears to be expansion of an unstable trinucleotide repeat and is remarkably similar to that seen in fragile X syndrome, spinal and bulbar muscular atrophy and myotonic dystrophy (see Chapters 1 and 4).

More recent work has shown a significant negative correlation between repeat length on the HD chromosome and age at onset (e.g. Snell *et al*,

1983). In addition, there is evidence for anticipation when HD is transmitted from the father (Roos *et al*, 1991) and this phenomenon seems to be associated with expansion of the unstable sequence, as in mytonic dystrophy and fragile X syndrome (Chapters 1 and 4). Further studies will also hopefully reveal how the HD mutation affects expression of the putative protein product named 'huntingtin' (*sic*) and how this may be modulated with a view to therapeutic intervention. The predicted structure of the polypeptide encoded by IT15 does not resemble any known protein. Determination of its function and the consequences of its dysfunction will also be important prerequisites for therapeutic advance.

### Predictive testing

The discovery of closely linked markers in 1983 allowed predictive testing for HD to be carried out for the first time. Broadly speaking, this is possible in two situations. First, individuals at risk for the disease can be tested and assigned either to a very high or to a very low risk category. Complete precision cannot be achieved because of the possibility of a cross-over between the marker and the disease gene. Secondly, prenatal exclusion testing of the offspring of an at-risk parent is possible. Here the risk to the foetus is determined either to be very low or to be the same as that of the at-risk parent (this depends upon the age of this parent but is usually close to 50%). It should be noted that prenatal exclusion testing does not alter the estimated risk of the parent, but does allow them to have children in the knowledge that, if they subsequently develop the disease, the risk to the offspring will remain low (Harper, 1986; Morris & Harper, 1991).

Predictive testing is based upon linkage analysis in the family of the consultand. It cannot be conducted without obtaining DNA from several members of the family. It therefore depends upon the cooperation of the relatives as well as the suitability of the pedigree structure and whether the markers are informative in the family. There are also a number of clinical and ethical problems associated with predictive testing, and careful assessment, explanation and counselling is required (Morris & Harper, 1991). Predictive testing in HD and the problems and pitfalls associated with it are discussed more fully in Chapter 12, as are the implications of the recent identification of the disease-causing mutation.

# Pick's disease

Pick's disease is a progressive dementing illness with peak incidence in the sixth decade of life. It can be distinguished from Alzheimer's disease by its neuropathology. Classically the brain exhibits distinctive atrophy particularly involving the frontal and temporal lobes bilaterally. Microscopy shows neuronal loss with gliosis, and 'balloon cells' may be seen containing argentophilic inclusions, so-called Pick bodies. There is no increase in the number of senile plaques and neurofibrillary tangles over and above that expected for the age of the brain examined.

Clinically it can be difficult, if not impossible, to distinguish Pick's disease from Alzheimer's disease especially in the later stages of dementia. In the early stages, Pick's disease may cause changes in character and disposition predicted from the early involvement of the frontal lobes. In contrast, Alzheimer's disease almost invariably presents with memory disturbance (see Lishman, 1987).

Evidence supporting a genetic contribution to aetiology has come from family studies showing increased risks of illness in the relatives of probands. Sjögren *et al* (1952) studied the relatives of 44 patients with certain or probable Pick's disease for which histological verification was available in 18 cases. The morbidity risk for parents was calculated as 19% and for sibs as 7%. Sjögren suggested that Pick's disease might be caused by a dominant major gene operating against a polygenic background. Heston *et al* (1987) reported a family study of the relatives of 18 probands with neuropathological evidence of Pick's disease. Fifteen secondary cases of dementia were discovered among relatives, and the risks were significantly greater for first-degree than for second-degree relatives. Heston *et al* do not speculate on the mode of transmission. However, they do point out that in only one family was there a pattern of inheritance consistent with autosomal dominance and complete penetrance. They remark that in most of their families the occurrence of secondary cases appeared to be irregular and in some probands cases seemed likely to be sporadic. There have however been reports of families with Pick's disease apparently showing a clear pattern of autosomal dominant transmission (Groen & Endtz, 1982).

# The spongiform encephalopathies

The spongiform encephalopathies are a group of rare neurodegenerative disorders which in humans consist of Creutzfeldt–Jakob disease (CJD), Gerstmann–Straussler syndrome (GSS) and kuru. They are so called because of the characteristic vacuolar, spongy appearance of the brain seen post-mortem. Spongiform encephalopathies are also seen in animals, the most studied being scrapie in sheep and currently the most notorious being bovine spongiform encephalopathy (BSE or 'mad cow disease'). As well as spongiform change, these diseases are all characterised by the abnormal deposition in the brain of a protease-resistant form of prion protein (PrP), sometimes in the form of amyloid plaques. Although an extremely rare cause of dementia, spongiform encephalopathy warrants mention because of its unusual and possibly novel pathogenesis, and because the pace of recent advances suggests that it will be the first cause of dementia to be understood at the molecular level.

Typically, CJD presents as a rapidly progressive presenile dementia occurring in the absence of a family history in the sixth decade of life. In addition, patients classically exhibit myoclonus and have a characteristic EEG with periodic triphasic discharges of 1–2 hertz (Lishman, 1987). There are a number of exceptions to this typical pattern. In particular, approximately 10% of cases have a family history. They tend to be younger at onset, but do survive for longer than the one or two years typical of sporadic cases. There are also a variety of other rarer clinical variants (Harrison & Roberts, 1991).

Gerstmann–Straussler syndrome is rarer than CJD and shows an apparently autosomal dominant pattern of inheritance. It differs from CJD in that cerebellar symptoms are prominent and dementia tends to be mild. The mean age at death is earlier than in CJD but the duration of illness is longer.

Kuru is an extremely rare disorder that is restricted to the Fore tribe of New Guinea. It is notable mainly for the fact that it was Gajdusek's (1977) study of this condition that established the transmissibility of the spongiform encephalopathies from its association with ritualistic cannibalism. Subsequently each of the human forms of spongiform encephalopathy has been shown to be transmissible by inoculation both to other species and iatrogenically from person to person via surgical and therapeutic procedures. The animal forms of the disease also show cross-species infectivity.

PrP is encoded by a normal cellular gene located on human chromosome 20. This gene is expressed and its encoded protein synthesised by cells including neurones and glia throughout life. Studies of familial cases of CJD and GSS have revealed that mutations of this gene segregate with the disease in a number of families (Owen *et al*, 1989; Hsiao *et al*, 1989). It seems likely that these mutations result in a protein with altered properties, so that it is abnormally deposited in the brain of the sufferer. It should also be pointed out that the disease has been transmitted to marmosets by inoculation of brain tissue from a member of one of these families, suggesting that the same disease can be at once both genetic and infectious!

The demonstration of transmissibility naturally led to a search for the causative agent. A number of studies have failed to detect the presence of a conventional infectious agent (Carlson *et al*, 1991; Hardy, 1991; Harrison & Roberts, 1991) and have led to the controversial and heterodox conclusion that it may in fact be an abnormal derivative of the prion protein. If true, this would represent an entirely novel pathogenic mechanism.

However, this conclusion is not accepted by everyone. Indeed, the evidence is by and large compatible with the view that PrP might be a receptor or other type of factor required for the infective agent to grow successfully within cells. Of course, this begs the question of the nature of the infective agent, which itself would have to be fairly unconventional to have escaped detection for so long!

# References

Akesson, H. O. (1969) A population study of senile and arteriosclerotic psychoses. *Human Heredity*, **19**, 546-566.

Amaducci, L. & Lippi, A. (1992) Pro and con for heterogeneity of Alzheimer's disease: a view from an epidemiologist. In *Heterogeneity of Alzheimer's Disease* (eds F. Boller, *et al*), pp. 74-80.Berlin: Springer.

Avila-Giron, R. (1973) Medical and social aspects of Huntington's chorea in the state of Zalia, Venezuela. *Advances in Neurology*, **1**, 261-266.

Bell, J. (1992) Ace (or PNMT?) in the hole. *Human Molecular Genetics*, **1**, 147-148.

Boyles, J. K., Zoellner, C. D., Anderson, L. J., *et al* (1989) A role for apolipoprotein E, apolipoprotein A-1, and low density lipoprotein receptors in cholesterol transport during regeneration and remyelination of the rat sciatic nerve. *Journal of Clinical Investigations*, **83**, 1015-1031.

Breitner, J. C. S. & Folstein, M. (1984) Familial Alzheimer dementia: a prevalent disorder with specific clinical features. *Psychological Medicine*, **14**, 63-80.

——, Gatz, M., Bergen, A. L. M., *et al* (1992) Use of twin coherts for research in Alzheimer's disease. *Neurology*, **43**, 261-267.

Brody, J. A. (1982) An epidemiologist's view of senile dementia – facts and fragments. *American Journal of Epidemiology*, **115**, 155-162.

Carlson, G. A., Hsao, K., Oesch, B., *et al* (1991) Genetics of prion infections. *Trends in Genetics*, **7**, 60-65.

Chartier-Harlin, M.-C., Crawford, F., Houlden, H., *et al* (1991*a*) Early-onset Alzheimer's disease caused by mutations at codon 717 of the beta-amyloid precursor protein gene. *Nature*, **353**, 844-845.

——, ——, Hamoudi, K., *et al* (1991*b*) Screening for the β-amyloid precursor protein mutation (APP: Val.Ile) in extended pedigrees with early onset Alzheimer's disease. *Neuroscience Letters*, **129**, 134-135.

Chase, G. A., Folstein, M. F., Breitner, J. C. S., *et al* (1983) The use of life tables and survival analayis in testing genetic hypotheses, with an application to Alzheimer's disease. *American Journal of Epidemiology*, **132**, 590-597.

Constantinidis, J., Garone, G., & De Ajuriaguerra, J. (1962) L'heredite des demences de l'age avance. *Encephale*, **51**, 301-344.

Corder, E. H., Saunders, A. M., Strittmatter, W. J., *et al* (1993) Gene dose of apolipoprotein E type 4 allele and the risk of Alzheimer's disease in late onset families. *Science*, **261**, 921-923.

Delabar, J.-M., Goldgaber, D., Lamour, Y., *et al* (1987) Beta-amyloid gene duplication in Alzheimer's disease and karyotypically normal Down's syndrome. *Science*, **235**, 1390-1392.

Esch, F. S., Keim, P. S., Beattie, E. C., *et al* (1990) Cleavage of amyloid beta peptide during constitutive processing of its precursor. *Science*, **248**, 1122-1124.

Estus, S., Golde, T. E., Kunishita, T., *et al* (1992) Potentially amyloidogenic, carboxyl-terminal derivatives of the amyloid protein precursor. *Science*, **255**, 726-728.

Farrer, L. A., O'Sullivan, D. M., Cupples, L. A., *et al* (1989) Assessment of genetic risk for Alzheimer's disease among first-degree relatives. *Annals of Neurology*, **25**, 485-493.

——, Myers, R. H., Connor, L., *et al* (1991) Segregation analysis reveals evidence of a major gene for Alzheimer disease. *American Journal of Human Genetics*, **48**, 1026-1033.

Gajdusek, D. C. (1977) Unconventional viruses and the origin and disappearance of kuru. *Science*, **197**, 943-960.

Glenner, G. G. & Wong, C. W. (1984) Alzheimer's disease: initial report of the purification and characterization of a novel cerebrovascular amyloid protein. *Biochemical and Biophysical Research Communications*, **120**, 885-890.

Goate, A. M., Haynes, A. R., Owen, M. J., *et al* (1989) Predisposing locus for Alzheimer's disease on chromosome 21. *Lancet, i*, 352-355.

——, Chartier-Harlin, M.-C., Mullan, M., *et al* (1991) Segregation of a missense mutation in the amyloid precursor protein gene with familial Alzheimer's disease. *Nature*, **349**, 704-706.

Golde, T. E., Estus, S., Younkin, L. H., *et al* (1992) Processing of the amyloid protein precursor to potentially amyloidogenic derivatives. *Science*, **255**, 728-730.

Goldgaber D., Lerman, M. I., McBride, O. W., *et al* (1987) Characterisation and chromosomal localisation of a cDNA encoding brain amyloid of Alzheimer's disease. *Science*, **235**, 877-880.

Groen, J. J. & Endtz, L. J. (1982) Pick's disease: hereditary second re-examination of a large family with discussion of other hereditary cases with particular reference to electroencephalography and computerised tomography. *Brain*, **105**, 443.

Gusella, J. F., Wexler, N. S., Conneally, P. M., *et al* (1983) A polymorphic marker limited to Huntington's disease. *Nature*, **306**, 234-238.

Hardy, J. (1991) Prion dimers: a deadly duo? *TINS*, **10**, 423-424.

—— & Allsop, D. (1991) Amyloid deposition as the central event in the aetiology of AD. *TIPS*, **12**, 383-388.

——, Chartier-Harlin, M.-C. & Mullan, M. J. (1992) Alzheimer's disease: the new agenda. *American Journal of Human Genetics*, **50**, 648-651.

—— & Mullan, M. (1992) In search of the solution. *Nature*, **359**, 268-269.

Harper, P. S. (1986) The prevention of Huntington's chorea. The Milroy lecture. *Journal of the Royal College of Physicians*, **20**, 7-14.

Harrison, P. J. & Roberts, G. W. (1991) 'Life, Jim, But Not as We Know It'? Transmissible dementias and the prion protein. *British Journal of Psychiatry*, **158**, 457-478.

Henderson, A. S. (1986) The epidemiology of Alzheimer's disease. *British Medical Bulletin*, **42**, 3-10.

Hendriks, L., Van Duijn, C. M., Cras, P., *et al* (1992) Presenile dementia and cerebral haemorrhage linked to a mutation at codon 692 of the β-amyloid precursor protein gene. *Nature Genetics*, **1**, 218-221.

Heston, L. L., Mastri, A. R., Anderson, V. E., *et al* (1981) Dementia of the Alzheimer type: clinical genetics, natural history and associated conditions. *Archives of General Psychiatry*, **38**, 1085-1090.

——, White, J. A. & Mastri, A. R. (1987) Pick's disease. Clinical genetics and natural history. *Archives of General Psychiatry*, **44**, 409-411.

——, Orr, H. T., Rich, S. S., *et al* (1991) Linkage of an Alzheimer's disease susceptibility locus to markers on human chromosome 21. *American Journal of Medical Genetics*, **40**, 449-453.

Heyman, A., Wilkinson, W. E., Stafford, J. A., *et al* (1984) Alzheimer's disease: a study of epidemiologic aspects. *Annals of Neurology*, **15**, 335-341.

Hsiao, K., Baker, H. F., Crow, T. J., *et al* (1989) Linkage of a prion protein missense variant to Gesstraun–Straussler syndrome. *Nature*, **338**, 342-345.

Huff, J. F., Auerbach, J., Chakravarti, A., *et al* (1988) Risk of dementia in relatives of patients with Alzheimer's disease. *Neurology*, **38**, 786-790.

Huntington's Disease Collaborative Research Group (1993) A novel gene containing a trinucleotide repeat that is expanded and unstable on Huntington's disease chromosomes. *Cell*, **72**, 1-20.

Ignatius, M. J., Gebicke-Harter, P. J., Pate Skene, J. H., *et al* (1986) Expression of apolipoprotein E during nerve degeneration and regeneration. *Proceedings of the National Academy of Science USA*, **83**, 1125-1129.

Jarvik, L. F., Ruth, V. & Matsuyama, S. S. (1980) Organic brain syndrome and aging: a six year follow-up of surviving twins. *Archives of General Psychiatry*, **37**, 280-286.

Joachim, C. L., Morris, J. H. & Selkoe, D. J. (1988) Clinically diagnosed Alzheimer's disease: autopsy results in 150 cases. *Annals of Neurology*, **24**, 50-56.

——, —— & Selkoe, D. J. (1989) Amyloid beta-protein deposition in tissues other than brain in Alzheimer's disease. *Nature*, **341**, 226-230.

Kallmann, F. J. (1956) Genetic aspects of mental disorders in later life. In *Mental Disorders in Later Life* (2nd edn) (ed. O. J. Kaplan). Stanford: Stanford University Press.

Kang, J., Lemaire, H-G., Unterbeck, A., *et al* (1987) The precursor of Alzheimer's disease amyloid A4 protein resembles a cell surface receptor. *Nature*, **325**, 733-736.

Larsson, T., Sjogren, T. & Jacobson, G. (1963) Senile dementia: a clinical, sociomedical and genetic study. *Acta Psychiatrica Scandinavia,* **39** (suppl. 167).

Levy, E., Carman, M. D., Fernandez-Madrid, I. J., *et al* (1990) Mutation of the Alzheimer's disease amyloid gene in hereditary cerebral hemorrhage, Dutch type. *Science*, **248**, 1124-1126.

Liddell, M., Williams, J., Bayer, A., *et al* (1994) Confirmation of association between the 4 allele of apolipoprotein E and Alzheimer's disease. *Journal of Medical Genetics* (in press).

Lishman, W. A. (1987) *Organic Psychiatry* (2nd edn). London: Blackwell.

Macdonald, M., Novelletto, A., Lin, C., *et al* (1992) The Huntington's disease candidate region exhibits many different haplotypes. *Nature Genetics*, **1**, 99-103.

Mahley, R. W. (1988) Apolipoprotein E: cholesterol transport with expanding role in cell biology. *Science*, **24**, 622-630.

Mann, D. M. A., Brown, A., Prinja, D., *et al* (1989) An analysis of the morphology of senile plaques in Down's syndrome patients of different ages using immunocytochemical and lectin histochemical techniques. *Neuropathology and Applied Neurobiology*, **15**, 317-329

Mant, R., Parfitt, E., Hardy, J., *et al* (1991) Mononucleotide repeat in the APP gene. *Nucleic Acids Research*, **19**, 4572.

Martin, R. L., Gerteis, G. & Gabrielli, W. F. (1988) A family-genetic study of dementia of Alzheimer's type, *Archives of General Psychiatry*, **45**, 894-900.

Masters, C. L., Simms, G., Weinman, N. A., *et al* (1985) Amyloid plaque core protein in Alzheimer's disease and Down's syndrome. *Proceedings of the National Academy of Sciences of the United States of America*, **82**, 4245-4249.

McGuffin, P., Sargeant, M. & Weppner, G. (1991) The genetics of Alzheimer's disease and the ethical implications for prevention. In *Ethical Issues of Molecular Genetics in Psychiatry* (eds R. J. Sram, V. Bulyzhenkov, L. Prilipko & Y. Christen), pp. 42-56. Springer.

McKhann, G., Drachman, D., Folstein, M., *et al* (1984) Clinical diagnosis of Alzheimer's disease: report of the NINCDS–ARDRA work group under the auspices of Department of Health and Human Services task force on Alzheimer's disease. *Neurology*, **34**, 939-944.

Mohs, R. C., Breitner, J. C. S., Silverman, J. M., *et al* (1987) Alzheimer's disease: morbid risk among first-degree relatives approximately 50% by 90 years of age. *Archives of General Psychiatry*, **44**, 405-408.

Morris, M. J. & Harper, P. S. (1991) Prediction and prevention in Huntington's disease. In *The New Genetics and Mental Illness* (eds. P. McGuffin & R. Murray), pp. 281-298. Oxford: Butterworth-Heinemann.

Mullan, M. J., Crawford, F., Axelman, K., *et al* (1992*a*) A pathogenic mutation for probable Alzheimer's disease in the APP gene at the N-terminus of β-amyloid. *Nature Genetics*, **1**, 345-347.

——, Houlden, H., Windelspecht, M., *et al* (1992*b*) A locus for early-onset Alzheimer's disease of the long arm of chromosome 14, proximal to the α1-antichymotrypsin gene. *Nature Genetics*, **2**, 340-342.

Murrell, J., Farlow, M., Ghetti, B., *et al* (1991) A mutation in the amyloid precursor protein associated with hereditary Alzheimer's disease. *Science*, **254**, 97-99.

Namba, Y., Tomonaga, M., Kawasaki, H., *et al* (1991) Apolipoprotein E immunoreactivity in cerebral amyloid deposits and neurofibrillary tangles in Alzheimer's disease and kuru plaque amyloid in Creutzfeld–Jakob disease. *Brain Research*, **541**, 163-166.

Naruse, S., Igarashi, S., Kobayashi, H., *et al* (1991) Mis-sense mutation Val-Ile in exon 17 of amyloid precursor protein gene in Japanese familial Alzheimer's disease. *Lancet*, **337**, 978-979.

Nee, L. E., Polinsky, R. J., Eldridge, R., *et al* (1983) A family with histologically confirmed Alzheimer's disease. *Archives of Neurology*, **40**, 203-208.

——, Eldridge, R., Sunderland, T., *et al* (1987) Dementia of the Alzheimer type: clinical and family study of 22 twin pairs. *Neurology*, **37**, 359-363.

Owen, F., Poulter, M., Lofthouse, R., *et al* (1989) Insertion in prion protein gene in familial Creutzfelt–Jakob disease. *Lancet, i*, 51-52.

Owen, M. J., James, L. A., Hardy, J. A., *et al* (1990) Physical mapping around the Alzheimer's disease locus on the proximal long arm of chromosome 21. *American Journal of Human Genetics*, **46**, 316-322.

——, Liddell, M. B., & McGuffin, P. (1994) Alzheimer's disease. An association with apolipoprotein e4 may help unlock the puzzle. *British Medical Journal*, **308**, 672-673.

Oliver, C. & Holland, A. J. (1986) Down's syndrome and Alzheimer's disease: a review. *Psychological Medicine*, **16**, 307-322.

Palsdottir, A., Thorsteinsson, L., Aolafsson, I., *et al* (1988) Mutation in cystatin C gene causes hereditary brain haemorrhage. *Lancet, ii*, 603-604.

Pericak-Vance, M. A., Yamaoka, L. H., Haynes, C. S., *et al* (1988) Genetic linkage studies in Alzheimer's disease families. *Experimental Neurology*, **102**, 271-279.

——, Bebout, J. L., Gaskell P. C., *et al* (1991) Linkage studies in familial Alzheimer disease: evidence for chromosome 19 linkage. *American Journal of Human Genetics*, **48**, 1034-1050.

Podlisny, M. B., Lee, G. & Selkoe, D. J. (1987) Gene dosage of the amyloid beta precursor protein in Alzheimer's disease. *Science*, **238**, 669-671.

Poirier, J., Davignon, J., Bouthillier, D., *et al* (1993) Apolipoprotein E polymorphism and Alzheimer's disease. *Lancet*, **342**, 697-699.

Roos, R. A. C., Vander Vlis, M. V., *et al* (1991) Age at onset in Huntington's disease: effect of line of inheritance and patients sex. *Journal of Medical Genetics*, **28**, 515-519.

Sandkuijl, L. A. (1989) Analysis of affected sib-pairs using information from extended families, in multipoint mapping and linkage based upon affected pedigree members. *Genetic Analysis Workshop 6* (eds R. C. Elston, M. A. Spence, S. E. Hodge, *et al*). New York: Alan R. Liss,.

Saunders, A. M., Strittmatter, W. J. & Schmechel, D. (1993) Association of apolipoprotein E allele 4 with late-onset familial and sporadic Alzheimer's disease. *Neurology*, **43**, 1462-1472.

Schmechel, D. E., Saunders, A. M., Strittmatter, W. J., *et al* (1994) Increased amyloid beta-peptide deposition as a consequence of apolipoprotein E genotype in late-onset Alzheimer's disease. *Proceedings of the National Academy of Sciences USA* (in press).

Schellenberg, G. D., Deeb, S. S., Boehnke, M. L., *et al* (1987) Association of an apolipoprotein CII allele with familial dementia of the Alzheimer's type. *Journal of Neurogenetics*, **4**, 97-108.

——, Bird, T. D., Wijsman, E. M., *et al* (1988) Absence of linkage of chromosome 21q21 markers to familial Alzheimer's disease. *Science*, **241**, 1507-1510.

——, Pericak-Vance, M. A., Wijsman, E. M., *et al* (1991*a*) Linkage analysis of familial Alzheimer disease, using chromosome 21 markers. *American Journal of Human Genetics*, **48**, 563-583.

——, Anderson, L., O'Dahl, S., *et al* (1991*b*) APP717, APP693 and PRIP gene mutations are rare in Alzheimer disease. *American Journal of Human Genetics*, **49**, 511-517.

——, Boehnke, M. L., Wijsman, E. M., *et al* (1992*a*) Genetic association and linkage analysis of the apolipoprotein CII locus and familial Alzheimer's disease. *Annals of Neurology*, **31**, 223-227.

——, Bird, T. D., Wijsman, E. M., *et al* (1992*b*) Genetic linkage evidence for a familial Alzheimer's disease locus on chromosome 14. *Science*, **258**, 668-671.

Selkoe, D. J. (1991) The molecular pathology of Alzheimer's disease. *Neuron*, **6**, 487-498.

Sjögren, T., Sjogren, H. & Lundgren, G. (1952) Morbus Alzheimer and morbus Pick. *Acta Psychiatrica Scandinavica (suppl.)* **82**, 9-51.

Skoog, I., Nilsson, L., Palmer, B., *et al* (1993) A population-based study of dementia in 85-year-olds. *New England Journal of Medicine*, **328**, 153-158.

Snell, R. G., Lazarou, L., Youngman, S., *et al* (1989) Linkage disequilibrium in Huntington's disease: an improved localisation for the gene. *Journal of Medical Genetics*, **26**, 673-675.

——, MacMillan, J. C., Cheadle, J. P., *et al* (1993) Relationship between trinucleotide repeat expansion and phenotypic variation in Huntington's disease. *Nature Genetics*, **4**, 394-397.

Snipes, G. J., McGuire, C. B., Norden, J. J., *et al* (1986) Nerve injury stimulates the secretion of apolipoprotein E by nonneuronal cells. *Proceedings of the National Academy of Sciences USA*, **83**, 1130-1134.

Sourander, P. & Walinder, J. (1977) Hereditary multi-infarct dementia. *Lancet, i,* 1015.

St George-Hyslop, P. H., Tanzi, R. E., Polinsky, R. J., *et al* (1987) The genetic defect causing familial Alzheimer's disease maps on chromosome 21. *Science,* **235**, 885-890.

——, Haines, J. L., Farrer, L. A., *et al* (1990) Genetic linkage studies suggest that Alzheimer's disease is not a single homogenous disorder. *Nature*, **347**, 194-197.

——, ——, Rogaev, E., *et al* (1992) Genetic evidence for a novel familial Alzheimer's disease locus on chromosome 14. *Nature Genetics*, **2**, 330-334.

Strittmatter, W. J., Saunders, A. M., Schmechel, D., *et al* (1993*a*) Apolipoprotein E: high-avidity binding to 3-amyloid and increased frequency of type 4 allele in late-onset familial Alzheimer's disease. *Proceedings of the National Academy of Sciences USA*, **90**, 1977-1981.

——, Weisgraber, K. H., Huang, D. Y., *et al* (1993*b*) Binding of human apolipoprotein E to synthetic amyloid peptide: isoform-specific effects and implications of late-onset Alzheimer's disease. *Proceedings of the National Academy of Sciences USA*, **90**, 8098-8102.

Sturt, E. (1986) Application of survival analysis to the inception of dementia. *Psychological Medicine*, **16**, 583 593.

Tanzi, R. E. (1991) Gene mutations in inherited amyloidopathies of the nervous system. *American Journal of Human Genetics*, **49**, 507-510.

——, St George-Hyslop, P. H., Haines, J. L., *et al* (1987*a*) The genetic defect in familial Alzheimer's disease is not tightly linked to the amyloid β-protein gene. *Nature*, **329**, 156-157.

——, Gusella, J. F., Watkins, P. C., *et al* (1987*b*) Amyloid β protein gene: cDNA, mRNA distribution, and genetic linkage near the Alzheimer locus. *Science*, **235**, 880-888.

——, St George-Hyslop, P. H., Haines, J. L., *et al* (1987*c*) The genetic defect in Alzheimer's disease is not tightly linked to the amyloid beta-protein gene. *Nature*, **329**, 156-157.

——, Bird, E. D., Latt, S. A. & Neve, R. L. (1987*d*) The amyloid β–protein gene is not duplicate in brains from patients with Alzheimer's disease. *Science*, **238**, 666-669.

——, Vaula, G., Romano, D. M., *et al* (1992) Assessment of amyloid β-protein precursor gene mutations in a large set of familial and sporadic Alzheimer disease cases. *American Journal of Human Genetics*, **51**, 273 282.

Tomlinson, B. E., Blessed, G. & Roth, M. (1970) Observations on the brains of demented old people. *Journal of Neurological Science*, **11**, 205-242.

Tournier-Lasserve, E., Iba-Zizen, M. T., Romero, N., *et al* (1991) Autosomal dominant syndrome with stroke-like episodes and leukoencephalopathy. *Stroke*, **22**, 1297-1302.

——, Joutel, A., Melki, J., *et al* (1993) Cerebral autosomal dominant arteriopathy with subcortical infarcts and leukoencephalopathy maps to chromosome 19q12. *Nature Genetics*, **3**, 256-259.

Van Broeckhoven, C., Genthe, A. M., Vandenberghe, A., *et al* (1987) Failure of familial Alzheimer's disease to segregate with the A4-amyloid gene in several European families. *Nature*, **329**, 153-155.

——, Haan, J., Bakker, E., *et al* (1990) Amyloid beta protein precursor gene and hereditary cerebral hemorrhage with amyloidosis (Dutch). *Science*, **248**, 1120-1122.

——, Backhovens, H., Cruts, M., *et al* (1992) Mapping of a gene predisposing to early-onset Alzheimer's disease to chromosome 14q24.3. *Nature Genetics*, **2**, 335-339.

Van Duijn, C. M., Van Broeckhoven, C., Hardy, J. A., *et al* (1991*a*) Evidence for allelic heterogeneity in familial, early-onset Alzheimer's disease. *British Journal of Psychiatry*, **158**, 471-474.

——, Hendriks, L., Cruts, M., *et al* (1991*b*) Amyloid precursor protein gene mutation in early-onset Alzheimer's disease. *Lancet*, **337**, 978.

Warren, A. C., Robakis, N. K., Ramakrishna, N., *et al* (1987) Beta-amyloid gene is not present in three copies in autopsy validated Alzheimer's disease. *Genomics*, **1**, 307-312.

Weeks, D. R. & Lange, K. (1988) The affected pedigree member method of linkage analysis. *American Journal of Human Genetics*, **42**, 315-326.

Wright, A. F. (1991) The genetics of the common forms of dementia. In *The New Genetics of Mental Illness* (eds. P. McGuffin & R. Murray), pp. 259-273. Oxford: Butterworth-Heinemann.

—— & Whalley, L. J. (1984) Genetics, ageing and dementia. *British Journal of Psychiatry*, **145**, 20-38.

Yamaguchi, H., Hirai, S., Morimatsu, M., *et al* (1988) Diffuse type of senile plaques in the brains of Alzheimer-type dementia. *Acta Neuropathologica*, **77**, 113-119.

# 12   Genetic counselling and ethical issues

*Genetic counselling • Using knowledge of genetics • Ethical issues*

The goals of genetic counselling are to mitigate the adverse effects, and to reduce the possible recurrence, of genetically influenced disorders. Its scope and consequences depend upon the degree to which the genetic mechanisms underlying the disease are understood, but they can include medical interventions, reproductive choices or prenatal or presymptomatic diagnoses. For the majority of psychiatric disorders at the present time, most counsellees will be concerned either with the potential risk to children or, in the case of unaffected relatives of patients, with their probability of developing the disorder. However, future advances in molecular genetics can be expected to alter this picture and may allow presymptomatic and prenatal diagnoses at least in some families, as well as other possibilities of medical intervention. Clearly, these developments raise a number of important ethical issues which we shall also discuss.

## Genetic counselling

It needs to be said at the outset that there is no place for public health campaigns persuading people with psychiatric disorder or a strong family history of psychiatric disorder not to have children. Still less is there a place for any attempts to legislate on this matter. However, an informed and responsible genetic counselling service has a small but definite current role, and this is likely to increase in the future. Most genetic counsellors in current practice adopt a non-directive, educational approach (Harper, 1988). Appropriate emphasis is therefore given to the personal autonomy of counsellees. In practice, much of the work of a genetic counsellor is to allay anxiety and to dispel mistaken beliefs, for example that all the offspring of a parent with serious mental illness necessarily have the same 'hereditary taint' or that all disorders with a genetic component are necessarily untreatable. However, it may be legitimate not only to lessen anxiety by providing information and reassurance, but also to raise the awareness of potential problems where this appropriate. The counsellor needs to help the counsellee assess the risk as accurately as possible and to understand the potential burdens. However, finally, after assessing the risk/burden ratio, the ultimate decision must be that of the counsellee.

Murphy & Chase (1975) have pointed out that the assessment of risk in genetic counselling can be derived from three sources:

218

(1) *empirical* information, consisting of estimates based on available research data
(2) *modular* information, which depends upon a clear understanding of the mode of inheritance of the disorder
(3) *particular* information, which is a compilation of all the data that can be used in assessing the risks to a particular family.

For the majority of common psychiatric disorders, most of the information imparted in genetic counselling should derive from empirical sources. A clear understanding of the mode of inheritance of psychiatric disorders is usually lacking, and it is important for anyone attempting genetic counselling not to confuse tentative hypothesis with proven fact. For example, as we have seen, it is possible to identify families in which functional psychosis appears to be segregating in a Mendelian fashion. However, such families could also occur as a result of multifactorial/polygenic transmission. While it may be perfectly valid to postulate the operation of genes of major effect for the purpose of linkage studies, it would be unwise, indeed unethical to do so for the purposes of risk prediction. However, in such highly loaded families one may wish to take account of particular information, bearing in mind that the risk to relatives increases according to the numbers of relatives already affected and decreases with the number of healthy relatives (Gottesman, 1991).

Whatever the type of information available, the role of the genetic counsellor is to educate and inform rather than to direct or advise. For example, a couple planning a family, one of whom has a schizophrenic parent, might beneficially be told that the average risk for each of their children displaying the disorder is about 3%, which although small is three times the rate in the general population. It must then be their decision rather than the counsellor's whether this low risk is acceptable.

# Using knowledge of genetics

Other than informing potential parents about the risks to their offspring, how might empirical knowledge about genetics be used in counselling individuals or families about prevention? One obvious answer is that for most psychiatric disorders it is a diathesis that is inherited and environmental stresses are necessary before the disorder becomes manifest. Sometimes, as in schizophrenia, the nature of the relevant stresses are controversial or unknown. Alternatively, as in depression, relevant environmental insults have been defined with some certainty. However, it is of little use advising someone with familial diathesis to depression to avoid threatening life events! On the other hand, it may be quite legitimate and useful to advise an individual with a strong family history of alcoholism that he may be more than usually susceptible to moderate use becoming immoderate. Similarly, the close relatives of patients suffering from schizophrenia should be informed that they especially should not 'experiment' with such street drugs as LSD, PCP and cocaine, because clinical evidence suggests that these substances can precipitate psychoses in those with a high genetic loading.

In the future, advances in molecular genetics should lead to greater accuracy in prediction. At present, Huntington's disease provides the best prototype. As we have seen presymptomatic and prenatal testing are available for Huntington's disease, allowing quite extensive risk prediction. These tests have been available in specialised centres for some years now, and there has been careful research and evaluation from which important results have been obtained (Morris *et al*, 1989; Morris & Harper, 1991).

In addition to expected problems such as reaction to adverse test results, with suicides having been recorded, many other difficulties have emerged. These include unintentional risk alteration, in which an individual who participates in a linkage study aimed at determining risk in a relative but who has not volunteered for predictive testing unintentionally has his/her perceived risk altered by testing. One of the most common problems is in fact inappropriate referral (Morris & Harper, 1991), which indicates that much more professional and family education is necessary. In some cases, adult patients at risk were referred by doctors without being told. It has been argued that this is inappropriate on two grounds (Morris & Harper, 1991). First, patients have a legitimate right to know what use will be made of their blood samples. Secondly, and more generally, it is a mistake to regard presymptomatic testing in the same way as other medical investigations, since the applicants are not generally medically ill and samples are required not only from the applicants but from key relatives. It is generally agreed that people should not be tested without their knowledge. There is international agreement that the testing of children, not uncommonly requested by parents or adoption agencies, is an inappropriate use of the test.

It is unlikely that future research with genetic markers will allow similar levels of predictive certainty for common disorders such as schizophrenia and affective disorders. However, predictive tests may soon have a place in subforms of early-onset Alzheimer's disease and in prion diseases, and here the ethical and psychological issues are similar to those in Huntington's disease. This work should not be attempted by centres without specialised expertise. In particular, such testing should only be offered in centres that can precede the test with expert counselling and can provide facilities for psychological support when the outcome is adverse.

The need and demand for expert psychiatric genetic counselling is likely to increase as the accuracy and value of such counselling increases. The rudiments of genetic counselling could usefully be covered in general professional psychiatric training. It might also be prudent to plan for the development of psychiatric genetic counselling services which could be set up on a regional basis within the next 5–10 years. Until this is achieved, genetic counselling for psychiatric disorders is likely to be carried out by general psychiatrists or geneticists. Since misinformation may be more damaging to the counsellee than no information at all, the main message for both groups is to be frank and open about the inherent complexities and ambiguities of psychiatric genetic counselling, and to be prepared to seek advice from colleagues with specialist knowledge.

# Ethical issues

We can consider ethical issues in psychiatric genetics under two broad headings relating first to research and second to clinical practice.

## Is research into psychiatric genetics unethical?

As we hope has been shown in the earlier chapters of this book, study of the genetics of psychiatric disorders currently offers one of the most exciting approaches to understanding causes and discovering cures for these common diseases. However, the concern persists that there is something slightly sinister about investigating the inheritance of abnormal behaviours.

It is not difficult to trace the historical roots of this disquiet. The first of these probably stems from a reaction to the eugenics movement in the early part of the century. Eugenics was based upon the optimistic notion that a knowledge of genetics could not only enable the abolition of certain diseases but could lead to improvements of human stock in general (Carlson, 1987; Roll-Hanssen, 1988). Some believed that this could be implemented on a national basis, and invalid beliefs about genetic and racial influences on IQ and other behavioural characteristics played a part in a way immigration policies were carried out in the USA (Kamin, 1974). However, as is well known, there was much worse to come. Eugenic arguments were commandeered by the German Third Reich in a way that blended an astonishing mixture of scientific *naïveté* and evil intent (Müller-Hill, 1988). Despite the fact that such policies were seen by most of the scientific community as not just morally repugnant but intellectually bankrupt, psychiatric genetics acquired a sort of guilt by association. Perhaps not surprisingly, a reactive antagonism to psychiatric genetics among politicians is still more evident in Germany than in other parts of Europe.

A less tangible but still potent source of antipathy to psychiatric genetics is the view that genetic explanations of psychological disorders are unacceptably mechanistic and demeaningly simplistic, often allegedly ignoring the obvious influences of poverty, child abuse, poor education, interpersonal relationships, and so on. This argument is often allied with another which claims that not only do genetic theories reduce the richness and complexity of human experience, but also that they offer only the prospect of therapeutic nihilism because genetic mechanisms must be impossible to treat and are certainly unlikely to be susceptible to psychological interventions. A related concern is that interest in molecular genetics could lead to neglect of non-biological, potentially remediable contributions to mental illness (Pelosi & David, 1989).

Fortunately, counterarguments are not too difficult to find. The main thrust of modern molecular medicine is towards precisely defining aetiology both at the molecular level and at the level of interplay between genes and environment. By so defining causes more precisely, we should be able in the long term to acquire knowledge which allows the development of rational therapies and preventative strategies. There are a number of examples already of genetic diseases where environmental manipulations form the basis of treatment such as phenylketonuria (see Chapter 4), and there is no necessary reason why finding that there are genetic influences on a disorder should rule out psychological or behavioural treatments. For example, two findings from the same unit at the Institute of Psychiatry, London, have shown that anorexia nervosa is substantially heritable (Treasure & Holland, 1991) (see also Chapter 7) but is responsive to psychotherapy (Russell *et al*, 1987). Other well known examples include the effectiveness of cognitive therapy in depression and the useful combination of drug plus family therapy in prolonging remissions in schizophrenia. However, it would be naïve to suppose that successful application of molecular genetics will not produce specific ethical problems relating to clinical practice, and it is to these that we shall now turn.

### Clinical practice

As we have already seen, Huntington's disease provides the best prototype for considering some of the ethical problems that are likely to arise in psychiatric genetics. At the outset we should note that the 10-year gap between the identification of linkage to markers on chromosome 4 (Gusella *et al*, 1983) and the identification of the mutation responsible for the disease (Huntington's Disease Collaborative Research Group, 1993) has led to considerable experience being gained in the application of linkage markers to presymptomatic and prenatal diagnosis. Now that the pathogenic mutation has been identified, it should soon be possible to identify gene carriers directly and this will have a number of new ethical implications, which we shall also consider.

Presymptomatic diagnosis of Huntington's disease with linked markers is possible with a high degree of accuracy because these markers are tightly linked to the disease locus, there is apparently 100% penetrance, and the great majority if not all cases result from mutations in the same gene on the short arm of chromosome 4. However, there are a number of problems. First, the test cannot be applied to everyone at risk; at least one living, affected grandparent must be available. In one study this criterion was fulfilled by only 15% of individuals at risk (Harper, 1986). Secondly, because there is up to a 5% chance of recombination occurring between the markers and the disease locus, the test is not 100% accurate.

However, young adults at risk of developing Huntington's disease, providing they have an informative family structure and relatives available for testing, can be told that their probability of developing this fatal degenerative disease is either less than 5% or more than 95%. Given that there is no cure or treatment for Huntington's disease, it is a matter of debate how to provide such a predictive service and indeed whether such a service should be provided at all. We have already considered some of the useful guidelines that have emerged as a result of early experience in predictive testing and it seems strongly advisable that such testing should only be offered in certain specialised centres.

As long as inappropriate referrals are rejected, that testing is preceded with expert counselling, and the counsellee's autonomy to decide whether to continue with the test is respected, it would seem entirely reasonable to provide such a service. Out of 238 initial serious enquiries for testing in one published series (Tyler *et al*, 1992) only 40 final results were given. While in 43 cases testing proved impossible because of unsuitable pedigree structure or laboratory factors, a decision to withdraw from the programme by choice occurred in 46 of the 143 individuals who proceeded to the first interview. This suggests that patients in this series felt able to exercise their autonomy by declining to be tested. We also know that the majority of those at risk of developing Huntington's disease do not request testing. In large measure this probably reflects the fact that no effective treatment is available. However, further research is required to understand in how many instances this decision is based upon adequate factual understanding of the presymptomatic test and its consequences.

The marker test is likely to be more useful for prenatal diagnosis, where the foetus now represents the third generation. However, in most cases the parent will not have reached the age of risk and the test will therefore only determine whether or not the foetus has the same 50% risk as the parent. The availability of this test provokes an obvious moral dilemma. If the foetus' risk is close to zero, no difficulty arises. However, if the result is adverse, the counsellee must decide whether or not to continue with the pregnancy when the child's risk of illness is approximately the same as the counsellee's own risk. Moreover, carriers of the disease gene can be expected to live quite healthily for upwards of 30–40 years.

Concern has been expressed that prenatal diagnosis will be applied to more common psychiatric disorders, such as schizophrenia and bipolar disorder. As we have pointed out, the complexity of the genetics in these disorders is such that it is unlikely that it will be possible to attain similar levels of predictive certainty. It is conceivable that rare families exist which represent single-gene subforms of these common disorders. If prenatal testing was possible in such families, we would suggest an extension of the approach that we have already advocated. This is based upon skilled counselling, consideration of the severity, age of onset and other aspects of the phenotype, allowing the counsellee to take a fully informed decision.

All experience relating to presymptomatic testing for Huntington's disease up until now has related to linked DNA markers. However, the identification of the pathogenic mutation now makes possible a specific test that will be largely independent of family structure, and it seems likely from consideration of other disorders that mutation testing will rapidly be brought into clinical practice and will become the principal basis for prediction. Mutational testing will have a number of advantages, including greater accuracy (it should be possible to assign risks of virtually 0 or 100% to individuals) and the feasibility of testing without the need to involve relatives, resulting in greater privacy. However, disadvantages can also be envisaged. These include inadvertent prediction (e.g. a parent being shown to have the mutation with the testing of their offspring), and pressure for testing without appropriate counselling due to the relative simplicity of the test. With regard to this latter point, it may be necessary for guidelines to restrict the availability of mutational testing to those centres with the ability to offer appropriate counselling. Greater accuracy may also prove to be a double-edged sword, and the psychological consequences of an adverse result be much greater.

Another problem arises once specific mutations are identified in Mendelian disorders. This occurs when clinicians wish to use genetic tests for diagnostic purposes, and this is relevant not only in Huntington's disease but also in some forms of early-onset Alzheimer's disease and in prion dementia. Clearly, tests for genetic mutations are not the same as many other diagnostic tests, in that their results have implications for other members of the family. Of course, it can be argued that the same is true for any other type of test that allows diagnosis of a Mendelian disorder. However, inadvertent risk alteration is a particular problem in diseases of late onset. We should therefore ensure that families are adequately counselled before genetic tests are used in diagnostic settings, and that clinicians are dissuaded from including genetic tests as part of 'routine' diagnostic screens.

Another general area of ethical concern relates to the question of availability of genetic information to third parties such as relatives, employers, and insurance companies. These issues may not be areas of immediate concern, but are likely to pose problems in the future, particularly as we identify susceptibility genes to common disorders such as cardiovascular disease, cancers, and mental illness. Areas that are already of relevance to some disorders such as Huntington's disease include the use of genetic testing in relation to life and health insurance (Harper, 1993) and the related issue of possible testing by employers. These issues are complex, but future developments need to be discussed and debated openly, not only by professionals but also by the public (Harper, 1992*a*, 1993). This will require an improvement in public education about science in general and genetics in particular. We shall also need to pay particular attention to issues of confidentiality and to ensure that individuals and families fully understand the implications of testing as well as retaining control over the disclosure of the results. Understanding the genetic basis of common disorders will have profound public health implications. Many of these relating to improvements in treatment and prevention will be beneficial. However, the excesses of the eugenics movement and the abuses of Nazi Germany are stark reminders of the dangerous consequences of individual interests becoming subordinated to broader, population-based goals, particularly in relation to mental illness (Holtzman, 1989; Harper, 1992*b*).

# References

Carlson, E. A. (1987) Eugenics and basic genetics. in H. J. Muller's *Approach to Human Genetics. History and Philosophy of the Life Sciences*, **3**, 57-78.

Huntington's Disease Collaborative Research Group (1993) A novel gene containing a trinucleotide repeat that is expanded and unstable in Huntington's disease. *Cell*, **72**, 1-20.

Gottesman, I. I. (1991) *Schizophrenia Genesis. Origins of Madness*. San Francisco: W. H. Freeman.

Gusella, J. F., Wexler, N. S., Conneally, P. M., *et al* (1983) A polymorphic marker limited to Huntington's disease. *Nature*, **306**, 234-238.

Harper, P. S. (1986) The prevention of Huntington's chorea. *Journal of the Royal College of Physicians*, **20**, 7-14.

—— (1988) *Practical Genetic Counselling* (3rd edn). Bristol: Wright.

—— (1992*a*) Genetics and public health. *British Medical Journal*, **304**, 721.

—— (1992*b*) Insurance and genetic testing. *Lancet*, **341**, 224-227.

—— (1993) Huntington's disease and the abuse of genetics. *American Journal of Human Genetics*, **50**, 460-464.

Holtzman, N. A. (1989) *Proceed with Caution: Predicting Genetic Risks in the Recombinant DNA Era*. Baltimore: Johns Hopkins University Press.

Kamin, L. J. (1974) *The Science and Politics of IQ*. Chichester: Wiley.

Morris, M. J., Tyler, A., Lazarou, I., *et al* (1989) Problems in genetic prediction of Huntington's disease. *Lancet*, **i**, 601-603.

—— & Harper, P. S. (1991) Prediction and prevention in Huntington's disease. In *The New Genetics and Mental Illness* (eds P. McGuffin & R. Murray), pp. 281-298. Oxford: Butterworth-Heinemann.

Müller-Hill, B. (1988) *Murderous Science*. Oxford: Oxford University Press.

Murphy, E. A. & Chase, G. A. (1975) *Principles of Genetic Counselling*. Chicago: Yearbook Publishers.

Pelosi, A. J. & David, A. S. (1989) Ethical implication of the new genetics for psychiatry. *International Review of Psychiatry*, **1**, 315-320.

Roll-Hanssen, N. (1988) The progress of eugenics: growth of knowledge and change in ideology. *History of Science*, **26**, 295-331.

Russell, G., *et al* (1987) An evaluation of family therapy in anorexia nervosa and bulimia nervosa. *Archives of General Psychiatry*, **44**, 1047-1056.

Treasure, J. L. & Holland, A. J. (1991) Genes and the aetiology of eating disorders. In *The New Genetics and Mental Illness* (eds P. McGuffin & R. Murray), pp. 198-211. Oxford: Butterworth-Heinemann.

Tyler, A., Ball, D. & Crawford, D. (1992) Presymptomatic testing for Huntington's disease in the U.K. *British Medical Journal*, **304**, 1593-1596.

# Index

*Compiled by Linda English*

The page numbers in bold type refer to definitions in the text.

additive gene effects **39**
adoption studies 35–36, 150
  adoptee's family studies **35**
  adoptee studies **35**
  affective disorders 114–115
  alcoholism 36, 165–166 &
    Table 9.3, 167
  conduct disorder 180
  cross-fostering studies **35**,
    92, 150, 167
  hyperactivity, childhood
    182–183
  schizophrenia 36, 90–92 &
    Table 5.2
affected relative pairs:
  linkage studies 60
affective disorders 110–127,
  155, 222
  adoption studies 114–115
  adversity and 119–120,
    219–220
  alcoholism and 49, 166–
    167
  anxiety and 120, 133, 134–
    135
  in childhood 178–179
  eating disorders and 139
  family studies 110–112 &
    Table 6.1, 118 Table 6.4
  linkage/association studies
    and molecular biology
    122–124
  modes of transmission
    115–117
  neurotic and endogenous
    depression 117–118
  schizophrenia and 93–94
  sex differences 121–122
  twin studies 34, 50 & Table
    2.4, 112–114 & Tables
    6.2–6.3, 118, 119 Table
    6.5
age correction 31 Box 2.1, 32
agoraphobia 131–132 &
  Table 7.2, 138
Aicardi syndrome 71 Table
  4.4
alcoholism 150, 161–173, 220
  adoption studies 36, 165–
    166 & Table 9.3, 167
  biological basis 168–170
  depression and 49, 166–
    167
  family studies 161–162 &
    Table 9.1
  subtypes 167

twin studies 163–164 &
  Table 9.2
  'normal' use 164–165
alleles **1, 37**
  marker: identical by
    descent (IBD)/by state
    (IBS) 60
allelic association *see*
  association studies
allelic heterogeneity **59**
Alzheimer's disease (AD) 59,
  192–205, 220, 224
  familial (FAD) 197–198
    chromosome 14 linkage
    204
    chromosome 21 linkage
    25, 78, 199–201 &
    Fig.11.1, 202
  genetic epidemiology 194–
    196
  mode of transmission 47,
    52, 198–199
  molecular genetics of 199–
    205
  senile plaques and
    neurofibrillary tangles
    192–193
  twin studies 196
amyloid precursor protein
  (APP) gene: link with
  Down's syndrome and
  Alzheimer's disease 78,
  193, 199, 202–204
aneuploidies **7, 77**
Angelman syndrome 14, 81–
  82
animal studies
  alcoholism 169
  gene expression in central
    nervous system 27,28
  genetics of normal
    personality 146–147
anorexia nervosa 139–140,
  141, 222
anticipation **14**, 76–77, 207–
  208
antisocial personality 149–
  151
anxiety
  depression and 120, 133,
    134–135
  disorders in childhood
    179–180
  neurosis 130–132 & Table
    7.2
  *see also* neurotic disorders

anxious personality 151
Apert's syndrome 70 Table
  4.2
Arginosuccinic aciduria 72
  Table 4.5
ascertainment of probands
  **31–32**
association studies 60–63 &
  Table 3.1, 123, 141–142,
  205
  classical markers:
    schizophrenia 100–101
  DNA markers in 26
ataxia telangiectasia 71
  Table 4.3
autosomes **1**
  anomalies of and mental
    retardation 77–78, 79
    Table 4.6
  disorders of and mental
    retardation 70–74 &
    Tables 4.2–4.3 & Table
    4.5

bacteria and molecular
  cloning 15–16 & Fig.1.7
Barr body **2**
base pairing rule and DNA 8
  Fig.1.4, 9, 15
*Bezugsziffer* 31 Box 2.1
biological markers
  infantile autism 177
  personality disorder 155
bipolar (BP) disorder 38, 47,
  52, 93, 94, 111–112 &
  Tables 6.1–6.2, 113 &
  Table 6.3, 115, 116–117,
  121, 139
borderline personality
  disorder 154–155
brain, study of gene
  expression in 26–28
Briquet syndrome 150–151,
  152–153
bulimia nervosa 44 & Table
  4.2, 139–141

candidate gene studies 24,
  25–26, 27, 124
  schizophrenia 103–104
carriers: sex-linked traits **38**
cell division 2–5 & Figs 1.1–
  1.2
central nervous system
  (CNS)
  response to alcohol 168

study of gene expression in 26–28
Charcot-Marie-Tooth (CMT) neuropathy 59
childhood psychiatric disorders 174–191
chromatin 1
chromosomal abnormalities 25, 155
cytogenetic techniques and 7–8
familial Alzheimer's disease and *see under* Alzheimer's disease, familial
mental retardation and 77–80 & Table 4.6
chromosomes 1–8
behaviour during cell division 2–5
cytogenetic techniques and application 5–8, 55
clinical practice: ethical issues 222–225
complementary DNA (cDNA) 15–16
concordance and twin studies 33–34
conduct disorder 180–181, 182
Creutzfeldt–Jakob disease (CJD) 206, 210–211
Cri du chat syndrome 79 Table 4.6
criminality 149–151, 155, 167, 180–181
cross-fostering studies 35, 92, 150, 167
crossing over (recombination) 4 Fig.1.2, 5, 55
Crouzon's syndrome 70 Table 4.2
cytogenetic techniques and application 5–8 & Fig.1.3, 55

deletions 7, 12, 20, 25
dementia 192–217
deoxyribonucleic acid (DNA) 1
classes of in genome 10–11
complementary (cDNA) 15–16
enhancer/promoter regions 11 & Fig.1.6
markers
in association studies 26
and disease 20–24
linkage studies with 24–26, 102–103
mutation and variation 12–13
probes 15–17
recombinant DNA technology and new genetics 14–19

sequencing 15, 18
structure 8–9 & Fig.1.4
unstable sequences 13–14, 76–77, 207–208
depression *see* affective disorder
diploid/haploid distinction and cell division 3
dizygotic (DZ)/fraternal twins 32–33
dominant disorders 38
autosomal, and mental retardation 70 Table 4.2
dominant traits 36–37, 39, 41
dopamine receptor genes
alcoholism and 170
schizophrenia and 102, 103
double back-cross matings 37, 55–56 & Fig.3.1
Down's syndrome (trisomy 21) 77–78, 79 Table 4.6
link with Alzheimer's disease and chromosome 21: 25, 78, 193, 194, 203–204
Duchenne muscular dystrophy 25, 59, 71 Table 4.4
duplications 7

eating disorders 44 & Table 4.2, 139–142, 222
Edward's syndrome 79 Table 4.6
endogenous depression 117–118
enuresis, childhood 183
environment 219–220
alcoholism and 164, 166–167
bulimia nervosa and 140–141
contributors to variance in 41–42
depression and 119–120, 121
path analysis and 42–45
twin studies and 34–35
*see also under* genes
epistasis 44, 134
equilibrium and allelic association 61
ethical issues 221–225
eugenics 221, 225
exclusion and linkage studies 57
exons and introns 9–10

familial Alzheimer's disease *see under* Alzheimer's disease
family studies 30–32
affective disorder 110–112 & Table 6.1
in childhood 178–179
alcoholism 161–162 & Table 9.1

conduct disorder 180
developmental reading disorders 183
family history method 30–31
family study method 31
hyperactivity, childhood 181
infantile autism 175–176
neurosis 128–129
obsessive–compulsive disorder 135–137
tics and Tourette's syndrome 184–185
foetal karyotyping 7
fragile sites 7, 75
fragile X syndrome 7, 14, 38, 74, 75–77, 178, 207–208
frame shift mutations 12

galactosaemia 72 Table 4.5
gametes 2, 3
Gaucher disease 73 Table 4.5
generalised anxiety disorder (GAD) 130–133 & Table 7.2
genes 1
and environment:
co-actions 44
covariance 45
interactions 44–45, 221–222
infantile autism and 177–178
neurotic disorders and 133–134
non-additive effects 44–45
gene–gene interactions 44, 134
structure and expression 9–10 & Fig.1.5, 11 Fig.1.6
study of expression in central nervous system 26–28
genetic counselling 218–221
genetic fingerprinting 13, 33
genetic linkage 5
*see also* linkage studies
genetic markers 55
classical 55, 100–102, 122–123, 141
informativeness of 23
*see also under* deoxyribonucleic acid
genetic marker studies
alcoholism 169–170
neuroses and eating disorders 141–142
personality 155–156
schizophrenia 25, 58, 100–103
*see also* association studies; linkage studies
genetics, formal: historical origins 36
genomic imprinting 14, 76, 81

genomic phenomena that decrease familial resemblance 13–14
genotype **36**
germ line mutations **13**
Gerstmann–Straussler syndrome (GSS) 210, 211

Hardy–Weinberg equilibrium **39**
Hartnup disease 72 Table 4.5
hemizygous, males as, and sex-linked traits **37–38**
hereditary cerebral haemorrhage with amyloidosis (HCHWA) 202, 203, 206
heredity
  chromosomal basis 1–8
  molecular basis 8–13
heritability of a trait **41**
heterogeneity
  genetic 59, 70
  and multiple thresholds 47–49
  phenotypic 70
  of schizophrenia 48, 95–98 & Table 5.3
heterozygotes **1, 36**
high-resolution banding and chromosomal analysis **6–7**
histocompatibility (HLA) antigens, marker studies with 55, 100–101, 123, 141
homocystinuria 72 Table 4.5
homosexuality 148–149
homotypia
  affective disorder and 111, 113
  schizophrenia and 96
homozygotes **1, 36**
human genome
  classes of DNA in 10–11
  mapping of 18, 24, 63
human karyotype **1**
Hunter syndrome 73 Table 4.5
Huntington's disease (HD) 14, 38, 207–209
  predictive testing 208, 220, 222–223, 224, 225
Hurler's syndrome 73 Table 4.5
hyperactivity, childhood 181–183
hysterical personality 152–153

idiopathic mental retardation 66–69 & Fig.4.1
imprinting, genomic 14, 76, 81
inbred populations **38**
incomplete penetrance 46, 58
independent assortment 3, **37** & Table 2.1
infantile autism 75, 175–178
insertions **12**

*in situ* hybridisation histochemistry (ISHH) 27–28
intelligence quotient (IQ) 43, 44 & Table 2.2
  and mental retardation 66, 67 Fig.4.1, 68–69, 80
intra-class correlation coefficient **33**
introns and exons 9–10
inversions **7**
iterative model fitting 49–50, 52

juvenile delinquency 149, 180–181

karyotype, human **1**
karyotyping 5–7 & Fig.1.3
Klinefelter's syndrome (XXY) 2, 79–80 & Table 4.6
kuru 210, 211

Laurence–Moon–Biedl syndrome 71 Table 4.3
Lesch–Nyhan syndrome 38, 71 Table 4.4
liability/threshold models 45–49 & Figs 2.6–2.8, 51–52 & Fig.2.9, 115–116, 153
libraries and molecular cloning **17**
life events and depression 119–120
lifetime incidence/expectancy **32**
lifetime prevalence **32**
likelihood ratio tests **51**, 59
linkage disequilibrium **61**, 63
linkage studies 22–24, 55–57 & Figs 3.1–3.2
  affective disorder 122–124
  Alzheimer's disease 199–205 & Fig.11.1
  with classical markers 55, 101–102, 122–123, 141
  and complex disorders 57–59
  with DNA markers 22–24, 102–103
  Huntington's disease 207–208, 222–223
  model-free 60
  schizophrenia 25, 101–104
lipid metabolism and connective tissue disorders 73 Table 4.5
locus, gene **1, 37**
locus heterogeneity **59**
lod scores **56**–57 & Fig.3.2
Louis Barr syndrome 71 Table 4.3
Lowe's syndrome 71 Table 4.4

mandibulofacial dysostosis 70 Table 4.2

manic depressive illness 58–59, 110–113 & Tables 6.1–6.3, 115, 120, 122–123, 139
maple syrup urine disease 72 Table 4.5
Marinesco Sjogren syndrome 71 Table 4.3
maternal age and increased risk 77, 78, 80, 194
meiosis 2–5 & Fig.1.2
Mendel, Gregor: laws of inheritance 36–42 & Table 2.1
mental retardation 66–86
  aetiology 66–68 & Fig.4.1 & Table 4.1
  chromosomal abnormalities 77–80 & Table 4.6
  idiopathic 66–69 & Fig.4.1
  single-gene defects 69–77 & Tables 4.2–4.5
messenger RNA (mRNA) 9, 10 Fig.1.5, 27–28
metabolism
  of alcohol 168
  inborn errors of 72–73 & Table 4.5
microcephaly, true 71 Table 4.3
microsatellite repeats **22**
mitosis **2**, 3 Fig.1.1
mixed-model inheritance 47, 51 & Fig.2.9, 116
model fitting 49–52 & Table 2.4, 99–100, 114
model-free linkage tests 60
molecular basis of heredity 8–13
molecular cloning **15–17** & Fig.1.7
molecular genetics
  application to study of disease 20–26
  'central dogma' 9
monozygotic (MZ)/identical twins **32**
  reared apart (MZA) 34–35
morbid risk **32**
mosaicism 77
mucopolysaccharidoses 73 Table 4.5
multifactorial inheritance **41**
multifactorial (MF) threshold model of disease transmission 45–46 & Fig.2.6
multi-infarct dementia (MID) 192, 206–207
multiple incomplete ascertainment **32**
multiple thresholds and heterogeneity 47–49
multipoint linkage analysis **57**
mutational testing 224
mutations 12–13
  amyloid precursor protein 202–204
  identification of 18–19, 20, 224

myotonic dystrophy (MD)
14, 76–77, 207, 208

nephrogenic diabetes
insipidus 71 Table 4.4
neurofibromatosis 46
neurotic depression 116,
117–118
neurotic disorders 120, 126–
145
anxiety and depression
120, 133, 134–135
in childhood 179–180
eating disorders 139–142
genetic marker studies
141–142
mode of transmission and
gene–environment
interactions 133–134
neurosis as a whole 126–
130 & Table 7.1
obsessive–compulsive
disorder 135–138 &
Table 7.3, 151, 179, 185–
186
specific phobias 138
specific syndromes 130–
132 & Table 7.2
twin studies, population
based 132–133
neurotic personality 151
neutral mutations 12–13
Niemann–Pick disease 73
Table 4.5
non-disjunction 77, 78, 79
non-recombinants 55–56 &
Fig.3.1
Norrie's disease 71 Table 4.4
Northern blotting 27
nucleotide bases and DNA 8

obesity 139, 141
obsessional personality 151-
152
obsessive–compulsive
disorder (OCD) 135–138 &
Table 7.3, 151, 179, 185–
186
oligogenic model of
inheritance 47

pair-wise concordance: twin
studies 33
panic disorder (PD) 130–132
& Table 7.2, 133, 134, 141,
179
paranoid schizophrenia and
HLA system 100–101
Paris classification of
chromosomes 6 Fig.1.3
Patau's syndrome 79 Table
4.6
path analysis 42–44 & Figs
2.4–2.5 & Table 2.2, 99
with model fitting 49–51 &
Table 2.4
penetrance 46 & Table 2.3
incomplete 46, 76

perinatal adversity 67 Table
4.1, 177–178, 182
personality
alcoholism and 167
depression and 120
normal, genetics of 43–44
& Table 2.2, 146–149
temperament in childhood
174–175
personality disorders 146–160
antisocial 149–151
anxious/neurotic 151–153
borderline 154–155
genetic marker studies
155–156
hysterical 152–153
obsessional 151–152
schizoid–schizotypal 94,
99, 153–154, 155
personality questionnaire
studies 147–148
phenocopies 38
schizophrenia and 96–98 &
Table 5.3
phenotype(s) 36
continuous 39–41 & Figs
2.1–2.3
irregular, and threshold
models 45–47 & Figs
2.6–2.7 & Table 2.3
phenylketonuria (PKU) 20,
38, 70, 72 & Table 4.5, 74,
177, 222
phobias 131–132 & Table 7.2,
138, 151
Pick's disease 209–210
pleiotropy 48, 62, 63, 95
point mutations 12, 20
point prevalence 32
polygenic inherited traits 41
polygenic threshold model
of disease transmission 45–
46 & Fig.2.6
polymerase chain reaction
(PCR) 18–19 & Fig.1.9, 20,
22–23 Fig.1.11, 24, 76
polymorphic, genetic
markers as 55
populations and heritability
42
positional cloning 24–25,
206–207
Prader–Willi syndrome 14,
80–81
premutation 76
prevalence and family
studies 32
prion dementia 26, 209–210,
220, 224
prion protein (PrP) 209, 210
probands 30
ascertainment of 31–32
proband-wise concordance:
twin studies 33
psychiatric genetics: twofold
task 30
psychophysiological studies:
normal personality 147

quantitative genetics 30–54
quantitative trait loci (QTL)
63, 142, 156, 169
quasi-continuous disorders
45

reaction ranges, phenotypic
45
reading disorders, developmental 183–184
recessive disorders 38
autosomal, and mental
retardation 71 Table 4.3
recessive traits 36–37
reciprocal translocations 7
recombinant DNA technol-
ogy and new genetics 14–
19 & Fig.1.7
recombinants 55–56 &
Fig.3.1
recombination 4 Fig.1.2, 5,
24, 55–57, 223
recombination fraction 56–
57 & Fig.3.2
Refsum disease 73 Table 4.5
relative risk and association
studies 61
renal (transport)
aminoacidurias 72 Table
4.5
research: ethical issues 221–
222
restriction enzymes 15–16, 21
restriction fragment length
polymorphisms (RFLPs) 21
Fig.1.10, 22, 55
retinoblastoma, hereditary
13
ribonucleic acid (RNA) 9, 10
Fig.1.5
risk alteration, unintentional
220, 224
Robertsonian translocations
7

sample stratification 62
schizoaffective disorder 93–
94
schizoid–schizotypal
personality 94, 99, 153–
154, 155
schizophrenia 87–109 &
Fig.5.1
adoption studies 36, 90–92
& Table 5.2
candidate gene studies
103–104
defining limits of 93–100 &
Fig.5.2, 153–154, 155
heterogeneity 48, 95–98
& Table 5.3
mode of inheritance 47,
52, 98–100
genetic counselling/ethical
issues 219, 220, 222,
223–224
genetic marker studies 25,
58, 100–103

twin studies 89–90 & Table 5.1
schizophrenia spectrum disorder 91 Table 5.2, 92, 153, 154
segregation 3, 37 & Table 2.1
segregation analysis 51–52 & Fig.2.9, 99, 116
sex cell division 2–5 & Fig.1.2
sex chromosomes 2
  anomalies 78–80 & Table 4.6
  pseudoautosomal region and schizophrenia 102–103
sex differences in psychiatric disorder 120–121, 166–167, 185–186
  multiple threshold models and 48–49, 121, 150, 166–167, 177
sex-linked traits 37–38
  see also X-linked disorders
sexual orientation 148–149
simple sequence repeats 22 Fig.1.11, 24, 103
single ascertainment 31
single-gene defects and mental retardation 69–77 & Tables 4.2–4.5
single major locus (SML) model of inheritance 46–47 & Table 2.3 & Fig.2.7
somatic cell division 2, 3 Fig.1.1
somatic mutations 13
somatisation disorder 150–151, 152–153
Southern blotting 17–18 & Fig.1.8
splicing out non-coding regions and gene expression 10, 11 Fig.1.6
spongiform encephalopathies 210–211
staining techniques and karyotyping 5–7

Tay Sachs disease 73 Table 4.5
temperament see personality
testing, predictive 7–8, 218, 223–224
  fragile X syndrome 76
  Huntington's disease 208, 220, 222–223, 224, 225
  phenylketonuria 20, 74
third parties, availability of information to 224–225
threshold models
  irregular phenotypes and 45–47 & Figs 2.6–2.7 & Table 2.3
  multiple, heterogeneity and 47–49 & Fig.2.8
tics and Tourette's syndrome (TS) in childhood 184–186
transcription/translation of genetic information 9–10 & Fig.1.5
translocations 12, 25, 77
transmitter males: fragile X syndrome 75, 76
triple X syndrome 79 Table 4.6
tuberous sclerosis 13, 59, 70 Table 4.2, 177
Turner's syndrome (XO) 2, 79 Table 4.6, 80
twin studies 32–35
  affective disorder 34, 50 & Table 2.4, 112–114 & Tables 6.2–6.3, 118
  alcoholism 163–165 & Table 9.2
  Alzheimer's disease 196
  conduct disorder 180
  developmental reading disorders 183–184
  eating disorders 139–141
  hyperactivity, childhood 182
  infantile autism 176
  neuroses 129–130 & Table 7.1

neurotic syndromes 132–133
  obsessional symptoms/traits 137–138 & Table 7.3
  personality questionnaires 147–148
  schizophrenia 89–90 & Table 5.1
  tics and Tourette's syndrome 185
'two-hit' hypothesis and mutations 13

uniformity 36, 37 Table 2.1
unipolar (UP) disorder 111–112 & Table 6.1, 113 & Table 6.3, 115

variation in quantitative traits, components of 41–42
variations affecting protein structure or expression (VAPSE) in genes 63, 104
Virchow Sekel dwarf 71 Table 4.3

Weinberg's shorter method of age correction 31 Box 2.1, 32
Wilson's disease 38

X-linked disorders 37–38, 121, 123
  and mental retardation 71 Table 4.4, 74–77, 82
  X-linked hydrocephalus 71 Table 4.4
XYY syndrome 79 Table 4.6, 80, 155

zygosity in twins, mistaken 33, 34